The 104th Field Artillery
Regiment of the New York
National Guard, 1916–1919

ALSO BY PAMELA A. BAKKER

*Eyes on the Sporting Scene, 1870–1930:
Will and June Rankin,
New York's Sportswriting Brothers* (McFarland, 2013)

The 104th Field Artillery Regiment of the New York National Guard, 1916–1919

From the Mexican Border to the Meuse-Argonne

Pamela A. Bakker

McFarland & Company, Inc., Publishers
Jefferson, North Carolina

LIBRARY OF CONGRESS CATALOGUING-IN-PUBLICATION DATA

Bakker, Pamela A.
　　The 104th Field Artillery Regiment of the New York National Guard, 1916–1919 : from the Mexican border to the Meuse-Argonne / Pamela A. Bakker.
　　　p.　cm.
　　Includes bibliographical references and index.

　　ISBN 978-0-7864-7915-3 (softcover : acid free paper) ∞
　　ISBN 978-1-4766-1567-7 (ebook)

　　1. New York (State). National Guard. Field Artillery Regiment, 104th.　2. World War, 1914–1918—Regimental histories—United States.　3. World War, 1914–1918—Campaigns—Western Front.　4. United States. Army. Infantry Division, 27th.　I. Title.
UA366.B35 2014
940.4'1273—dc23　　　　　　　　　　　　　　　2014016275

BRITISH LIBRARY CATALOGUING DATA ARE AVAILABLE

© 2014 Pamela A. Bakker. All rights reserved

No part of this book may be reproduced or transmitted in any form or by any means, electronic or mechanical, including photocopying or recording, or by any information storage and retrieval system, without permission in writing from the publisher.

On the cover: The Officer's Training School at Gun Drill, Camp Wadsworth, South Carolina, 1917 (National Archives)

Printed in the United States of America

McFarland & Company, Inc., Publishers
　Box 611, Jefferson, North Carolina 28640
　　www.mcfarlandpub.com

In memory of Sergeant Andrew B. Rankin, Jr.,
Battery F, 104th Field Artillery Regiment, NYNG.
Dedicated to his children Andrew, Ruth and Lois,
and to their children,
grandchildren, and
great-grandchildren.

Table of Contents

Acknowledgments	ix
Preface	1
ONE. Formation of the 1st Field Artillery Regiment, 12th Infantry, New York National Guard (1867–1915)	5
TWO. The Mexican Punitive Expedition (June 1916–February 1917)	14
THREE. Camp Wadsworth, Spartanburg, South Carolina (April 1917–May 1918)	60
FOUR. Camp Stuart, Newport News, Virginia (May 1918–June 1918)	85
FIVE. The School of Fire of Camp de Souge, Bordeaux, France (July 1918–August 1918)	93
SIX. St. Mihiel Salient Offensive (September 12, 1918)	108
Seven. The Meuse-Argonne Offensive (September 26–October 6, 1918)	119
EIGHT. The Meuse-Argonne Offensive (October 7–November 11, 1918)	143
NINE. Mustering Out (1919)	170
Appendix I: Deaths	181
Appendix II: Awards and Citations, World War I	183
Chapter Notes	197
Bibliography	207
Index	213

Acknowledgments

This book began with my grandfather's letters and photographs from 1916 to 1919 as he served in the 1st Field Artillery Regiment, 12th Infantry, New York National Guard, which became the 104th Field Artillery Regiment during the Great War. The story soon outgrew one man's accounts. A special thank you goes to the daughters of Sergeant Andrew B. Rankin, Jr., Ruth and Lois, for their comments and recollections. Family members sharing their memories and items in their possession contributed greatly to an understanding of how individual men serving within the period of conflict handled the stress of engagements. Thanks also go to my siblings for insights and editing, especially Kitti Canepi who patiently reviewed each page using her skills in library science. I am also indebted to my children Alissa and David, and daughter-in-law Ashley, for their encouragement.

The Spartanburg County Historical Association in Spartanburg, South Carolina, has kept extensive records on Camp Wadsworth's brief stay in their city during the Great War. Jonathan K. Brooke was particularly helpful in researching their records on the regiment, which were thin. He spent a great deal of time, and sent a photograph. I am grateful for his many emails to me.

Jim Gandy, the associate librarian/archivist for the New York State Military Museum, also pointed me in helpful directions during my research for the book. Extensive material on the 104th Field Artillery Regiment appears to be lacking. However, his interest in accumulating more information on this particular regiment helped the project feel more like a collaborative work, with my research contributing to a greater body of knowledge. I'm grateful for the copy of the 52nd Field Artillery Brigade's Meuse-Argonne Offensive barrage map which he supplied. It helped me place the regiment on the ground during the battle.

The National Archives and Records Administration in College Park, Maryland, did three searches for photographs and rosters on the regiment. They contributed a few photographs from Camp Wadsworth and of the regiment's return trip to the United States after the war. Many photographs of the regiment appear to be missing. This book is helpful in collecting scattered records of the heroic work done by the 104th Field Artillery Regiment, and hopefully will add to the testament of the 27th Division's extensive contribution to the American Expeditionary Forces.

Preface

My initial draw to the 1st Field Artillery Regiment in the New York National Guard was through my grandfather. His given name was Andrew Brown Rankin, VI, but he went by the names of Drew and Andrew Jr. He had served in the New York National Guard from 1915 to 1919, in Battery F, ending with the rank of sergeant.[1] During World War I his regiment became the 104th Field Artillery Regiment in the 52nd Field Artillery Brigade of the 27th Division, American Expeditionary Forces (A.E.F.). While studying their activities, there arose a need to collect material which appeared to be widely scattered, in order to get a clear picture of the regiment for the period of 1916–1919.

The New York National Guard was federalized twice during this period as it served the American army. The first time was to assist as border patrol in Texas during the Mexican Punitive Expedition in 1916. New York sent an entire tactical 6th Division to the border, serving in three small towns as they watched

Sergeant Andrew B. Rankin, Jr., served in Battery F, 1st Field Artillery Regiment, New York National Guard, from 1915 to 1919. He was a private during the Mexican Punitive Expedition, a corporal during World War I, and became a sergeant right after Armistice while in France (courtesy Andrew B. Rankin, Jr., Collection).

for Pancho Villa's forces. The regiment, called the 1st New York Field Artillery Regiment, camped at McAllen, Texas, with the division's headquarters. They trained at the gunnery field at La Gloria, Texas, and suffered through 120-degree weather, relentless hikes with insufficient water, a para-typhoid "A" epidemic, and a gulf hurricane. Europe was already at war while the men were in Texas, and everyone contemplated whether the United States would go to war with Mexico or Germany first. Mexico was a very real possibility for the men stationed near it.

There have been many books written on the Mexican Punitive Expedition. Most, however, are focused on the activities of General Pershing and his army in Mexico. The divisions at the border are briefly mentioned without a clear view of what they were doing while guarding and patrolling the border. One chapter in Major-General John F. O'Ryan's book *The History of the 27th Division* focuses on that period, but it addresses the entire 6th Division, and only mentions the artillery sporadically. Henry Hagamen Burdick's book *New York Division, National Guard, War Record 1916 by the Officers and Men of the Division* did focus on their time at the border. Six pages in it are on the 1st Field Artillery, but it did not give a complete view of all of their activities. It was more of a personal remembrance by Lieutenant William P. Welsh who served in the regiment. The New York State adjutant general reports to the legislature gave some information and the division's newspaper had articles which mentioned activities. Drew Rankin wrote a long newspaper article for a Long Island newspaper in 1916 that has not been widely circulated. He also had a collection of photos and letters. These items were combined to give a more detailed view of that period at the border from start to finish.

Even though the United States initially remained neutral in the Great War, ultimately it was drawn into it in 1917. A few months after their service at the southern border had ended the New York Division was on trains bound for Camp Wadsworth in South Carolina. The 1st Field Artillery Regiment was renamed the 104th Field Artillery Regiment within the 27th Division during World War I. The division would be nicknamed O'Ryan's Roughnecks. The men were trained extensively in conditions similar to France with miles of trenches. French, British and Canadian veterans of the war served as instructors. While their own officers were being trained by the Regular Army off site, they were trained in camp by members of the Regular Army. In addition, their commander, Major-General O'Ryan, was sent to France during this period to inspect conditions and meet with divisional and corps leaders in Paris. While he was gone, the men at camp slept in tents and trenches, experiencing a combination of heat and cold, rain and snow, and practiced under live fire with gas launched. The artillery trained at the gunnery field at Glassy Mountain.

Bits of information on the artillery's service during the Great War from short regimental and brigade field diaries were included in one chapter of Major-General John O'Ryan's book. Out of a 1,157-page book, he wrote only six pages which addressed the field artillery during the war. His focus was largely on the infantry because he served with them. O'Ryan was commanding the infantry under the British and Americans in Belgium and then in Flanders, France, covered by British and Australian artillery. The 52nd Field Artillery Brigade, under which the 104th Field Artillery Regiment served, was not attached to its own division during the war. The 52nd Field Artillery Brigade served under the French and Americans, and was attached first to the 33rd Division as their artillery, and then to the 79th Division as their artillery for the entire Meuse-Argonne Offensive. They were located near Verdun on the other side of the Hindenburg Line. The brigade commander, Brigadier-General Wingate, contributed six pages from his brigade diary to O'Ryan's book; the commander of the 104th Field Artillery Regiment, Colonel Merritt H. Smith, contributed a seven-page diary. Three divisional reports included some mention of brigade activities, but the two divisions under which they served were focused on their own infantry. When they mentioned the artillery, they were often called "divisional artillery," which often sounded as though they were members of that division. In addition, each regiment in the brigade wrote small books following the war. The histories of the 105th and 106th are widely available, but there are only a few copies of the 72-page book on the 104th Field Artillery Regiment's history during that period, kept mostly in military libraries.

Current writers seem to also be focused on the work done by the infantry of the 27th Division during the war rather than the artillery. Usually they at least indicate that the artillery did not serve with the division. Some authors have placed them in the wrong location, and some have left out one of the two divisions under which they served. Requests for information from organizations which should have had material on the 104th Field Artillery Regiment resulted in referrals to other organizations which found nothing. Even the New York State Military Museum and the National Archives had difficulty, although all expressed an interest in learning more about the regiment, encouraging me to help the individual repositories enlarge their own collections.

This book is a result of perseverance as it follows the 1st Field Artillery Regiment from New York to the extreme heat of Texas during the Mexican Punitive Expedition; through heavy snowstorms in the mountains at Camp Wadsworth in South Carolina to mosquito-infested Camp Stuart in Virginia, to the rainy countryside of the School of Fire of Camp de Souge near Bordeaux, France. It explains the structured training of the 104th Field Artillery Regiment with descriptions of their field pieces and the way the pieces functioned in both offensive and defensive situations. The field diaries are enlarged with comments made by artillerymen to help the reader see and feel the events through the eyes of the men engaged in the action.

At the front, the 104th Field Artillery Regiment was under constant shell fire, bombing, and gassing from the enemy nestled securely in the high places along the Meuse River. Through it all, in an exposed position, they fulfilled each order given in an accurate manner, enabling the infantry to make its advances as scheduled. They succeeded in "doing their bit" for their country, and received little praise or recognition for their sacrifices. Few remember them now. As we approach the centennial of that war, their voice is one that needs to be recorded so that others may experience this period of great struggle. The artillery was an important part of why the infantry had such great success. They were protective, supportive, and used in both offensive and defensive moves, often suffering with those making the advances as they came under direct fire.

The 27th Division as a whole, because of its excellent stateside training prior to the war, was subsequently raided by the War Department, to intersperse members within a number of divisions. This contributed greatly to the A.E.F.'s success in ways that seem to be missing in other retellings of events. Their commander had a very real fear that the 27th Division was being completely dismantled. They also were blocked from recruiting replacements at one point. When again allowed carefully defined recruiting, they had to work extra hard to bring the new members up to strength, and they did. That story needs to be shared as well.

The men of that generation did not talk in great detail about the daily experiences of war. The experiences were horrific and most men sought to put them behind them. Still, letters home were written, short articles typed, and photos collected which help us hear and see the men during their time of service. It was a period of great change in both the National Guard and in the Regular Army as the United States moved towards what we consider modern warfare. The 104th Field Artillery Regiment changed with the technology, while world events were happening around them. Following the war, members of the 104th Field Artillery Regiment gathered annually to remember. A bond was established that would never be broken by those who had served together blasting the Boche, and protecting the Doughboys.[2]

CHAPTER ONE

Formation of the 1st Field Artillery Regiment, 12th Infantry, New York National Guard (1867–1915)

New York State's militia dates back prior to the Revolutionary War. The militia, called provincials in the thirteen English colonies, was composed of conscripted males sixteen years or older. Enrollment was compulsory and the men were expected to bring their own muskets. They were fined if they did not. In 1702, Queen Anne declared the required ages to be 16–50; if an invasion was imminent, the age of those called would then be 15–60.[1]

During the Revolutionary War, New York State contributed three groups of infantry. The militia consisted of about 68 organizations which served three months at a time when called, although they could be called repeatedly during a given year. The line was composed of nine organizations which served under General George Washington, including artillery. The levies which were drafted from different militia regiments and local citizens included seven organizations which served entirely outside New York State. There were also privateers who would capture and loot enemy ships. Henry Knox was the chief of the Continental Artillery, and he used confiscated British nine pounders taken from Manhattan at first.

After the Revolutionary War, the militia contained both volunteer and independent companies, each with its own organization and supplying its own weapons with individuals bringing a musket and blanket. It was still compulsory for males. The companies tended to reflect different ethnic groups, economic classes and, in some cases, religious affiliations. The militia had an annual training day once a year, but it was not well organized. They could also be called by local sheriffs to stop things like public riots, serving as a type of posse.

The state's Volunteer Militia Artillery dated back to 1786. By spring of 1806, there were four companies of artillery in the New York State Militia. The term "National Guard" is actually tied to the artillery of New York. In July of 1825 the 2nd Battalion, 2nd Regiment of Artillery turned out in New York City to welcome the Marquis de Lafayette, the French aristocrat who had helped the American patriots in the fight for independence from the British. To honor him, the battery took on the name of "National Guard" after the Garde Nationale de Paris commanded by Lafayette during the French Revolution. Following the Civil War, more states began using the term "National Guard." In 1903, legislation made the name official.[2]

The 12th Infantry Regiment in New York City, to which the 1st Field Artillery Regiment would be attached, had served during the Civil War for a few months at a time in the years 1861, 1862, and 1863 in the 2nd Brigade of the 1st Division of the New York State Militia. The infantry regiment defended the nation's capital during those years. There had been 380 men in the infantry regiment, but the numbers were raised to 1,000 with new recruits who entered service carrying muskets but wearing street clothes. They marched down Broadway towards Mercer Street with crowds waving.[3] However, most of the work of the National Guard within the state was suppressing riots: Astor Place in 1849, the Orange Riot July 1871, and the Railroad Riots in July 1877. The number of regiments within the state militia was lowered after the Civil War with preference given to cities and large villages.[4]

The 1st Field Artillery Regiment began as Battery K, 1st Regiment of Artillery, New York National Guard, on April 3, 1867. Civil War veterans of Company K, 9th Militia New York National Guard were responsible for its formation. Company K had entered federal service during the Civil War as the 6th New York Battery, Horse Artillery serving with the 2nd Cavalry Division.[5] Horse Artillery had all men riding on horses with the cavalry, and pulling light guns attached to limbers, or caissons with ammunition.[6] They would dismount and deploy the guns when needed. Mounted Artillery had men walking beside the heavier cannons. They moved to "mount" the cannons when in battle. Company K served for four years during the Civil War until July 8, 1865, at engagements such as Chancellorsville and Gettysburg.

The artillery in the newly formed battery used Delafield guns, which were considered light artillery, and also 24-pound brass Howitzers. The men carried Springfield muskets as well. The Delafield Branded Iron Rifle was a 3.67-inch gun. It used a Delafield Malleable Shell with a cast iron base with five cast flanges which matched the cannon's rifling. Major-General Richard Delafield (1798–1873), a military engineer from New York after whom the gun is named, is considered the father of American seacoast artillery. He had studied the use of artillery in Europe. He served in the Union Army during the Civil War and as the superintendent of the United States Military Academy at West Point, New York. Thirteen guns designed by him had been delivered to the commissary general of the state of New York in 1862. Interestingly, there were 13 Delafield guns in good working order, plus three not in good order, in the 1st Field Artillery Regiment's armory review in 1868.[7] It appears the guns given to the commissary general were held by the regiment.

During this early period, a standard field artillery battery had six guns. Each was attached to a limber and pulled by six to eight horses with drivers on the left side of the horses. They controlled the horse to their right as well. A caisson was also attached to a limber and pulled by six horses. It carried the ammunition and a spare wheel. A battery carried about 1,200 rounds of ammunition. In battle, the gun was removed from the limber by the cannoneers. Each battery had a captain, two lieutenants (one in charge of the caissons and one in charge of the guns and crews), a sergeant in charge of a gun, corporals in charge of a caisson and as a gunner to aim the field piece, men taking care of the horses and equipment, and cannoneers with different numbers and tasks. One cannoneer swabbed the bore and rammed the load; one inserted the charge and shell; one covered the vent to protect it from flying embers; one primed and fired the piece; one carried ammunition from a point close to the cannon to the one inserting the shell; one was in charge of the limber; and one brought ammunition from an ammunition dump to the one carrying it to the person inserting the shell. Each concentrated only on their specific task in the process of firing.[8]

Battery K, 1st Regiment of Artillery was disbanded on December 10, 1869, but the battery was retained as a separate Battery K. It served during the Railroad Riots in July 1877. The riots began in Martinsburg, West Virginia, and spread to a few states as workers united against autocratic leaders attempting to cut their pay. The battery went through a series of name changes as the National Guard tried to consolidate and evaluate regiments. On December 17, 1881, the name was changed to 1st Battery. The battery served the state in Brooklyn during the Motormen's Strike in January 1895. The motormen and conductors of the Brooklyn Rapid Transit Company trolley car lines were given long hours of labor for low wages. Marches and a riot resulted. The guard was sent in to bring order.

In 1912, the battery tumbled through transitions. The New York State Militia had served during the Mexican War, Civil War and Spanish-American War under the governor, who was the commander-in-chief, and his appointed adjutant general. Things had begun to change in 1898 when the New York National Guard, under a new military law championed by New York Governor Frank Swett Black (1853–1913), was changed to a division under a major-general instead of an adjutant general. The governor was still the commander-in-chief. Major-General Charles Roe was the first major-general, serving until his retirement on May 1, 1912. On April 16, 1912, Major-General John Francis O'Ryan (1874–1961) took his place as the second major-general to lead the New York Division. O'Ryan had enlisted at age 23 as a private in the National Guard while attending New York University. He became an attorney in 1898 while continuing his service and attended the Army War College, graduating in 1914 with the highest grade point average recorded up to that point. O'Ryan had served as a captain of the 1st Battery, Field Artillery in 1907, and then as a major in the 2nd Battalion, Field Artillery in 1911 prior to accepting the commission as major-general of the New York National Guard. The division did not have all of its units at that early stage.[9] Major-General O'Ryan had been appointed to this particular field artillery regiment prior to his new role as division commander. The transition in leadership accounts for some of the reshuffling that happened within the 1st Field Artillery Regiment during this period.

In 1912, the 1st Regiment, Field Artillery, was organized from the 2nd Battalion composed of Batteries D, E and F, with a Separate Battery A, on May 28, 1912. On October 26, 1912, Battery A, located in Syracuse, was detached and became a separate battery. Batteries A, B and C had been attached to the 2nd Field Artillery. At the same time Battery A was detached, the Headquarters of 1st Battalion, 1st Field Artillery, with Batteries A, B and C, was transferred into 1st Field Artillery. It was renamed the 1st Battalion. Battery C, located in Binghamton, was then detached and designated a separate battery on November 26, 1912. The new Battery A was also detached and designated as Separate Battery B on December 16, 1912. Two additional batteries formed from Battery B were organized within 1st Field Artillery Regiment to replace the missing Batteries A and C, now detached.[10] The remaining batteries were located in New York City.

The year 1913 brought still more changes. On May 19, 1913, Battery E, 2nd Field Artillery was detached from that regiment and transferred to the 1st Field Artillery as Battery A, 1st Field Artillery. A new battery was formed at the same time to be Battery B. Prior to 1916, these batteries were moved and reshaped every few months. If a battery did not attain its objective, it was dropped or shifted until it did.

The 28-year period between the Spanish-American War (1898) and World War I (1914–1918, with our involvement beginning in 1917), was relatively short. During that period the military made some much needed changes to bring itself into the modern age of warfare. Reorganization and evaluation of America's protection needs would go on with the establishment of the Peekskill Camps for summer regiment training, and Pine Camp for training of the New York State Militia. Maneuver camps such as Pine Camp instructed men in the use of arms in both theory and practice.

Many European powers had not looked upon the United States as a serious military threat, since they had not adopted the modern tactics which many European countries already had in place. This began to shift, however, with the birth of the arms race. Countries moved to enlarge their armies and navies. Experiments were held with more deadly weapons, stronger guns and, in some countries, the use of chemicals. The United States had been largely focused on self protection. It sought first to strengthen its navy to defend the coasts and on coastal artillery. The navy had been successful during the Spanish-American War. The building of the Panama Canal across the Isthmus of Panama had been begun in 1881 and would be completed in 1914. This 48-mile channel would offer United States Navy ships more freedom of movement between the Atlantic and Pacific Oceans. Naval bases would be set up in places like Hawaii, annexed in 1898. On the other hand, the army desperately needed to make a number of technological changes. Rifles and artillery needed updating; hand arms were difficult to use. The manually operated Gatling Gun of 1866 needed to be replaced with rapid-fire machine guns. Unfortunately, Congress only approved enough money for a limited number of machine guns for the Regular Army, plus a few for the National Guard. In 1916 they would finally vote for $12 million for machine gun procurement, but the War Department did not spend the money until 1917 because they were undecided upon which weapon would best serve their needs.[11]

The military also began to look at sanitation. During the Philippine-American War many men had died in the Philippines of disease. It became a top priority. Antibiotics were not yet available; so the focus was on preventative care. Health and fitness were encouraged during this period. Methods of training shifted as well. Major-General O'Ryan believed in Spartan-type training for his men to condition them both physically and psychologically for the difficulties of warfare. His goal was to move away from the ceremonial functions of the National Guard to create men capable of endurance under pressure during war.

The Militia Act of 1903, known as the Dick Bill, after the sponsoring senator, had separated the state militia into two units: the Organized Militia, known as the National Guard, and the Reserve Militia. Organized Militia would get state funding for training of their officers at army facilities; for army personnel to train enlisted National Guardsmen; for summer encampments in addition to the guard's regular weekend and weeknight training; and to update equipment. Reserve Militia were all men ages 18 to 45 in a given state. United States Senator Charles W. F. Dick, a major-general in the United States Army and member of the Ohio National Guard, and chair of the Committee on the Militia, was the sponsor. The National Guard was to be patterned after the Regular Army, and was to drill at least twice a month with its annual training periods. Legislation passed in 1908 and 1914 gave the President the right to decide the length of federal service for the National Guard and to appoint all officers of the guard while under federal service, with the consent of the Senate.[12]

Part of the reason for these changes was because the United States had begun to feel pressure at its southern border as trouble began brewing in Mexico in 1910. Francisco I. Madero, Jr., decided to run against 30-year Mexican dictator Porfirio Díaz who was quite old. Madero was very popular with the Mexican people, especially those in rural areas, so Díaz had him put in jail until the election was final. Madero fled to the United States and called for a revolution in November of 1910. Back in the mid–1800s, the United States had been embroiled in the Mexican War. United States soldiers had occupied Arizona, California and New Mexico. The Treaty of Guadalupe Hidalgo was signed in February of 1848, ending that war. As part of the treaty, Mexico gave the United States California, Nevada, Utah, most of Arizona, parts of Colorado, New Mexico and Wyoming. Mexico recognized Texas down to the Rio Grande as part of the United States and was given $15 million for the exchange. In the Gadsden Purchase of 1853 the United States also bought southern Arizona and New Mexico. The 1910 revolution meant unrest at the United States' southern border in areas heavy with Mexican populations resentful of the Anglos. The Unites States government was understandably concerned.

In 1911, Mexico was still in the midst of internal conflict. President William Howard Taft (1857–1930) attempted to strengthen the boarder patrols during the summer, concentrated mainly at San Antonio, Texas. He sent about sixteen thousand troops to Texas in April of that year. They were led by Major-General Leonard Wood. They were called the Maneuver Division and ordered to train and prepare for possible problems with Mexico. In May, Díaz was finally forced from office. By June, Madero was elected president, and the Maneuver Division was disbanded by August 7, 1911.

The Stimson Plan was then created by the Secretary of War, Henry L. Stimson, which divided the United States into Eastern, Central, Southern and Western Departments. Each department was assigned Regular Army units along with a number of National Guard units from at least 32 of the states. The Coastal Artillery was re-organized into three units as well: Northern Atlantic Coast Artillery District, Southern Atlantic Coast Artillery District, and Pacific Coast Artillery District.

On February 19, 1913, the new Mexican president Francisco Madero was arrested and forced to resign by General Victoriano Huerta (1850–1916). On the 22nd Madero was assassinated and General Huerta declared himself the leader. Civil War erupted as Huerta's forces battled those of General Venustiano Carranza (1859–1920), a constitutionalist and state governor, and Pancho

Villa (1878–1923). Madero's followers wanted Carranza to take Madero's place. Villa's military group, called the "Division of the North," took control of the mountains of northern Mexico. Newly-elected United States president Woodrow Wilson (1856–1924) and his administration sided with Carranza. They felt that Heurta had taken power in a corrupt manner. The United States instituted an arms embargo and the Texas border was strengthened. About 7,000 officers and men from the United States Army served along the border.

In early 1914, Wilson lifted the arms embargo against Mexico in order to assist Carranza. United States Navy warships had been protecting the Mexican oil field, and were stationed at the ports of Tampico and Veracruz. On April 9, sailors from the U.S.S. *Dolphin* went ashore at Tampico for supplies. Huerta's troops arrested them and detained two men. Things became tense when Huerta refused to give a formal apology by way of a twenty-one-gun salute as requested by the United States flag ship and instead requested the salute be done for him. President Wilson ordered the United States Navy Atlantic Fleet to the Gulf Coast to strengthen the existing ships and occupy the city of Veracruz. Navy men held and administered the city of Veracruz for several months.[13] A German ship, delivering arms to Huerta, was due in port on April 21. The United States seized the guns. Carranza's forces occupied Mexico City and Huerta was forced to leave the country.

By September, divisions were occurring between Carranza and former supporter Pancho Villa. Francisco "Pancho" Villa was named Rancho de la Coyotada at the time of his birth on June 5, 1878. He grew up on a large hacienda at del Rio Grande in the state of Durango where he had seen the discrepancy between rich land owners and poor workers first hand. His father, Agustin Arango, and mother, Maria Micaela Arambula, worked a portion of the ranch as sharecroppers. His father died when he was just five years old. Villa had four siblings. In September 1914, Villa published his *Manifesto for the Mexican People* which went against Venustiano Carranza as the first chief of the revolution. At 180 lbs. and light complexion, Villa had a thick mustache with dark hair and a "winning" smile. He "married" a number of girls and had many children by them. He wore bullet holsters across his chest, and donned a Mexican sombrero, while carrying a long rifle and sitting atop his black horse. He was a dashing figure to many Mexicans. He had controlled Chihuahua for two years during the Mexican Revolution. That area had a number of rangers and cowboys. Pancho Villa, now against Carranza, began to accumulate followers along with the radical Emiliano Zapata. Zapata had wanted Madero to distribute the large estate lands to the poor peasants. He influenced the south. Because the United States supported Carranza, Pancho and Zapata began a series of small raids across the border into United States territory. There was a very real potential for war with Mexico, until Europe began to erupt.[14]

The Great War, now called World War I, began in Europe on June 28, 1914, with the assassination of both Austria's Archduke Franz Ferdinand and his wife, Sophie, by Gavrilo Princip (1894–1918) in Sarajevo, Bosnia and Herzegovina. Princip was just a teenager, but Ferdinand was heir to the Austro-Hungarian Empire.[15] The empire linked Princip to a Serbian terrorist organization and used that as a reason to declare war on Serbia. The Russians were in an alliance with Serbia and rushed in to help the Serbs. Germany was in an alliance with the Austro-Hungarian Empire and declared war on Russia and France. The system of alliances became complex. The Germans invaded France in August of 1914, crossing through Belgium and Luxemburg. Under what was called the Schlieffen Plan, the Central powers, those linked with the Austro-Hungarian Empire, swept into France from the north in a surprise attack, and then also invaded from the east. Belgium tried to resist, but the forces against them were very great. The Central powers sought control over the coal and iron mines of their neighbors. Great Britain then declared war on Germany and partnered with France to repel the invasion. The war spilled into European colonies in Africa, Asia and the Middle East. The Central powers in 1914 were made up of those countries which supported the Austro-Hungarian Empire. Germany, Bulgaria and the Ottoman Empire joined them. France, Britain, and Russia supported Serbia. They were called the Allies. More nations joined the Allies but not all sent troops. Nations like Belgium, Serbia, Montenegro, Japan, Italy, San Marino, Romania, and Portugal would all be part of the Allies by 1916. More countries would join them in 1917.

The United States, however, tried to keep its distance between 1914 and 1917. Americans were of differing European origins, and it was difficult to determine which way the public would go. The United States, in an attempt to help both the French and German citizens who were starving due to blockages, developed trade using her farms and factories. To stop the United States from supplying the Germans, the British and French mined the North Sea, but agreed to pay the United States for material.

During 1914–1917, the 1st Field Artillery Brigade of the 12th Infantry had its armory at 1988 Broadway in New York City. The armory had been built between 1889 and 1892 and would be razed in 1929. The location was between 67th and 68th Streets near what is now Lincoln Square, just north of Lincoln Center. In 1915, the New York National Guard Field Artillery used the Army Field Artillery School at Tobyhanna, Pennsylvania, for target and field artillery firing. The Tobyhanna Artillery Target Range, in Coolbaugh Township, Monroe County, Pennsylvania, had been designed between 1912 and 1913 to service both army and National Guard in the northeast. The isolated broad rocky area was home to a permanent camp. The day for enlisted men ran from 5:15 a.m. to 6:15 p.m. Officers trained until 9:30 p.m. Since

Major-General O'Ryan had been an artilleryman, he made sure the artillery under his command had sufficient army training under the new guidelines. National Guard members fired alongside the Regular Army men, and both officers and non-commissioned officers attended the school of instruction there.[16] He also began his own training of officers prior to the President of the United States' call for troops, knowing that the guard might very well be called to serve in the near future.

Everyone in the United States was closely watching Europe. An added danger came with the German U-boats prowling the shipping lanes. "U-boat" was a shortening of the German Unterseeboot (under sea boat). On May 7, 1915, a U-boat sank the *Lusitania,* an English passenger liner. Over 1,000 civilians were killed, 128 of which were Americans. American ships were also sunk by the Germans. America still tried to remain neutral, although it was becoming more difficult. England and Germany had been vying for supremacy of the seas for some time, but the U-boats were changing naval warfare. Then, the Germans used gas against the British at the second Battle of Ypres in the spring of 1915. It would change the face of warfare forever.

CHAPTER TWO

The Mexican Punitive Expedition (June 1916–February 1917)

While keeping a close eye on what was happening in Europe, America was still experiencing troubles with Mexico. In June of 1915 the United States had about 486 officers and 14,354 men near the border, and had stopped a German shipment of guns in 1914 to Carranza's enemies. By October 19 the United States officially recognized the government of Venustiano Carranza. Pancho Villa took offense at these actions, seeing it as a personal insult to himself and his followers who were set against Carranza. Villa's followers, called Villistas, sought retaliation for the interference of the United States in Mexican politics. Villistas began attacking American property and citizens in northern Mexico. Pancho Villa also led raids on a number of border areas belonging to the United States which largely involved stealing cattle. His men preyed on those who were isolated.

On January 6, 1916, a resolution had been adopted by the United States Congress which listed President Wilson's "precautionary measures" with the intent "to protect American lives and property."[1] Before it could be enacted, however, Villa's next moves pushed the United States into a more formal position. Engineers from the American Smelting and Refining Company had been invited by the Carranza government to come to Mexico as American mines were reopened. On January 11, 1916, ten American employees of that company on their way from Chihuahua City to the La Cusi Mine were removed from a train near Santa Isabel in Chihuahua, stripped, and executed by the guerrilla forces under Pancho Villa. The murder caused great concern in America for the safety of those working in Mexico.

The 1916 border between the United States and Mexico had been divided into patrol districts. The Columbus District was under the command of Colonel Herbert J. Slocum, with his headquarters at Columbus, New Mexico. Columbus was a small town with only one hotel, a few stores, and a cluster of adobe houses. The total population of Anglos and Mexicans was only about 350. Camp Furlong, with the 13th United States Cavalry Regiment, was located there since September 1912. Slocum's forces included headquarters, machine gun troops, and seven rifle troops of the 13th Cavalry with a total of 21 officers and 532 enlisted men.[2] There were more military members than townsfolk. There had been numerous rumors in early March 1916 of a possible forthcoming raid, but disinformation given by paid Mexican informants led the officers to believe that Villa would simply surrender at Columbus. This was accepted as fact and those pointing to a coming raid were considered unreliable. Major-General Frederick Funston (1865–1917), Commander of the Southern Department, did try to strengthen vulnerable points in the area, but Villa arrived with a force of between 500 and 1000 men. He crossed into the territory, about 3 miles west of the border at 4 a.m. on March 9. His men looted the town. The 13th Cavalry repulsed the attack. In the end, there were 24 American casualties; 14 military, and 10 civilian. Of this number, 18 Americans died. Two troops of the 13th, under Major Frank Tompkins, pursued Villa south of the border for about 12 miles. The Villistas lost 100 men, and seven were wounded and captured. The town of Columbus had been burned, horses and mules stolen, as well as machine guns, ammunition, and merchandise.

Major-General Funston sent a telegram on March 9 to the War Department requesting more troops. President Wilson directed Secretary of War Newton Baker to organize a Punitive Expedition. They were given strict instructions in order to avoid a full scale war: capture Villa, prevent further raids, and have the utmost regard for the sovereignty of Mexico. A war plan was submitted on March 10 stipulating no occupation of Mexican cities or towns. The President of the United States sent the message, through his agencies, that the Mexican Punitive Expedition was to capture Villa "dead or alive." Major-General John J. Pershing (1860–1948) was put in charge of the military action, which was officially to begin March 14, 1916, though the actual start date was March 16.

John J. Pershing had distinguished himself during the Philippine-American War of 1899 that had directly followed the Spanish-American War of 1898. Filipinos had launched a revolution against Spanish rule, much as the Cubans had. The United States had sent about 11,000 ground troops to the Philippines to help them from 1901 to 1903. Pershing was sent to the Philippines to use his gifts in diplomacy to help stabilize the area, in his promotion to Brigadier-General. The United States had also interacted against German interests while in the Philippines, which would contribute to their adversarial relationship later.

Major-General Pershing was nicknamed "Black Jack." It may have originally been used as a derogatory title, referring to the "colored" unit he led; the 10th Cavalry of Buffalo Soldiers. Some scholars indicate his students at West Point gave him the name. He also had taught African Americans in a school near Laclede, Missouri. The name eventually became a point of pride for him. For the Punitive Expedition, Pershing led the 7th, 10th, 11th, and 13th Cavalry Regiments along with the 6th and 16th Infantry. Most of his officers were veterans of the Philippine War, as well as earlier Indian Wars. In early March 1916, they traveled south towards Mexico. The area into which they were going was largely unknown with no reliable maps and guides who often led poorly. The 5th Cavalry, 17th and 24th Infantry joined them, along with several other units. A total of 4,800 men crossed into Mexico. Pershing was under orders to respect Mexican sovereignty, but was hindered by resentful Mexicans along the way. It took a great deal of restraint on the part of the army to avoid additional conflicts. He reached Parral, 400 miles south of the border, but Villa escaped. There were minor skirmishes with small bands, but not with Villa's regulars.

The units tried to use new technology, such as airplanes, for the first time in a military action. The Curtiss JN-3 airplane, nicknamed Jenny after the "JN," was enlisted but ran into difficulties in the mountains. It could not achieve the altitude necessary, and there were no parts for repairs when it broke down. The automotive trucks also suffered from lack of parts. The roads in Mexico were mostly little more than trails. The few roads available needed to be rebuilt by the Army Corps of Engineers. As a result, Major-General Pershing largely used pack mules, horses and wagons to carry material, since the military was not given permission to use the Mexican railroad. Most of the military action took place on foot or horseback.

By the middle of March, the Army was 400 miles into Mexico. Their headquarters were set up in Colonia Dublán near the Casas Grandes River. The mountains were filled with Villa's forces. They were largely protected by the local citizens. The Americans did not continue deeper into Mexico, and the first battle was on March 29 at San Geronimo Ranch near Guerrero. The 7th Cavalry launched the last true cavalry charge in United States history. It was a five hour battle during which 75 Villistas were wounded or killed, and five Americans.

On April 12, 1916, 100 men of 13th Cavalry were attacked by 500 Mexicans near Parral. They were forced to retreat to a fortified village. Two Americans were killed, and six wounded. The Mexicans lost somewhere between 14 and 70 men. On April 22, Villistas at Tomochic fought the 7th Cavalry. The 7th Cavalry lost two men, with four wounded; about 30 Villistas were killed.

On May 5, the 11th Cavalry fought at Ojos Azules, killing 41 Villistas. The same day, Mexican bandits attacked Boquillas, as well as Glenn Springs, Texas. Sixty Mexicans crossed the United States border to Glenn Springs, Brewster County, Texas, looting stores and homes. The spring, located on the Glenn Draw, was an important source of water. A three hour battle was fought against them by a small force of American solders but buildings had been burned, and the general store and a local silver mine were robbed by the bandits. Four Americans were killed, one civilian and three soldiers, and two taken as hostages. Two Mexicans also were killed. The intruders were driven out. They were called Villistas, however some felt that the raiders were not all Villa's forces. A number of the members had been identified as Carranziatas, followers of Carranza, which made the situation more complex. These actions resulted in complaints by local Americans to the federal government.

All of these skirmishes, and the ones that followed, resulted in the National Guards from Texas, Arizona and New Mexico being called into service on May 8, 1916, by the Secretary of War. Because United States borders had been crossed, many felt that war was inevitable. There was a high level of alertness in the National Guard units as they patrolled their assigned territories. Throughout May and June, Pershing's troops in Mexico engaged in struggles and skirmishes, including being ambushed.

On June 3, Congress approved the National Defense Act in which the National Guard would take a double allegiance to both state and federal authorities. This expanded the usage of the guard for federal purposes. Most of the New York National Guard officers were already at the Infantry School of Application at Peekskill, New York, for training during May and June. All officers were sent there for a week of training by Regular Army personnel. Major-General John O'Ryan was there as well. There was a planned meeting for all of the commanding officers of the division called for June 19 to iron out an upcoming July maneuver.[3] The state assembly had appropriated $500,000 for mobilization costs on May 20, 1916, in anticipation of what they saw coming. On June 18, President Wilson formally called 110,000 National Guardsmen from the remainder states, and from Washington, D.C., to border protection duty. The call was received by the commanding generals of the Eastern, Central and Western Departments. They were instructed to not cross the border, but be a show of force, and to be on alert against bandit raids. In addition to the Villistas, the Mexican Army clashed with the Americans at Carrizal on June 21, 1916. The 10th Cavalry was nearly decimated. The unrest of events in Europe was the only thing preventing the United States from a declaration of war against Mexico.

New York State was to send to the Brownsville District, Hidalgo County, Texas, one full tactical division of three brigades with three regiments each of infantry. They would serve in what was nicknamed "Magic Valley." Brigadier-General James Parker was the District Commander. Once there, they were known as the 6th Division. There would also be officers with them from the Regular Army by order of the governor of New York including Colonel William C. McNair, Colonel Harry H. Bandholtz, Colonel Gordon Johnston, Colonel William N. Haskell, Colonel Daniel W. Hand, Lieutenant-Colonel George H. White, and Lieutenant-Colonel William Welsh with others additionally serving on temporary duty. The headquarters of the division included 1st Brigade New York Infantry with the 7th, 12th, and 14th Infantry; 2nd Brigade with the 1st, 23rd, and 71st Infantry; and 3rd Brigade with the 2nd, 3rd, and 74th Infantry. The Brigade Field Artillery was made of the 1st, 2nd, and 3rd Field Artillery and would be called, respectively, 1st Regiment of New York Field Artillery, 2nd Regiment of New York Field Artillery and 3rd Regiment of New York Field Artillery once at the border. The division also included 1st Cavalry; Squadron A and Machine Gun Troop; 22nd Engineers; and 1st Battery, Signal Corps. The accompanying trains included the Military Police, Ammunition Train, and Supply Train. The Sanitary Train included the Headquarter Ambulance Company with 1st, 2nd, 3rd, and 4th Ambulance Companies. The Headquarters Field Hospital included 1st, 2nd, 3rd, and 4th Field Hospital. The full New York 6th Division had a total of 15,289 officers and men assembled, but they were still under full strength. The men were told to assemble in uniform on June 19. The mobilization center was supposed to be at Camp Whitman on the Green Haven tract by the state farm in Dutchess County. The plan had the men assembling locally and then transferring to Green Haven to be equipped and trained, but the urgency of getting troops to the border meant that many units assembled near their armories and then entrained directly to Texas. The engineers had been busy mapping and designing water systems at Camp Whitman. Individual regiments were already doing rifle practice at Peekskill and marching thirty miles to Camp Whitman prior to the call.

By June 23, the National Guard units were to be transferred to the Mexican border, as soon as they were fit for field service. Recruits were accepted, with about half of the enlisted men who entered that conflict having had no former service or training. The commanders had limited experience as well.[4] Recruits were to come with hair cut very short, bathed and with clean underwear. Men were allowed light hand baggage with toiletries, two towels, six handkerchiefs, and two changes of underwear with the understanding that the civilian clothes would be sent home after they were in uniform. No suitcases were allowed but things could be bundled. They could also bring postcards or stamped envelopes for their family communication.[5]

It is interesting to note that the letter sent by the New York State governor stipulated "organizing *militia* to be employed in the service of the United States." They were to "assemble forthwith at their respective home stations." The older name was still the more familiar, though now largely forgotten. Major-General Funston liked the idea of using the new National Guard for this mission. He felt that because officers in the guard were paid $500 a year, then considered a large sum, they would attract more competent men. He chose the New York Division's location for strategic reasons. They were to protect the area from raids on the railroad line; at Hidalgo there was a ferry which ran to Reynosa, Mexico, which needed coverage; irrigation pumping stations used for agriculture like the one at Madero, Texas, needed protection; and there was an old military road along the border which could be used if the conflict escalated. Men were quickly mustered into the service of the United States. There was little warning, and the units did not even have the proper forms to fill out for requisitions. Correspondence to and from division and headquarters took 10 days.[6]

An allotment of $8.33 had been made for clothing for each man for the New York National Guard, which was adequate, but there was no provision made for the increase in the amount of soldiers needed to secure the border. New York State had excess funds for the minimum strength National Guard, but not enough for war strength. Clothing and equipment were also not stored in New York, but at the Federal Supply Depot in Philadelphia, Pennsylvania. Three years prior to this, Major-General O'Ryan had requested supplies be sent from government depots and arsenals to mobilization camps so that in an event of an emergency it would be accessible. The request had not been met and this resulted in delays and excessive inventory assignments. Shipments were often sent to the wrong location and property was lost. The olive drab woolen uniforms worked well in colder climates, but there was not enough olive drab cotton or khaki issued for the 120 degree climate of summer in Texas. The cotton uniforms had been discontinued in 1914, and there was a scramble to re-issue them.[7] The uniforms finally came in boxes.

When the division was called, the 1st Field Artillery Regiment, in the 12th Infantry New York National Guard, had its armory at 1988 Broadway in New York City. The regiment had outgrown its facility and with the large number gathered it necessitated the use of the city parks for assembly prior to departure. The maximum enlistment strength for a battery of the light field artillery at the time was set at 171, with 1,128 for a regiment. With all of its batteries, the regiment only had 35 officers and 755 men.[8] It needed to be brought up to strength quickly, and men were recruited.

Lieutenant-Colonel Merritt H. Smith (born May 21, 1862) would be in command of the entire 1st New York Field Artillery Regiment at the border until Colonel Henry H. Rogers was able to arrive from Japan on July 22, 1916.

Rogers, unfortunately, arrived in poor health and would later need an extended leave of absence. Colonel Rogers had served in the 22nd Engineers and on staff of the 1st Brigade before becoming an artilleryman. Engineering was helpful to the work of the artillery. Rogers had served as an adjutant in the 1st Field Artillery and as a battery commander. He called himself an industrialist in civilian life, but was also heir to his father's vast Standard Oil fortune. His family was close personal friends of people like Mark Twain. Lieutenant-Colonel Smith, in civilian life, was the chief engineer of the New York City water supply. These professional skills would serve the regiment in their duties at the border.

There were two battalions in the 1st Field Artillery Regiment. The 1st Battalion was commanded by Major Charles Robert Seymour and was composed of Batteries A, B, and C. Battery A was commanded by Guido Fridolin Verbeck with 1st Lieutenants William Henry Thomas and Irvine A. Williams, and 2nd Lieutenant Richard J. Bush. Battery B was commanded by Captain Walter Cecil McClure with 1st Lieutenants James Harrison Giles, and William Peter Welsh.[9] Battery C was commanded by Captain Charles Gray Blakeslee with 1st Lieutenants Arthur Edward Kaeppel, Stelle Wotkyns and Albert James Sinnock, and 2nd Lieutenant Philip B. Weld. The 2nd Battalion with its three batteries was commanded by Major James Edward Austin. Battery D was commanded by Captain Sylvester Simpson with 1st Lieutenants Frederick Jacob Koch and Fred A. Petersen, and 2nd Lieutenants John Farr, Jr., and Henry B. Stimson. Battery E was commanded by Lieutenant-Colonel John Thomas Delaney and Captain Robert Law Russell with 1st Lieutenants Channing Rust Toy and Matthew S. Weir, and 2nd Lieutenants Harold LeRoy Whitney and John W. Pulleyn. Battery F was commanded by Captain George Billings Gibbons with 1st Lieutenants Francis P. Gallagher and Harold Lawson, and 2nd Lieutenants Edwin S. Bettleheim and James Park. The Battery Headquarters Company had Captain James H. Kenyon with 1st Lieutenant Walter E. Hegeman. The Battery Adjutants were Captains Benjamin Van Raden and Arthur W. Hofmann. Supply Company was commanded by Captain Clarence Gayler Michalis with 1st Lieutenant William James Volkland. The chaplain for the regiment was 1st Lieutenant Herbert Shipman.

The 2nd New York Field Artillery Regiment was commanded by Colonel George A. Wingate with Lieutenant-Colonel Franklin Harrington Hines and Major DeWitt Clinton Weld, Jr. It initially had 38 officers and 627 enlisted men. The 3rd New York Field Artillery Regiment would be commanded by Lieutenant-Colonel John D. Howland with Major Louis Henry Eller. It was newly formed for this service at the border from the 65th Infantry of Buffalo, New York. They used the 4.7-inch Howitzer guns. They would not be sent to the border until October, at which point they had 39 officers and 646 men.[10]

The Clerk of Battery F, 1st New York Field Artillery Regiment busy at work making reports on the regiment in Texas (courtesy Andrew B. Rankin, Jr., Collection).

The combined Field Artillery Brigade of the 1st, 2nd and 3rd Regiments New York Field Artillery would train under Brigadier-General William S. McNair of the Regular Field Army once they reached their assigned post. Brigadier-General McNair had been a classmate of Major-General John F. O'Ryan at the Army War College between 1913 and 1914. O'Ryan specifically chose McNair to train the artillery regiments due to his gifts in this area. McNair was known to have a great deal of common sense, was considered fair, and had a "cool, quiet temperament."[11] Major-General O'Ryan, at age 42, was the youngest divisional commander to lead his division all the way through the Great War. In civilian life, he practiced law in New York City. His intelligence was continually reflected in the way he prepared his men.

In the fall of 1916, Private Drew Rankin, a member of Battery F in the 2nd Battalion of the 1st New York Field Artillery, published an article for *The Owl* newspaper of Long Island, New York, about his service on the Mexican border. He had joined the National Guard in 1915. The article was a long piece broken up into sub-sections. In the first section, titled "THE CALL," he detailed his experiences on Monday, June 19, 1916, when he read President Wilson's declaration calling out the militia while riding on the train. The National Guard had been mobilized to rush to the southern border. Members of the 1st New York Field Artillery Regiment headed for the armory, arriving at 3:00 p.m. By 6:00 p.m. the cannon and ammunition carriages were parked behind division headquarters.[12]

The New York National Guard was so large that they could not use the camp at Peekskill as a mobilization center which was why Camp Whitman was being developed. Peekskill only fit about 1/8th of the division. Instead, the division was spread out during the mustering-in process. The Municipal Building in New York City became division headquarters. They also worked with the Eastern Department Headquarters on Governors Island under Major-General Leonard Wood. Major-General Wood is credited with having helped them cut through many cumbersome government regulations which would have made it impossible for them to have prepared in time. The 3rd Regiment of Infantry was camped at Pelham Park; members of the 2nd New York Field Artillery Regiment, based in Brooklyn, used Prospect Park; the 1st Regiment of Cavalry was on the Bliss Estate in Bay Ridge; the Coast Defense was nestled in their armories and set to do joint training exercises at Fort H. S. Wright in New York. In addition, a battery of engineers was sent to the Belvoir Tract in Virginia for field service; a machine gun regiment was sent to Fort Ethan Allen in Vermont; and a number of regiments, including Troops A and B, Cavalry and the 1st New York Field Artillery Regiment, were stationed at Van Cortlandt Park in the Bronx.

The 1st New York Field Artillery was tented at what was called "Camp

Some of the horses given to the artillerymen in the New York Division by the army were wild. They needed to be branded, shoed and broken-in. Six to eight horses were needed to pull one field gun (courtesy Andrew B. Rankin, Jr., Collection).

Van Cortlandt" for the first ten days following the president's call to muster. According to Lieutenant William P. Welsh, a member of the regiment, the B, D, E, and F batteries of the 1st Field Artillery and members of the 2nd Field Artillery were spread across the polo field, which was the most attractive part of the park. A and C left later from Camp Whitman. At the park there were many spectators watching the assembly process which was frustrating to the men. They seemed to trip over the gawkers.[13]

On June 20, the 69th Infantry and two battalions of engineers were sent to Green Haven, New York. They cleared the land and set up a water system there. It was to be used later for summer maneuvers. Meanwhile, on June 21, information and guidance was given to the newer recruits. Many soldiers took the newly established oath to both state and federal authorities instituted by the National Defense Act of June 3, 1916. The new recruits did not have uniforms, so they largely trained in street clothes with street shoes.

The biggest hindrance to training was the lack of horses. In ordinary times the division only had enough for the units to share during drills. The same horses that pulled the 1st Battery into mobilization were needed for each of the three other batteries, Headquarters Division, and Hospital Corps. They only had enough horses for each unit to do their individual night drills using the same animals, and the call to action revealed this major shortfall. Field artillery had to have horses to move their caissons and guns. The National

The 1st New York Field Artillery Regiment, 6th Division, New York National Guard, traveled on this train to McAllen, Texas. They were stationed there during the Mexican Punitive Expedition in 1916 (courtesy Andrew B. Rankin, Jr., Collection).

Guard did not have authority to order horses for this assignment, so additional horses were ordered by the federal government. Some of the horses were said to have been "seized from a shipment intended to go to another government," although which government was not specified.[14] The horses were unloaded at piers near 125th Street and 130th Street on the Hudson River but they were far from tame. It took six men per horse to lead them down the pier. Cowboys accompanying the horses helped with the process, but it still resulted in a mass of confusion as the frightened animals bucked and tried to bolt. Some kicked and jumped on passing cars and the majority of them, some 80 percent, were ultimately rejected by the army. The rest had to be branded, shoed and broken-in at Van Cortlandt Park, before being used. Mules were also put into service to pull the heavy artillery.[15]

Lieutenant William P. Welsh commented that the government had purchased the horses from the "Northwest" and they were unloaded in New Jersey first, and then ferried across the river and herded onto the piers. They were then to be moved from the pier to the park by guardsmen. Each battery was represented at the pier, and a man was assigned to each horse to halter them and lead them away, with the unexpected results listed above. He added that some of the horses had caught influenza and some had distemper. Most of the field artillery's time at Van Cortland Park was spent breaking-in, watering, feeding, and grooming horses. The horses were later tied to a picket line and

The 1st New York Field Artillery Regiment field guns were loaded onto and off of the train on planks of wood (courtesy Andrew B. Rankin, Jr., Collection).

harnessed. Major William R. Wright of Squadron A, Cavalry, also at Van Cortland, commented that the horses often broke free and had to be continually returned. Welsh stated that three months later when they were reviewed by General Funston in Texas, the only comment Funston made was on the "wonders" the men had done with those horses.[16]

On June 26, the soldiers participated in long muster-in rolls. Many of them lacked even elementary military training. There was an endless grind of paperwork and compiling of inventories. Officers complained that they needed to address battle plans and the sudden expansion of their regiments with untrained recruits, instead of spending all their time filling out papers for the government.[17] The government insisted that every piece of equipment had to be accounted for. On June 27, army medical staff examined the troops and rejected only three members of the 1st New York Field Artillery Regiment. Physical exams were supposed to include vision, hearing, teeth, and diagnosis of disabilities, but authorities complained that that full of an exam required at least 10 minutes per person to complete properly, and there was only one regular medical officer. The exams would have taken twenty days if done thoroughly with that many men. So corners were cut.

A June 28 telegram had been sent requesting the formation of the 3rd Regiment of Field Artillery. It was quickly formed. Colonel Daniel W. Hand from the 65th Infantry in Buffalo was given this assignment as he was also a

The horses needed to be watered, fed and exercised each day on the trip to Texas. This stop was at Ennis, Texas (courtesy Andrew B. Rankin, Jr., Collection).

captain in the Regular Army. Hand organized the 3rd New York Field Artillery Regiment from members of the old 65th Infantry Regiment. With so many guardsmen leaving, the state of New York needed substitutes to fill in for those guardsmen called into federal service. The new recruits were to be used largely as depot units to protect utilities and the state's water supplies from possible acts of sabotage by enemies of the United States. Recruitment began right away in earnest.

On June 28 at 4 p.m. the tents of Batteries B, D, E and F 1st New York Field Artillery were taken down and the "green" horses were packed in box cars lined with hay at Yonkers, New York, along with the guns and caissons; old horses would be left behind.[18] Those batteries were the New York City batteries. Battery B left with the Hospital Corps. There were about six guns and caissons per flat car. The artillery was loaded and unloaded by being rolled onto and off of wooden planks. Mature horses were driven to Yonkers hitched to their guns and caissons. Automobiles were also loaded onto the flat cars. The men left at midnight. Their official entrainment is listed as June 29. The adjutant general for 1916 lists Batteries B, D, E, and F of 1st New York Field Artillery Regiment as having been mustered in on June 28 at Van Cortlandt Park. However, Major-General O'Ryan states that the entire 1st Field Artillery Regiment was federalized at the Plattsburgh Camp on that day.[19] Perhaps Batteries A and C were federalized in Plattsburgh since they were from upstate New York and at Camp Whitman. It seems likely they might have been there since those two regiments left for the border later, on July 9 and July 16 respectively. The 2nd Field Artillery Regiment also left New York in July. Since the 3rd Field Artillery Regiment was still newly forming, they were mustered in at Camp Whitman on August 5, 1916, and trained there by Captain Daniel W. Hand until October. They followed the other two artillery regiments by three months, but needed the additional training since they would be using different artillery pieces requiring different handling. By the time the artillery reached Texas, the 1st New York Field Artillery Regiment had 42 officers and 1,030 men; 2nd New York Field Artillery had 47 officers and 1,068 men; and 3rd New York Field Artillery would have 34 officers and 695 men.

The guardsmen of 1st New York Field Artillery 2nd Battalion were moved to a special slow moving train at Poughkeepsie on the New York Central line. The process of entrainment was organized by the assistant quartermaster, Captain James T. Loree, Q.M.C., who in civilian life was the general manager of the Delaware and Hudson Railroad Company. "The train consisted of nineteen cars; seven flat cars with guns, carriages and escort wagons, four cars of horses, two box cars full of supplies, one baggage car converted into a kitchen, one passenger car and four Pullman tourist cars, which are combination sleepers and day coaches."[20] Each man took their assigned berth and kept it tidy. As the 1st New York Field Artillery Regiment traveled, the men were awakened by villagers in upstate New York blowing whistles. They had stayed up all night

McAllen, Texas, was very rural in 1916, and a semi-tropical desert. It had just been incorporated in 1911. It had inadequate water, telephone and telegraph lines. All were improved by the New York Division. Bridges and canals were also constructed (courtesy Andrew B. Rankin, Jr., Collection).

to show their respect for the division passing through. The same happened in Syracuse and Utica. The train passed through the Midwest with little notice, as the local people had not been told about their coming. When they did come into a station, those present responded with thanks. It is important to remember that in 1916 there were only certain areas of the United States with train rails. In order to move from point A in New York to point B in Texas, the trains had to follow existing lines and make connections wherever possible.

The trip from New York took a total of eight days. Men wrote letters, played cards or read. They slept in their seats. The kitchen on the train was primitive. According to Welsh, "the stoves had to be taken down, reinforced and put up again at least once a day." Folding tables under the seats were set up for meals. The horses also needed to be watered, fed, and walked each day, so the train had to stop for those activities. It was not an easy process with untrained and tired animals.[21]

In San Antonio, the men of the 1st New York Field Artillery were greeted with "sandwiches and fruit presented by a ladies organization." However, three men of the regiment decided to see the Alamo without permission and the train left while they were gone. They found a car to take them to the next stop, where they were arrested. One of the fathers had to wire one hundred dollars to pay the fine.[22] All were said to be quite embarrassed.

The guns, baking in the open sun on the train flat cars, needed to be unloaded but were too hot to handle. Men wrapped grain bags around their hands to move them. The temperature registered between 115 and 120 in the shade (courtesy Andrew B. Rankin, Jr., Collection).

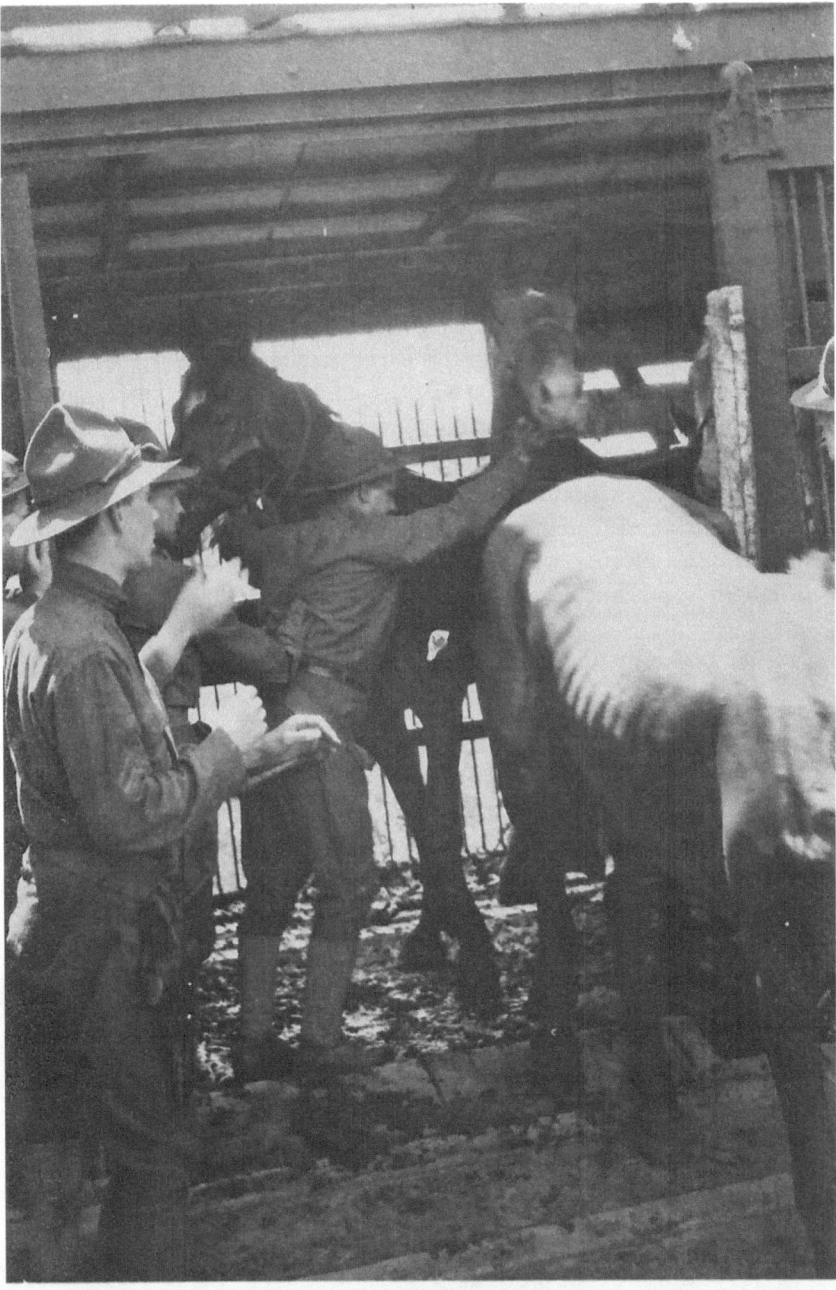

The 1st New York Field Artillery Regiment unloading horses from the hot train from New York at McAllen, Texas. Many of the animals were sick from the extreme heat and angry after the long ride (courtesy Andrew B. Rankin, Jr., Collection).

The New York 6th Division was placed in the Texas towns of Mission, McAllen and Pharr, with Harlingen as the supply base. Beginning from the west, Mission was five miles west of McAllen. McAllen was three miles west of Pharr, and Pharr was 32 miles west of Harlingen. These were towns parallel to each other, on the border, nestled along a single railroad track called the St. Louis, Brownsville and Mexico Railroad line. The track was flat with a gradual slope from Mission to the east and south.[23] The trains shrieked their whistles at night. There was a junction at San Benito with the San Benito and Rio Grande Valley Railway. Each camp was set up on a level plain in a grid fashion with pup tents low to the ground. Some members of the New York National Guard had arrived July 1 and began the daunting task of clearing brush and cactus for the camp, although it was still very rough when the regiments arrived. The 1st Ambulance Company and the 1st, 2nd, 14th, and 69th Infantry Regiments were at Mission. The 2nd Ambulance Company and the 3rd, 23rd, and 74th Infantry Regiments were at Pharr along with the 3rd Tennessee Infantry which had Colonel Cary F. Spence, United States Army, as commander. The Tennessee Infantry would later become part of the 30th Division, A.E.F., fighting side by side with the New York Infantry Division during World War I. The 6th Division Headquarters was in McAllen with the rest of the regiments, including the 1st New York Field Artillery Regiment.

The McAllen camp was ½ mile east of the railroad station on the south side of the track. It extended at a right angle from the Pharr-McAllen-Mission highway which ran south to the Rio Grande River. There were 10,000 men and 3,500 animals in the small town. An irrigation ditch, fed from the river,

The view of Camp McAllen from the train track (courtesy Andrew B. Rankin, Jr., Collection).

was located south of and parallel to the camp line. The encampment from north to south was as follows: 2nd Brigade under Brigadier-General Dyer with the 7th, 12th, and 71st Infantry Regiments; 1st and 2nd New York Field Artillery Regiments; 23rd Engineers; 1st Cavalry and Squadron A; Brigade Headquarters; Field Hospital; 1st Ambulance Company; and the Signal Corps on the eastern flank of the camp.[24]

Batteries D, E and F of 1st New York Field Artillery Brigade entered the desert country around McAllen at 11:30 a.m. on July 5, 1916. Battery B would follow the next day and Batteries A and C would join them on October 19. McAllen was only about six miles north of the Mexican border near the southern part of Texas near the Rio Grande River in Hidalgo County. To the southwest, near the Gulf of Mexico is Reynosa, Mexico. McAllen had just been incorporated in 1911. It was 1,540 miles from Washington, D.C., and 283 miles from the Texas capital. The weather was considered a semitropical desert, with about 26 inches of rain per year. A small population began living in the area in the mid–1700s, but it wasn't until John McAllen arrived in 1850 that the town began to develop. In 1904 it was formally established as West McAllen. Another site formed in 1907 was called East McAllen, and by 1910 they joined together, having about 150 residents. It was then just called McAllen. Hidalgo County had called itself the "Republic of Hidalgo" during the 19th century when it felt neglected by the state as cattle rustlers and bandits made their raids. Texas Rangers had been sent in. But, the evidence of bandits was everywhere along the border when the New York Division entered.

It was a rural area which was very hot. Most of the soldiers from New York had never experienced heat that intense before. It ranged in temperature during July from 112 to 120 degrees in the shade. Drew Rankin commented, "We felt as if we were on a frying pan."[25] They unloaded the horses and tied them to the picket line, watering and feeding them. The horses were not sheltered from the sun and later some members of the division would use their own money to protect them with canvas. Many of the horses were sick on arrival with distemper and under weight. They suffered greatly from the heat. Unfortunately, so did the National Guardsmen who arrived in wool uniforms. It took a while for cotton ones to be issued. And to make it worse, they then had to unload the artillery caissons off of the flat cars of the train on the Gulf Coast Line which had been sitting in the hot sun while the train spewed out "ear-splitting shrieks."[26]

The artillery pieces had to be moved about one mile south of the train station. It was the only train line, so they could not leave things until it became cooler. "The guns and caissons, which are made of armor plate steel, were so hot after their long exposure to the sun, that it is without exaggeration that I say they were too hot to handle with the bare hand, and that we were oblige

There was no shelter initially for the horses which stood in the heat at the picket line. The caissons were placed by them (courtesy Andrew B. Rankin, Jr., Collection).

to wrap empty grain bags around our hands before we could touch them."[27] Men were stripped to undershirts and some to the waist, and many were sunburned by day's end. All were sweating profusely with no time off for recovery.

The water in the camp was bad; warm and rust colored. "The final and most important step is the flavor, which is obtained by dissolving a piece of soap in the glass. Tastes differ here, some people liking more soap than others. Personally I find that half a cake is sufficient. Some of the fellows insist that the laundry soap must be used, but this is entirely unnecessary; toilet soap will do quite fine."[28] Obviously, the quality had to be improved. Additionally, the length of the pipes was inadequate to reach the entire camp. This had to be addressed right away; fortunately Lieutenant-Colonel Merritt H. Smith of the 1st Field Artillery was also the chief engineer of the water supply system for New York City. He diagnosed the problem. Captain Ernest F. Robinson of the 22nd Engineers was a hydraulic engineer and Major James M. Hutchinson of the 71st Infantry had done municipal construction. Together, they designed and installed a new system at minimal cost to the guard.[29] Water was sterilized with calcium hypochlorite, which had a strong chlorine scent. The 1st New York Field Artillery Regiment and Squadron A, Cavalry, dug their own wells and installed tanks with pumping systems to be independent of the town supply. Their water was a higher quality than what the town used.

Some of those labeled "Mexican" at McAllen were actually American Indian. Some were descendants of the Lipan Apache and Comanche. They spoke Tex-Mex, and little or no Spanish (courtesy Andrew B. Rankin, Jr., Collection).

The first few weeks were spent building the camps. The men arrived well disciplined but the work was miserable. They had to clear the burned cactus and underbrush before they could pitch their tents. The cactus often left them with sores.[30] The ground proved difficult. "The first inch or so is easy enough, then comes a foot or so of gumbo that is so rubbery that a mattock all but bounces when you hit it, and after that is hard pan that makes one think he is working in a quarry."[31] It was back breaking work under a tropical sun. The soil was a combination of clay and sand that had mineralized and often repelled water. The area had suffered a long drought prior to the arrival of the New York Division. The climate was extremely dry with a rainy season the end of June into August punctuated by thunderstorms and cloudbursts. At night it was cool or even cold. The vegetation was cactus with spines and thorns, giant pitahaya 50 feet tall, yuccas, mesquite, and agaves. There was very thin grass during the rainy season, but it was sparse. Lizards slithered about, and there were warnings about snakes, spiders, tarantulas, and scorpions in the division newspaper. The fear of infection was often repeated.[32] There were no floors for the tents initially and there were no cots for some time. The men had to sleep on their ponchos and blankets on the ground. Some used their own money to purchase floor boards and cots from local vendors. There were no screens for the kitchen and mess shacks initially either. Showers had to be built, though many used metal tubs and sprinkling cups. There were not a great number of mosquitoes, but they did breed quickly wherever there was standing water. The latrines were open and mosquitoes bred there as well as in any standing pools. Flies were abundant and everywhere.

It was unclear to the men just how long they would be in Texas. Rumors placed it into September, but the site appeared to many to be a permanent site for the army, due to the quality of the construction going on. Men of the various batteries were busy building showers and stalls. The telephone and telegraph wires were improved in the area. The Signal Corps had laid field lines and erected poles. The 22nd Engineers also repaired area roads, dug canals and laterals with ditches, built bridges, and mapped the area. The improved water mains, drainage ditches, permanent kitchens, two Y.M.C.A. buildings, and field hospitals all pointed to an extended duration.[33]

Logistics proved a problem, too, with roads not really adequate for trucks or airplanes, called "aeroplanes." There was a lack of parts for wagons, planes, and trucks which often were just left in disrepair. It was hot for the horses and they had little upon which to graze. The guard also needed horseshoers for the horses. The heat made the marches miserable for everyone with an inad-

A native home in McAllen, Texas, with the New York National Guard tents set up behind it (courtesy Andrew B. Rankin, Jr., Collection).

equate amount of water for travel. The field hospital filled with men suffering from dysentery and heat prostration. The division needed a base camp hospital with cots, but had to make do with men lying on stretchers or blankets. Those who were seriously sick were sent by train to the base hospital at Fort Sam Houston in San Antonio.

The local Mexicans were leery of the Americans at first and often gave misinformation. Relationships between the two governments were strained and there were many rumors of war. The American consuls in Mexico had been warned of that possibility. Even Major-General Funston felt it was inevitable. In addition, the area occupied by the New York National Guard in Mission, McAllen and Pharr had been in disputed territory between the United States and Mexico during the Mexican War of 1846 with the United States claiming the Rio Grande as the border and Mexico claiming the Nueces River.[34] Americans had set up ranches, but most of the population was part Mexican and part American Indian. Many of them spoke little Spanish, even though the division offered Spanish lessons and made the books readily available. Most of the citizens spoke "Mex," a dialect of Spanish often called Tex-

A typical "Mexican" style home in McAllen, Texas (courtesy Andrew B. Rankin, Jr., Collection).

Mex, which combines English and Spanish words. The Indians in the area were largely descended from Lipan Apaches who had fled Comanche from their territory in Colorado and New Mexico, and Comanche had followed them to southern Texas. The families were large with a main diet of goats' milk, tortillas and beans. The locals proved to be very skillful with tools. Some natives lived in huts and camps, but most lived in the brush.

The town was estimated by some as having about 500 "Americans" and about 1,500 "Mexicans." The Mexican section of town was said to be one of "misery and poverty."

> One place was about twelve by twelve feet and had an extra habitation in the form of a ragged piece of canvas stretched from a near by tree to the "house." 18 individuals huddled around a small fire. Most 'houses' consisted of one room with a bed in one corner. There were no chairs as people sat on the floor. No decorations like pictures hung from the walls, and no books. If an extra room is wanted they build some kind of a lean-to with thatched roof and sides. When they expect to stay in one place for any length of time they make a wall by weaving long poles basket fashion and plaster the outside with mud, which dries in the sun and becomes quite hard. Old pieces of tin are used for the roof, if they can get it, otherwise thatch is used. Donkeys and burrow are tied outside, and not allowed in the house. I don't know why; certainly not for sanitary reasons, for pigs, dogs and chickens have the run of the place. One house in particular has a little brown hen which may be seen nearly always perched on the foot of a brass bed [24].[35]

Coming from the New York area, a number of the men reflected astonishment at viewing a culture which lived on so little. They were apt to say people lived like animals, which showed a common misunderstanding of issues involved in poverty such as lack of education and opportunity. The American ideals of self improvement and industry seemed to clash with a people content to live as their ancestors had lived. The officers of the 6th Division did, however, make attempts to get to know the locals, visiting natives in their humble homes. For those who did, the experience would lead to greater understanding of others. Others merely complained about the braying of burros.

Although the National Guard troops mostly drilled and patrolled during their time at the border, on July 31 an American Soldier from another division and a United States customs inspector were killed at Fort Hancock, Texas. Another soldier was wounded. Three Mexicans were killed during the struggle and three were captured by Mexican government troops. Everyone was on high alert on the border with the very real threat of war hanging over them with the possibility of a "big push" into Mexico. Discipline was kept tight and the guardsmen on the border lived under very strict rules. Saloons were off-limits as a means to help curb venereal disease. They were part of the "G.O. 7." ruling. General Orders Number 7 stated that men were not allowed intox-

Field guns often were stuck in the mud after one of the frequent thunder showers. Learning how to free them was part of the process of training (courtesy Andrew B. Rankin, Jr., Collection).

icating liquor in any form on duty at the border during this expedition. They were not to have it in their possession at all. Military police were set up near saloons such as La Esmeralda, the main saloon in McAllen, and places of prostitution resulting in dissatisfaction by locals hoping to earn easy cash from the soldiers in exchange for these pleasures. The result was a very healthy military force with almost no signs of sickness or venereal disease.

The 6th Division trained new recruits at camp at the School of the Soldier. Members of the 1st and 2nd New York Field Artillery Regiments began training under Brigadier-General William S. McNair the second week, by which point other batteries had arrived, even though the field artillery range was not yet complete. Both battalion commanders of the 1st New York Field Artillery Regiment, Majors Seymour and Austin, taught alternating weeks of the Officer's Training School.[36] There was also a School of Instruction in Defense, and a school which taught the men how to assemble and disassemble their rifles and pistols. There was much to learn, including target practice with pistols over by the irrigation canal by McAllen where 50 targets were set up across the canal from the men. The division was limited to 100 rounds per rifle and 50 pounds of ammunition for each pistol or revolver.[37] There was also a range at Sharyland for the troops at Mission and one mile southeast of Pharr. They learned both slow and rapid fire. Machine gun units were trained at the Ordinance Depot at Harlington for several weeks.

There were a number of men in the regiments who had never even been

The horses needed to be harnessed prior to a regimental march. They worked in pairs on either side of a limber pole which pulled either caissons or field guns (courtesy Andrew B. Rankin, Jr., Collection).

on a horse before. They were city boys. Elementary exercises in horsemanship were offered. The majority arriving did not know how to use a 3-inch field piece either, although those who had enlisted earlier had used the guns before. It was hot work with the temperature registering between 114 and 120 degrees in the shade of the tents as they pulled guns and greased shells. Men also learned the importance of guard duty with river patrol and there were daily hikes in all directions, as well as mounted drills. The training for the entire New York 6th Division was intentionally intense with O'Ryan's favorite "Spartan-style" approach, meant to help the men endure the hardships of warfare. Most washing was done in metal tubs until the cold showers were complete. The goal was to strengthen these men both physically and psychologically so that they would be able to maintain their assignments under adverse conditions with little complaint.

The 1st and 2nd New York Field Artillery Regiments both used the 3-inch Model 1905 Field Gun made of nickel steel. It was a three-inch gun weighing 788 pounds at 7 feet in length. Its muzzle velocity was 1,700 feet per second and its maximum range was 8,500 yards. If it was elevated 15 degrees, then it only reached 6,000 yards. It had a continuous-pull firing mechanism which required no cocking. The gun was able to recoil 45 inches on its carriage which had wheels, an axle, trail and elevating mechanism. The 3-inch field gun fired 15 pound shells which could be explosive or filled with shrapnel. On average

The guns were apt to tip over if a corner was taken too quickly. Helping horses and drivers judge a proper turning radius was part of training (courtesy Andrew B. Rankin, Jr., Collection).

it could fire 15 rounds per minute, which was considered quick. The gun was the standard field piece of the United States Army until 1917, but there were only about 600 of them in total. It was considered a light field gun that would be phased out by the 1920s.

The carriage for the guns also had shields to protect the soldiers, ammunition carriers, road brakes and axle seats. The carriage weighed 2,520 pounds when loaded and was 60 inches wide and 45 inches long. The caisson was made of metal, except for the spokes and felloes of the wheels. When fully loaded with the gun, carriage and limber, it weighed 4,560 pounds.[38] The care and cleaning of the field pieces took a great deal of time. Every bit of dust and moisture had to be removed before it could be put away. Each piece was oiled, dusted, and cleaned with great care. Separate lubricants were used for different functions. Each part of the gun, as well as its separate field telescope, required a different type of oil depending upon its usage. Some were light oils and some heavy. Shells were also greased. Leather horse harnesses and bits also needed special cleaning, as did horse blankets, using specified soaps for each. Maintaining this equipment was all part of the men's day.

The horses needed to be watered and fed, groomed, and trained in pulling heavy field pieces by the designated men known as drivers. The off lead harness went on the front horse. The off wheel harness went on the horse pulling the field piece. They were teamed in pulling and needed to work together with other animals they did not initially know. They also needed to learn to turn slowly in wide circles to avoid tipping the field equipment behind them, and to travel in stifling heat over sandy and muddy ground on field hikes without stumbling. The first mounted review was held on July 23 after only a few weeks of drills.

The 1st New York Field Artillery Regiment had a long march on August 3, 1916, from McAllen to Sterling Ranch about nineteen miles away, then to La Gloria Ranch three miles further and back. Sterling Ranch was little more than a long flat desert but it had a water source which served as a type of oasis and the ranch owner rigged up a type of shower system for the soldiers. There was a bosque between the two encampments. The road leading to La Gloria was a wagon trail with dense groupings of cactus and mesquite. La Gloria was not a settlement. It initially had a broken windmill which was repaired by the division engineers so that it pumped about one and one-half gallons of water per minute, with a back-up portable four horse-power gasoline engine and a pump jack for auxiliary power. Standing water holes in the area were cleared of mosquitoes. Radio transmissions were made to headquarters during the marches via one radio platoon pack.[39] Men watched for snakes, wild cats and coyotes as well as stinging insects. An ambulance "motor car" also followed. Considering the heat and distance with little water, having medical assistance

All of the regiments had long forced marches and camped along the way. These were meant to train and harden the men and also to help the Supply Company learn how to provide for the men (courtesy Andrew B. Rankin, Jr., Collection).

was prudent. A number of the men did fall ill from the heat. Some units marched between 12:00 a.m. and 2:00 a.m. to avoid the issue. Most marched in the early morning and late afternoon. Four p.m. was a common time to start, marching until 7:30 p.m. Each formulated their own rest periods and use of water. War diaries kept by the officers provided much information about activities of the regiment.

In mid–August all infantry regiments had a 100 mile march covered over twelve days. The 12th Infantry also had a march on August 28, 1916, from McAllen directly west six miles to Mission, named after the ruins of the St. Peter's Novitiate Mission. They bivouacked and then marched north seven miles to Alton, north six miles to Sterling Ranch, and northwest three miles to La Gloria. Then they marched east three miles back to Sterling Ranch, then northeast ten miles through the dessert to Laguna Seca Ranch, still farther north six miles to Young's Ranch, back south six miles to Laguna Seca, southwest ten miles to Sterling Ranch, and directly east fourteen miles on a dusty road to Edinburg, which was the county seat and a small town. Like La Gloria, Laguna Seca had a windmill. Young's Ranch was a large ranch with space for grazing animals; there was a swimming hole there. The pigs there unfortunately gave some soldiers trouble as they marched into tents.

One day's rations and a change of clothes were carried in each 60 pound haversack for these extremely long marches. Each man wore their regular

In the photograph, one can see the driver on the "near" horse who also controlled the reins of the "off" horse next to him (courtesy Andrew B. Rankin, Jr., Collection).

equipment minus ammunition. They had instructions in individual cooking, route sketching, field orders, and the recording of things of military value. They marched between three and fourteen miles at a time in the heat, and they were instructed to take no "souvenirs" along the way. They were also to leave no evidence of their presence at the camp sites. Water was not to be wasted; it was rationed. Rifles were never to be placed on the ground when at rest; they were to be oiled, cleaned and piled at an appropriate place. Those riding on horses were told not to slouch, but to "sit squarely in the saddle." Each hike was to be done as though in enemy territory with an advance and rear guard. The humor writer of the *Rio Grande Rattler,* the 6th Division's newspaper at the border, joked in the first issue, "They told us this was going to be a 'punitive expedition' but for the life of us we can't think what we are being punished for."[40]

New York State pay for National Guardsmen had been $1.25 per day for a private, but the Regular Army pay was only $.50 a day. All pay was done in

The men learned field cooking on their marches. A number of men reportedly were proud of their newly learned domestic skills (courtesy Andrew B. Rankin, Jr., Collection).

coinage, no paper money. Officers were paid in gold. The enlisted men received a 50 cent piece; a corporal earned 70 cents instead of $1.40; sergeants earned $1 instead of $1.60; and 1st sergeants earned $1.50 instead of $2. Officers earned the same pay as the National Guard, but the state paid them 25 cents extra for each year of service. States were under federal authority at the border and men received federal pay. The states were under no legal obligation to make up the difference.[41]

The 1st New York Field Artillery Regiment members complained in August of having never been paid. They were supposed to get $15 a month, but had not seen any pay from June 19 to August 12. They would not receive pay until later in August. At 12 a.m. on August 17, the division thought they were under attack when they heard shots near the water troughs at McAllen half-a-mile away. The buglers sounded *Turn Out the Guard* and *To Arms;* everyone assembled and harnessed horses in rapid speed only to discover that members of the 2nd New York Field Artillery Regiment were celebrating their first pay check.[42]

A serious problem existed for married men; no provision had been made for the dependents of soldiers. This left those with children in a particularly

The marches during the summer months were almost unbearable with the excessive heat. The regiments usually marched in the morning and late afternoon and camped along the way. Some regiments marched between 12 a.m. and 2 a.m. (courtesy Andrew B. Rankin, Jr., Collection).

difficult position since they took a cut in pay while in service. Some civilian employers continued paying them while they were away, but others did not. Initially men were allowed to claim exemption from service due to having dependents, but so many flocked to claim that exemption that it was withdrawn. Mrs. Cornelius Vanderbilt, as chair of the Women's Auxiliary Committee, took on the task of trying to help families of servicemen who were at the border. She quietly funded the relief and enlisted others to the cause. Other private organizations also stepped in to assist. Mr. R. E. Horn of the First National Bank of McAllen also allowed officers to make advanced cash payments for four days before the bank had confirmation of funds.[43]

The army allowance at that time was $.07 per meal as compared to $.50 meals in New York. This was very low, and if the amount exceeded that, the captains had to pay for it out of their own wages. This resulted in a careful watch over expenses.[44] There were a number of complaints about the food. Some of the fresh meat spoiled on the way to camp in the extreme heat; quite a few lunches were composed of string beans, potatoes, and bread with jelly. Sugar seemed to be hard to find, as well as fruit and vegetables. New Yorkers discovered that they did not like Mexican beans. The men were often hungry and, due to the heat, craved lighter foods. Heavy meals contributed to diarrhea, which was a problem. Rations did improve over time.

The town did well during the soldiers' encampment there, although the soldiers tended to feel that the locals were "not friendly" by charging the highest prices possible.[45] Soldiers could still walk into stores and purchase what they needed. Film and cameras like the Eastman Kodak, could be purchased at the McAllen Drug Company on Main Street, a Rexall Store. The town had a Royal Ice Cream Parlor and the McAllen Creamery. C.P. Wright sold fatigue uniforms.[46] Men could buy fruit at D. Guerra and Sons three blocks west of Main Street, which advertised itself as being the nearest store to the McAllen camp. Soldiers could buy White Rock Mineral Water "from New York," Post Toasties Flakes sealed in wax paper, or Grape-Nuts Cereal, and wash it down with Welch's Grape Juice, specially ordered "from Westfield, New York." If they desired a meal, there were delicious pies at Delmonico Jr. Café next to the Commercial Hotel, perhaps following a lovely dish of chicken-a-la-king, planked steak, or a tasty ham sandwich. Helen's Palm Café was also frequented. The Amuseum Airdome Picture Theatre offered silent films, though the division had a type of circus tent in which films were shown. The Hammond Lumber Company, F. G. Crow Lumber, and Gregory and Cardwell Hardware stores prospered as the military constructed buildings and individual soldiers looked for items to improve their tent spaces. Eureka Laundry would take bundles of dirty clothing left at their office next to the division camp exchange and return them clean within three days, though most washed their own, deeming the

The men from New York suffered financial hardships during their term at the border. A private went from $1.25 a day New York National Guard pay to $.50 a day federal pay. No provisions were made for those with dependents. This unnamed cook above earned $38 a month under federal service at the border. In civilian life, he was the night chef at the Hotel Knickerbocker and earned $250 a month (courtesy Andrew B. Rankin, Jr., Collection).

facilities offered poor.[47] Extra blankets could be purchased at Zachry and Cawthon for $1.50. The ever-important military mail came via the McAllen Post Office, changing their regular 7,300 pieces of mail per month to 72,700 pieces of mail delivered by truck loads.[48]

When the men first arrived, they found the weather very changeable with frequent downpours. The locals swore that it was unusual. Water tended to gather in the low area at McAllen anywhere from 18 inches to 2 feet deep. When it rained, the west flank of the camp became a lake.[49] The men built dikes around their tents up to 18 inches high and then cut a deep trench from the center of camp to the irrigation canal. The 1st New York Field Artillery Regiment had higher ground for their camp than the rest of the brigades, perhaps because of their commander's expertise in water works.[50] This would prove a gift during the frequent rain storms. The weather was generally hot and humid, and then great dark clouds would send a brief downpour, followed by the sun coming out again, adding to the humidity. The soil was generally sandy and in some places soaked up most of the water quickly, but lower ground repelled the water and caused flooding. Everything became muddy. The rainstorms came on "suddenly in torrents, like the hardest thunder storms at home. This continues for about fifteen minutes and stops as suddenly as it commenced, and the sun is again shining as if nothing had happened. This happens several times a day, and is apt to happen at any time, not according

Camp McAllen after a thunderstorm. The soil in many areas repelled the water since it had mineralized. The division was hit with a gulf hurricane in August (courtesy Andrew B. Rankin, Jr., Collection).

to schedule, but always when it is least expected. And they say it never rains in Texas."[51]

A wind storm hit the division on August 5 and then on August 18 a Gulf hurricane. Nineteen sixteen was one of the most active hurricane and tropical storm seasons the United States has ever experienced. Eleven hurricanes and three tropical storms developed. Six of them were Category 3, and nine struck the United States at various locations from Texas to New England. When members of the 1st New York Field Artillery Regiment had arrived, on July 5, a Category 3 hurricane made landfall on the Mississippi coast. But this large Category 3 hurricane on August 18 landed at Brownsville, Texas, after crossing from the Caribbean Sea and Gulf of Mexico,[52] impacting the men directly. Both the 71st and 14th Infantry Regiments were on marches when the hurricane hit and it lasted for fourteen hours with 100 mile per hour winds. The 14th Infantry "stood and took it without shelter," meaning all their tents were taken down. The 71st found shelter, but it blew down the windmills at Laguna Seca.[53] All the telephone and telegraph lines were down in the district for four days. They had been warned about the coming storm via radio.

The men at camp in the towns tried to keep things from blowing away hunkered under their tents. Due to the efforts of the men, the division lost relatively little. Locals offered the drenched soldiers baths and places to recover. The official report on the storm found it necessary to state that the storm

View down Battery Street, Camp McAllen. These men of the 1st New York Field Artillery Regiment are doing cleaning at camp (courtesy Andrew B. Rankin, Jr., Collection).

postponed the marches by two days. Another serviceman stated that the combination of "tropical rains, deep mud, hurricanes blowing down tents, intense heat, choking dust, occasional cold and little water of poor quality ... would prove to be a great lesson in preparation for France."

In the midst of the weather issues, the division carried on its regular functions. On August 31, the 1st Brigade of 1st New York Field Artillery Regiment had a review at Jenning's Field. Between August and September, the entire 6th Division did field maneuvers from the division camps south to the Rio Grande River with simulated combat themes directed by Major-General O'Ryan on horseback. The division used 75,000 rounds of blank ammunition during these training events. These included repelling an invasion, retiring before a larger force, and defending a convoy. Some of the maneuvers also involved reinforcing a brigade and using a small force of cavalry and infantry to cover a larger force. The Rio Grande had some dangerous places along the river with quicksand where the river seeped underground. On either side of the river there were woods and willow thickets in places where natives build crude homes.[54] Irrigation canals had been cut into the muddy river on both sides prior to their arrival. Guard duty included careful patrolling of these areas as well as the many trails which ran south of the Military Road. The division set up eight detached posts covering 28 miles along the old Military Road. The line of resistance against a possible enemy covered a total of 52 miles along the river with armed patrols. Some groups also practiced crossing the Rio Grande near Hidalgo, just south of McAllen on the American side, and Reynosa on the Mexican side using a flatboat ferry. They had permission to do this from the Mexican government. The New York soldiers were delighted to be able to see real cowboys and Texas Rangers at Hidalgo.

A major epidemic hit the division at the end of August lasting until the middle of September. Paratyphoid "A" fever centered around the camp at Mission with 200 cases reported. The field hospital was not equipped for this massive epidemic. Severe cases had to be transported to the train station where those with high fevers made the hot and uncomfortable trip to the base hospital. Five men died from the disease. It was blamed by some on the irrigation ditch at Mission. Addressing illnesses would be a learning experience which would help the division later as they sought to avoid even greater threats.

To alleviate the misery of the heat and general boredom of the men, entertainment was offered. Each of the camps at McAllen, Mission and Pharr had an entertainment platform, which was elevated five feet and included lights. A prize ring was set up, with a piano in the corner covered by rough tent. Saturday night was the weekly sporting night. The chaplain at McAllen, Captain Herbert Shipman, organized the event. Major-General O'Ryan was a big fan of boxing, as were a number of the men. Prize fights were not yet legal in New

These horses are being watered at the Rio Grande River. The New York 6th Division practiced various scenarios of defense and offense by the river including repelling an invasion (courtesy Andrew B. Rankin, Jr., Collection).

York State. The most popular boxer at McAllen was Norman Selby of the 71st Infantry, nicknamed "Charles Kid McCoy."⁵⁵

The Y.M.C.A and Knights of Columbus had buildings at McAllen. At the Y.M.C.A. hut, the men could use stationery with its two American flags crossed behind a triangle. The return address on the stationery listed the Army and Navy Department of the International Committee Young Men's Christian Association with general office on 124 East 28th Street, New York, U.S.A. The hut also had magazines and books. Newspapers from New York were read with great interest, and sports were followed with eagerness. Soldiers played baseball, softball, football, soccer and some played bridge, chess or craps.⁵⁶ If a man had leave, he could hop on the Gulf Coast Lines and visit places like Corpus Christie for $10, swim in the gulf for $10, or visit San Antonio or Galveston for a few dollars. H.W. Pinnick was the general agent in the train's Passenger Department at McAllen. Considering their low pay, it took a while to be able to afford trips like that. Worship services also were offered each Sunday, and they were well attended.

New Yorkers like their newspapers and the 6th Division had their own called *The Rio Grande Rattler*. Major Franklin W. Waterbury, Division Ordinance Officer and designer of the rifle range, was the managing editor. He would become a major fixture for the New York National Guard readers. The paper had professional journalists from the division writing and included contributed copy from nine volunteer war correspondents from the New York

The 1st New York Field Artillery with limbers pulling field pieces and caissons on a march. The terrain was rugged, water limited and the heat relentless (courtesy Andrew B. Rankin, Jr., Collection).

area newspapers and upstate New York dailies. The paper also took subscriptions from people back in New York.[57] *The Rio Grande Rattler* was published in a small printing office at Mission, Texas. It was filled with news and information on the European developments, and also contained local ads and funny stories. The newspaper was published between August and December 1916, and then again on August 8, 1917. The newspaper was 15 inches wide by 21 inches high. It usually had 8 pages, except for issue 18 which had 12 pages. The subtitle of the newspaper was: "The Strength of the Wolf is the Pack, but the Strength of the Pack is the Wolf." In 1917 the paper morphed into the *Wadsworth Gas Attack and the Rio Grande Rattler* at Camp Wadsworth, South Carolina, shortened to *The Gas Attack*. Each issue cost 5 cents. Crawford and Rudolph were the official photographers for the New York Division.

The rifle range at La Gloria had been completed by mid–July with targets set at 50 to 100 yards. It was eighteen miles north of McAllen, requiring a march. The range was a 1,200 yard area which was one-half cactus and chaparral, and one-half open; both sections were used.[58] The rifle range was designed by Major Fred M. Waterbury and built by the 22nd New York Engineers. The range officer was Major George F. Chandler, Adjutant of the 1st Brigade with Lieutenant Percy E. Barbour of the 22nd Engineers serving as the assistant range officer. The course was set up with a tactical combat problem

The 1st New York Field Artillery Regiment at the gunnery field at La Gloria, Texas. They used the three-inch field guns which were standard army light artillery pieces at the time (courtesy Andrew B. Rankin, Jr., Collection).

which needed to be solved. The men learned how to advance on an enemy under fire using a limited supply of ammunition. They fired standing, kneeling and in a prone position on the ground. Six pits were set up in which range personnel knelt. The pits were connected by telephone to officers on ladders who directed the lifting of 100 targets at unexpected times. The targets represented the enemy which would appear as an individual, a squad, or company. Each group had a given situation and there was competition between regiments for high scores. Regiments also weaved through thick brush following assignments. Men seemed to enjoy the challenges presented there. "The intention was to make the combat exercises tactically correct, to teach the meaning of fire superiority and to show that the individual shot must subordinate himself to the unit of which he is only a part."[59]

Modern trenches were constructed by the Engineer Corps in a field adjoining their camp site. The men practiced assaulting an enemy trench. The trenches were connected to dressing stations, latrines, and shelters. They were protected by obstacles and barbed wire with trip wire installed. When the wire was tripped, flares exploded with reflectors and there was fire from the trenches. Mortars were set with illumination bombs and the entire field became "day." Men attempted night raids but the defense system was successful and used as a school of defense. The men became "well seasoned" in the 18–30 mile "hikes" to the range. Regiments usually arrived early in the morning and shot for that day and the next before returning to camp. It was done in "all weather." Each brigade received a final score. In fact, "the New York Division was the only one on the border which was practiced in individual rifle and pistol work, as well as in group and field firing with ball ammunition."[60]

The artillery did not practice firing their pieces until the artillery range one mile north of La Gloria was complete on September 28. It was called a "desolate place" by the men of the division.[61] There was a shortage of equipment and prior to that the horses were in poor condition for pulling field pieces long distances. By early September, the horse situation seemed better. Colonel Henry H. Rogers, commander of the regiment, took thirty days leave at the beginning of September to try to regain his health. It would later be extended. Lieutenant-Colonel Merritt H. Smith took command again for the month, and would later lead the men in France. Most of the batteries of the 1st New York Field Artillery Regiment had arrived in Texas by September and joined the 2nd Field Artillery in live action training on the three-inch field guns. The artillery fired in the remote location which was also located six miles above Sterling Ranch. The artillery field training for all units was set within a six day period. Each battery marched two days to the range, fired for two days addressing a simulated problem, and then marched back two days. Everything was covered in dust and dirt once the guns fired. The combination of

The 1st New York Field Artillery on a march. The men were trained in the "Spartan-style" to harden them so that they would complete their tasks with little complaint (courtesy Andrew B. Rankin, Jr., Collection).

blasted earth and the winds blowing sand around often made it uncomfortable, causing men to joke about using alkali dust for talcum powder. The 1st and 2nd New York Field Artillery Regiments were busy at La Gloria throughout the fall and by October, Battery A and C of 1st Field Artillery had joined them.

On October 1, Lieutenant-Colonel Smith took 30 days leave, and Col. Rogers had an extension to his leave, which placed Major Charles R. Seymour in command. He organized target practice. General McNair supervised fire and Captain Verbeck gave instruction on a tactical problem. Officers erected observation ladders and stood on them giving direction to one gun of the battery. The men would be told to shift the trail of the field piece in a direction right or left, and then the others would shoot parallel to that. General McNair would then critique what had happened and give the correct way to resolve any problem. A group called the Range Party would then check the data. Each day two batteries fired for two days with the third doing Range Party duty for one day, and then it was repeated. Each officer in a battery fired during at least two tactical problems. Battalion 1 returned to McAllen as Battalion 2 hiked to Sterling Ranch and they repeated what had been done by Battalion 1.

The 3rd New York Field Artillery then arrived in Texas, and began their practice at La Gloria on the 4.7-inch howitzer field gun, Model 1906. It was a 4.7-inch gun weighing 2,688 pounds with a maximum range of 11,000 yards, much farther than the three-inch guns. The howitzer, considered heavy artillery, was made of gun steel and some of nickel steel. It fired ordinance like heavy explosive shells and shrapnel balls. Everyone became more efficient in their preparations and fire, and began to understand the rhythm of their pieces, simplifying their work. This increased their speed significantly. There was also a 110-mile practice march which included the rifle range at La Gloria, Texas, in the early fall of 1916.[62]

An issue surfaced with regards to the uniforms. The shoes, Russet Marching Shoes, which covered the ankle, were not constructed to take the combination of water, mud, sand, and unstable roads. They simply were not strong enough for extended hikes through rough terrain and replacements were needed. Foot inspection became part of military discipline with many men complaining about fallen arches and crumbling leather. The army would later go through two styles of boots: the 1917 Trench Boot; and the 1918 Trench Boot, nicknamed the Pershing Boot or "Little Tanks."[63] The division learned much during these hikes about endurance, providing equipment for large assemblies of men, and care of equipment and animals. Officers also learned how to pace and protect their men in an unfriendly environment.

To alleviate the fatigue of the men, the division held a celebration called Frontier Day beginning on September 30 and lasting three days. It was a huge

The New York 6th Division Brigade Artillery on parade near Sharyland, Texas. They were reviewed by Maj.-General Frederick Funston, U.S. Senator James W. Wadsworth, Jr., and New York State Governor Charles S. Whitman (courtesy Andrew B. Rankin, Jr., Collection).

success. The festivities were located on the drill field of the 7th Infantry. The entire 6th Division was present with over 6,000 in attendance: soldiers, cowboys, rancheros, townspeople, and Mexicans. The canteens were open and popcorn and peanut stands set up. In the morning, exhibitions and athletic events were held and prizes given. In the afternoon, the military held mounted events with cavalry and artillery. There were also artillery demonstrations, and even a jousting event using streamers and wooden swords. A Wild-West show included bronco busting. The best in that event turned out to be Privates Hathaway of 2nd New York Field Artillery Regiment and Joe Hooker of the 1st Cavalry. In the evening, the 22nd Engineers launched fireworks using new trench lighting.[64] A vaudeville show and two boxing bouts ended the affair at 11 p.m. The band of the 3rd Tennessee Infantry played as well as divisional bands. Over the three-day-period a horse show was held, as well as races, including rescue races and a four-mount relay.[65]

Although less fun, reviews were part of training. The division had a total of six. Regiments and brigades had additional reviews as well. "White House Field," three miles southeast of McAllen, was often used for reviews. On September 22 Major-General O'Ryan reviewed the division. Brigadier-General James Parker, who commanded the Brownsville District, reviewed the division the following day. October 1 Major-General Frederick Funston, commanding the Southern Department and the troops at the border, reviewed the troops on a large plain south of Sharyland, northwest of McAllen. Sharyland contained small farms and modern bungalows. United States Senator James W.

The New York 6th Division Infantry on parade near Sharyland, Texas, on October 1. It was the first time a complete division, with all its regiments and support systems, had paraded since the Civil War (courtesy Andrew B. Rankin, Jr., Collection).

Wadsworth, Jr., was also there with Governor Charles S. Whitman of New York. It was the first time a complete tactical division had done a review since the Civil War. "The formation with nine regiments of infantry, three regiments of field artillery and a regiment and one separate squadron of cavalry, together with engineers, signal troops, sanitary units and trains, was most impressive."[66] Pershing, in Mexico, was actually functioning under Funston. The governor of New York, the Honorable Charles S. Whitman, reviewed the division on November 16. November 20 the Honorable James W. Wadsworth, Jr., Senior United States Senator of New York reviewed. He would spend each Thanksgiving with the division all the way through the war to come. Then on December 12 Brigadier-General Edward M. Lewis, who would later command the 30th Division which would serve next to the 27th Division Infantry during World War I, reviewed. All of these reviews were done in the heat of the middle of the day.

By October 2 the long hikes were completed, but it was still between 90 and 120 degrees. Dust kicked up from the ground that was said to have choked the men. During rainy periods it was replaced with mud up to the ankles. All of this slowly hardened the men to the weather and helped them learn to negotiate their caissons and horses. They simply did as they were told and ignored their surroundings. The First Battalion of the 1st Field Artillery Regiment returned to New York on October 19, and the Second Battalion returned on October 27, 1916. On November 15, 1916, a number of the men were mustered out of federal service, remaining in the National Guard. The 2nd Field Artillery Regiment did not return to New York until December 30 and the 3rd Field Artillery Regiment, which had not arrived until October 3, did not return home until March 6, 1917.[67] They had been sent to train at Point Isabel 75 miles south of headquarters in December. It required a march.

For those remaining at camp, voting for the general election was held. The mess halls had voting booths set up and the men were given an extremely long and narrow ballot upon which to make their choice. The ballot was then collected back at their tent and placed in a sealed box. The box was then taken to headquarters where the ballots were counted and the final report sent to the New York State Board of Elections. The result of the election in the United States was a win by Democrat Woodrow Wilson over Republican Supreme Court Justice Charles E. Hughes. Later in the month, men used up remaining ammunition at the rifle range, and on Thanksgiving Day the troops had a turkey dinner and church services with lots of sports. One of the events was a point race by the 12th New York Infantry. It was a three mile cross-country race on foot with full pack and 100 rounds of rifle ammunition. Their unit would not return to New York City until February 26, 1917.[68]

In December, the men had an opportunity to see Charlie Chaplin's Bur-

Members of the New York 6th Division relax by the Rio Grande River during maneuvers. The possibility of war with Mexico was very real. Events in Europe contributed to American restraint (courtesy Andrew B. Rankin, Jr., Collection).

1st New York Field Artillery Regiment tent inspection. There were no floors for the tents, and no cots. The men slept on the ground on their blankets. Those with money were able to purchase floor boards and cots at local stores for higher prices (courtesy Andrew B. Rankin, Jr., Collection).

lesque on Carmen which was showing in a local theater. In an attempt to control disease, an order came down that the theaters were not to allow over crowding. Military Police would insure that the men were located in well ventilated theaters.[69] The local news was largely focused on Carranza in Mexico who had called together a convention to prepare a new constitution. It would be adopted in 1917 giving the government control over education, oil properties, farm properties and even the Roman Catholic Church. Labor unions were recognized with the president limited to a single term of office.[70]

The total cost of the Punitive Expedition has been numbered at $3,287,649.82.[71] Those who crossed the border did not necessarily win a decisive victory, and those at the border did not engage the enemy in what would be considered a battle, though it was a show of strength. The New York National Guard Division did suffer losses while there however; there were about 22 deaths due to injury and disease during their stay. Injuries included being kicked by a horse, gunshot wounds and drowning in an irrigation canal. The diseases were things like pneumonia, tuberculosis, the paratyphoid epidemic, and meningitis. There were intestinal issues and a cardiovascular issue which might have been intensified by the excessive heat. Those moving forward in their lives had been hardened by their service in the uncomfortable climate with poor food. They prepared to return to New York with all of its sophisticated entertainment. It was time to return to normal life, at least for a few months.

CHAPTER THREE

Camp Wadsworth, Spartanburg, South Carolina (April 1917–May 1918)

On December 30, 1916, the remainder of the 2nd New York Field Artillery Regiment returned from active border patrol in Texas. They were mustered out of the Federal Army on January 12, 1917, although still in the New York National Guard. Some members of the 6th New York Division remained in Texas a little longer with the last group, the 4th Field Hospital, leaving March 12, 1917. The guard noted an increase in applications for enlistments following the border service, but the National Guard units were ordered to reduce their size, so many of the men serving were honorably discharged only to be called up again a few months later.

On January 18, 1917, General Funston told General Pershing that his units would be withdrawn from Mexico. Pershing had previously recommended removal from Dublan, Mexico, no later than January 28. The Mexican Punitive Expedition, however, officially ended on February 7, 1917. National Guard units left Palomas, Chihuahua, in Mexico, and returned to Columbus, New Mexico. The expedition had been a difficult campaign, requiring a great deal of "forbearance and discretion" on the part of the United States troops to avoid unnecessary clashes with locals. A small force was maintained in Texas, Arizona, and New Mexico as a preventative measure. The 3rd New York Field Artillery Regiment remained until March 6. Although not actually controlling political lawlessness in Mexico, the expedition had regained control of the American border. Minor clashes continued between 1917 and 1919 in places like Texas and Arizona. The period at the border also served as a training ground for some of the military forces, and Pershing relied on this experience when facing a new front as he took command of the American Expeditionary Forces during the Great War, using many of the same men from the Mexican Punitive Expedition.[1]

Camp Wadsworth, Spartanburg, South Carolina

Top: Members of the 1st New York Field Artillery enjoy an afternoon drive in Texas (courtesy Andrew B. Rankin, Jr., Collection).
  Bottom: The men of 1st New York Field Artillery relaxing by their limbers in Texas (courtesy Andrew B. Rankin, Jr., Collection).

Back at home, the State Militia was now officially called the National Guard, following federalization in 1914 that enabled them to serve both the state and the federal government. By 1917 these changes in the guard resulted in the State of New York amending the state education requirements to included physical exercise for students in elementary and secondary school. This change was requested by the Military Training Commission (M.T.C.). The M.T.C. was composed of the president of the University of the State of New York, the major-general of the New York National Guard, a member appointed by the Board of Regents of the University of the state, and a gubernatorial appointee. Boys age 16–19 who were not still in school were expected to train for the military three hours a week, or its equivalent, from September 1 to June 15. State military camps were set up for field training of these boys. Few boys attended high school in New York State during this period as most were working in trades, although some went to high school at night after work at one of the evening high schools for boys. While men were serving in the New York National Guard in places like Texas, plans had been underway to ensure that teens were introduced to the modern principles of armed service. A common belief was that military character promoted moral character and good citizenship. Military character was, in fact, considered moral character. Following his term of service at the border, Colonel Merritt H. Smith, the commander of the 1st Field Artillery Regiment, was busy at the Plattsburg Camp training student officers.[2] The 1st Field Artillery Regiment, along with the 105th Field Artillery Regiment, was made an instructional detachment and placed at the camp.

Called the Preparedness Movement, this nationwide effort to train young men was sponsored by people like General Leonard Wood, ex-president Theodore Roosevelt, Elihu Root and Henry Stimson, all of whom saw the need for updating and strengthening the military. The pattern for the later Citizen's Military Training Camp (CMTC) was modeled on the Plattsburgh Camps. The Plattsburgh Camps had been in use the summers of 1915 and 1916 and would later hold summer training for men from 1921 to 1940 as authorized by the National Defense Act of 1920. Some members of the New York Division would be re-federalized for service in the Great War from that location.

With the close of the one conflict to the south, America looked at the other across the sea. Europe, along with its attached colonies and alliances, was in turmoil. When the Archduke of Austria-Hungary was assassinated in 1914, it set off outrage in that empire which resulted in the empire seizing the Balkan territories with heavy Serbian populations. A domino effect resulted as Russia mobilized to defend Serbia. Serbia shared a border with Germany. Germany then declared war on Russia and on France, its ally. Germany moved troops through Belgium into France, violating an international treaty. The

Members of the 1st New York Field Artillery relax by their tents in Texas (courtesy Andrew B. Rankin, Jr., Collection).

British then declared war on Germany in defense of France. The alliance system drew in many nations. Most countries were extremely competitive and nationalistic at this time. The war spread continent-wide from the North Sea to Switzerland. Trenches and barbed wire, complete with machine gun nests and artillery, ran throughout boundary lines. The British had also sided with the Arabs of Arabia and Palestine against the Ottoman Empire. They invaded Jerusalem and Damascus. African colonies belonging to the Germans were also invaded. The Germans, in turn, went after British and French ships.[3] The international scene was complex and the fighting was brutal.

The sinking of the ship R.M.S. *Lusitania* in May of 1915 off the coast of Ireland began the process of drawing the United States towards the war in Europe. It had resulted in the loss of 1,200 civilians lives; 128 were American. The United States was not yet involved in the war, yet German tactics had threatened American lives. Then, on January 16, 1917, a pivotal communication between Germany and Mexico was intercepted by the British. The note was signed by the German Foreign Secretary, Arthur Zimmerman (1864–1940), and it was addressed to the German Ambassador to Mexico. In it the Germans proposed an alliance between Germany and Mexico, if war should erupt between the United States and Germany. It also hinted that Japan might be invited to join in, something for which the Japanese later insisted they had no knowledge. Financial aid and American territorial annexation was promised to the Mexicans, granting them United States territory recently lost: Texas, New Mexico and Arizona. The Germans were attempting to draw Mexico, at the United States' southern border, into the European war. They were encouraging an adversarial relationship immediately following the recent threat of war during the Mexican Punitive Expedition. A key inflammatory point was that they were promising United States territory to Mexico.

Despite having previously promised to obey international law on the seas, on January 31, 1917, the Germans announced their new submarine policy giving them unrestricted naval warfare rights as of February 1. They would enforce this in all waters surrounding enemy countries. Only one United States ship per week would be allowed to sail through a prescribed course to Falmouth, England. U-boats would sink all vessels, neutral or allied alike, without warning.[4] Kaiser Wilhelm III of German was setting forth an aggressive policy, attempting to dominate the seas. It was the last straw that forced the American president's hand.

On February 3, the passports of the German Ambassador, Count Johann Heinrich von Bernstorff (1862–1939), and the United States Ambassador in Berlin, New York City born James Watson Gerard (1867–1951), were recalled. Von Bernstorff was the ambassador to the United States from 1908 to 1917. President Wilson encouraged all other neutral countries to do the same. There would be no negotiations with Germany until their U-boat policy was rescinded. Some historians have speculated that because the Germans had negotiated a tentative peace with the Russians in 1917, they may have thought they would only have to fight on a single front in France and could afford more risks. At this point the French were close to collapse and the British exhausted. America was not taken as a serious threat. If they could draw Mexico into the conflict to keep America's weak army busy defending its southern border, Germany would be successful in their enterprises.

Congress with no cessation of German hostility officially declared war on Germany April 6, 1917, with President Wilson announcing, "The world must be made safe for democracy." The May 19, 1917, *The New York Times* front page announced President Woodrow Wilson's (1856–1924) call to arms of the previous day. Registration for service was set was to begin June 5. At this time, the Regular Army only had about 137,000 men. The National Guard had another 181,000. The combined figures left the U.S. Army as the 17th largest in the world. The United States did not have a large reserve either.[5] As the United States entered the war in support of the Allies, so too did China, Liberia, Greece, Siam, Panama, Cuba, and Brazil. Before war's end Guatemala, Haiti, Honduras, Costa Rica and Nicaragua would also join them.

The American Army may have begun relatively small, but in the end about 5 million men served. This gave the Allies the manpower needed to win. Three groups of American forces would be fighting in the American Expeditionary Forces (A.E.F.): the Regular Army, Divisions numbered 1–8; the National Guard, Divisions 26–42; and the National Army, Divisions 76–93. The National Army was made of conscripted men and volunteer forces. Combined, they became the American Army. The need for training delayed their appearance on the battlefield. The commanding officer wanted an independent American offensive, and did not want his men to merely function as a supplementary infantry within British and French Divisions.

The commander of the combined American forces was Brigadier-General John J. Pershing. Major-General Frederick Funston had seniority over General John J. Pershing. He oversaw Pershing's activities during the Mexican Punitive Expedition and was in line to command the American Expeditionary Forces, should America become involved in the European arena. However, Major-General Funston died suddenly of a heart attack on February 19, 1917, which ultimately opened the way for General Pershing to take command.

On July 3, New York State Governor Charles Seymour Whitman (1868–1947) called the New York National Guard into service again. Whitman was governor from 1915 to 1918. The guard was drafted on July 9, and ordered to assemble the following day. At the beginning of their assembling, the New York Division had 991 officers and 27,114 enlisted men. Major-General John F. O'Ryan would lead them once again. On July 12, 1917, President Woodrow Wilson called out the entire National Guard of the United States to serve the country against the Central powers in Europe. The New York Guardsmen were already assembled. The guard, which had served as the 6th Division in the Mexican Punitive Expedition was renamed the 27th Division on July 20, 1917, to fit within the numbering assigned to National Guard units. The 27th Division had originally included the following brigades and regiments: 1st Brigade had been composed of the 7th Infantry Regiment, 12th Infantry Regiment, and 14th Infantry Regiment; 2nd Brigade had been composed of the 1st Infantry Regiment, 23rd Infantry Regiment, and 71st Infantry Regiment; and 3rd Brigade had been composed of the 2nd Infantry Regiment, 3rd Infantry Regiment, and 74th Infantry Regiment. Accompanying them was the Brigade Field Artillery composed of the 1st Field Artillery Regiment, 2nd Field Artillery Regiment, and 3rd Field Artillery Regiment;1st Cavalry Regiment; Squadron A and Machine Gun Troop; 22nd Engineers; and 1st Battalion Signal Corps. The trains were Military Police, Ammunition Train, Supply Train, Engineer Train and the Sanitary Train, including the Headquarters Ambulance Companies 1st, 2nd, 3rd, and 4th, and the Headquarters Field Hospital 1st, 2nd, 3rd, and 4th.

Limbers left at rest after a long day in Texas. Members of 1st Field Artillery had returned to New York from federal service on October 19, 1916, and regrouped to their regular formation in the New York National Guard. However, they would be federalized once again for the Great War (courtesy Andrew B. Rankin, Jr., Collection).

The division would be re-formed at camp: it was squared by fall with four infantry regiments while a few regiments were dropped and others were renamed. At that point it included the 53rd Infantry Brigade, composed of the 105th Infantry Regiment and the 106th Infantry Regiment; the 54th Infantry Brigade, composed of the 107th Infantry Regiment and the 108th Infantry Regiment; the 52nd Field Artillery Brigade, composed of the 104th Field Artillery Regiment, the 105th Field Artillery Regiment, the 106th Field Artillery Regiment, and the 102nd Trench Mortar Battery; Divisional Machine Gun Brigade, composed of the 104th Machine Gun Battalion assigned to the division, the 105th Machine Gun Brigade assigned to the 53rd Infantry Brigade, and the 106th Machine Gun Battalion assigned to the 54th Infantry Brigade; and the 102nd Divisional Trains Headquarters. The 102nd Divisional Trains Headquarters was composed of the 102nd Ammunition Train, 102nd Supply Train, 102nd Regiment of Engineers, 102nd Sanitary Train, 105th Ambulance Company, 106th Ambulance Company, 107th Ambulance Company, 108th Ambulance Company, 102nd Field Signal Battalion and the 27th Military Police Company.

The combined artillery of the New York 27th Division was named the 52nd Field Artillery Brigade and initially placed under the command of Brigadier-General Charles L. Phillips along with Major Leonard B. Smith. Later, command was given to Brigadier-General George A. Wingate of 2nd Field Artillery Regiment. The 1st Field Artillery Regiment, a detachment of the 12th Infantry, was now renamed the 104th Field Artillery Regiment. Existing and new officers comprised the staff serving under Colonel Merritt Haviland Smith as commander and Lieutenant-Colonel John Thomas Delaney. The 1st Battalion was commanded by Major Charles Robert Seymour; Battery A was commanded by Captain Guido Fridolin Verbeck with 1st Lieutenants Irvine A. Williams and William Henry Thomas, and 2nd Lieutenant Richard J. Bush; Battery B was commanded by Captain Walter Cecil McClure with 1st Lieutenants James Harrison Giles and William Peter Welsh; and Battery C was commanded by Captain Charles Gray Blakeslee with 1st Lieutenants Arthur Edward Kaeppel, Albert James Sinnock and Steele Wotkyns, and 2nd Lieutenant Philip B. Weld. The 2nd Battalion was commanded by James Edward Austin; Battery D was commanded by Captain Sylvester Simpson with 1st Lieutenants Frederick Jacob Koch and Fred A. Petersen, and 2nd Lieutenants Henry B. Stimson and John Farr, Jr.; Battery E was commanded by Captain Robert Law Russell with 1st Lieutenant Channing Rust Toy, and 2nd Lieutenants John W. Pulleyn and Harold LeRoy Whitney; and Battery F was commanded by Captain George Billings Gibbons with 1st Lieutenants Harold Lawson and Francis P. Gallagher, and 2nd Lieutenants James Park and Edwin S. Bettleheim. The Medical Corps for the regiment included Major Straford

F. Corbett, First Lieutenant James F. Coughlan, and 1st Lieutenant Russell J. McGraw with six privates first class and fourteen privates. Headquarters Company was commanded by Captain James H. Kenyon with 1st Lieutenant Walter E. Hegeman. The Battalion Adjutant consisted of Captain Arthur W. Hofmann and Captain Benjamin Van Raden. Supply Company was commanded by Captain Clarence Gayler Michalis with 1st Lieutenant William James Volkland. The chaplain for the regiment was 1st Lieutenant Herbert Shipman. Student officers were trained by Captain George B. Gibbons of 104th Field Artillery at the 3rd Officer's Training Camp at Camp Wadsworth.

The 2nd Field Artillery Regiment, a detachment of the 14th Infantry, was now renamed the 105th Field Artillery Regiment first under Colonel George A. Wingate, and then under Colonel Dewitt C. Weld, Jr. The 3rd Field Artillery Regiment, a detachment from the 1st, 71st and 74th Infantry, became the 106th Field Artillery Regiment and served under Lieutenant-Colonel John D. Howland and then under Major Lewis H. Eller. Troop I, 1st Cavalry, became the 102nd Trench Mortar Battery first under Colonel Charles I. DeBevoise and then Captain Charles Person, Jr. The 104th Field Artillery initially had 42 officers and 1,240 men. The 105th initially had 41 officers and 1,244 men. The 106th Field Artillery initially had 30 officers and 1,016 men. The 102nd Trench Mortar Battery initially had 52 officers and 1,471 men.

Battery F, 1st New York Field Artillery, outside at the mess hall in Texas. Drew Rankin is under the arrow (courtesy Andrew B. Rankin, Jr., Collection).

The 102nd Trench Mortar Battery, which had been a proud cavalry unit, was forced to release their horses and become foot soldiers. There was no need for cavalry in this war. Troop I, 1st Cavalry were called "highly trained," and of "above average intelligence." The majority of them were college graduates.[6] The 102nd Ammunition Train was also a member of the brigade.

The New York 27th Division was primarily made of soldiers who had seen hard service on the Mexican border, unlike a number of divisions just beginning to be formed. The Mexican Punitive Expedition was said to have served to "weed out officers and men who lacked the capacity to be efficient soldiers." It also had helped to "harden and endure officers and men to the fatigue and hardships of service in the field." The state of New York would end up furnishing the most men from the United States to the Great War, with a total number of 367,864 serving; next came Pennsylvania with 297,891. The National Guard had already federalized 77,000 men in 1916. On July 25, 1917, they were called into service for the great cause. The combined National Guards of the United States would ultimately send 16 divisions with the designated numbers from 26 to 42. The Regular Army only sent seven divisions. In the spring of 1917, the total male population in the United States was 54,000,000; 26,000,000 men ultimately registered to serve during World War I, or nearly half. That was a high representation. The best conditioned men

Battery F, 1st New York Field Artillery inside after the construction of the mess hall in Texas (courtesy Andrew B. Rankin, Jr., Collection).

were said to have come from New York, New England and California. However, there was not enough equipment, uniforms, or ships for transporting the vast numbers of men entering the war.[7]

On July 9, 1917, the New York National Guard was drafted. Recruiting continued until late August to increase their numbers. Most of the guardsmen were federalized at 9:00 a.m. on July 16, excepting for those guarding utilities.[8] The guard gathered at their home stations once again. The 27th Division then entrained and traveled to Camp Wadsworth, near Spartanburg, South Carolina. The 12th Infantry arrived September 16 and the 1st Field Artillery Regiment, now 104th Field Artillery Regiment, arrived October 15. They had been training students. The 3rd Field Artillery Regiment had arrived September 28 and the 2nd Field Artillery Regiment had arrived September 30.

Camp Wadsworth was close to Asheville and the Blue Ridge Mountains. It was largely a textile center set in the South Carolina Piedmont, and surrounded by cotton fields and cotton mills in a heavily wooded area. The camp was located on a large plateau with rolling hills and a few small creeks. The Piedmont and Northern Electric Railroad went through the camp, making it ideal for military transport. Parallel to those tracks and farther north ran the Southern Railroad with its depot on Magnolia Street.[9] The camp had been named after the Union Army Brigadier-General James S. Wadsworth, a New Yorker. This had been Confederate territory and there were said to be aged Confederate soldiers still living in the surrounding area when the Yankees arrived. Wadsworth, Jr., was a New York State Senator and an officer in the New York National Guard. James Wadsworth had served as a 1st Lieutenant of the 1st New York Cavalry when the guard was called to Texas. He had contemplated relinquishing his Senate seat in order to serve with the guard but was dissuaded from that. He did, however, spend every Thanksgiving with the division throughout this period, from Texas on into France.

There were no barracks at Camp Wadsworth. The officers lived on Quartermaster Road and the enlisted men lived in large eight-man pyramidal tents. Flooring was added and wooden walls, but the canvas top let the cold night air in, and the daily heat was unbearable during warm weather. They were in the mountains. In the winter to come, heavy snows would cause the temperatures to plummet. The men were only issued "two blankets, an over coat, and woolen underwear" with a little stove for the cold weather. It would "harden them for what was ahead."[10]

The field artillery bunked on the left or west side of the camp along Black Stop Road, forming the left perpendicular wall of a large letter "L." The 102nd Trench Mortar were in area number 20 on the south, then moving north came the 106th Field Artillery in area 21, the 105th Field Artillery in area 22, the 104th Field Artillery in area 23, the 102nd Ammunition in area 24, and the

102nd supply train in area 25. Each regiment filled about a quarter of a mile squared. All were in a neat column facing the common area. Extensive trenches were in the center and northern part of the camp. Forming the lower horizontal side of the "L" were the infantry who were to the east, facing the common area and the trenches. Along side of them was the base hospital, the engineers, the machine gun battalions and others. The camp was given the nickname of "Camp Mud" due to the conditions in the trenches and fields. Mud would take on an entirely new meaning in France.

A number of wooden buildings were built at camp including the mess halls, baths, latrines, and places used for training and entertainment. There were seven Y.M.C.A. huts, a Knights of Columbus Hall, Salvation Army, and the Jewish Welfare Board. Canteens and the Camp Post Exchange at the base hospital sold soda, souvenirs and snacks, although there would later be a ban on junk food enforced by the Military Police. In fact, junk food would be prohibited within 500 yards of camp with guards set by stores. During free periods, athletics were offered such as baseball, football, soccer, boxing, wrestling, polo, tennis, fencing, cross country running, and more. Once again, boxing proved very popular with the New York boys and their commander. Group sports were encouraged to develop team work. The men could also watch a constructed scoreboard to follow New York and Brooklyn baseball games.

In a blatant display of racism, African American servicemen were not permitted to enter the service organization clubs on base. Segregation was strictly enforced in the South. Most of the African Americans in the town were poor sharecroppers with little power. Many whites also were largely tenant farmers. A Black Soldier's Club was finally built in early 1918, but the very presence of the 15th New York Infantry, an African American unit in the 27th Division, caused such shock in the community that they were sent quickly to France as the 369th Infantry in order to avoid a riot. Some of the locals had enjoyed their band music, but most others treated them with great contempt. The New York National Guard had previously faced the issue of prejudice back in 1916. A number of men who were Jewish had tried to enlist in certain regiments and been told that those regiments were full, only to watch non–Jewish men accepted. A ruling was then made that enrollment should only be based on fitness and not on race or religion. The twelve companies called "colored regiments" of the 15th Infantry had been organized after that ruling on June 29, 1916.[11] They ultimately were attached to the French 4th Army overseas, and distinguished themselves during the war. The regiment earned the French Croix de Guerre medal. The Germans called them "The Harlem Hell Fighters."[12] Training for "colored officers" was held at Fort Des Moines, Iowa.

The 27th Division, as proper military, had a combined military band. It was fortunate to have some professional musicians from New York City in its ranks, which enhanced the level of playing greatly. They were conducted by 2nd Lieutenant Francis W. Sutherland of the 104th Field Artillery Regiment. He assembled them at Spartanburg. They later played during the final review of the 27th Division in Montfort, France. The 104th Field Artillery Band also played in the Meuse region of France during the war. The American Doughboys were often called the "singing army," which was true. Music played a large role in building moral and expressing humor and irony. Favorites of the men were tunes like *Hail, Hail the Gang's All Here; In the Artillery; Over Hill, Over Dale; Where Do We Go from Here, Boys?; Beautiful K-K-K-Katy; Oh, How I Hate to Get Up in the Morning.* They did tend to prefer more racy versions of the lyrics. Major-General O'Ryan said that his division did not sing when companies were marching because the line was just too long to keep it all together, but platoons did sing as they marched. Their particular favorites were *The Long, Long, Trail; Joan of Arc; Pack Up Your Troubles in Your Old Kit Bag and Smile, Smile, Smile*; and the divisional song, *My Heart Belongs to the U.S.A.* The divisional song had been written by two enlisted men. In addition, the division sang at band concerts conducted by Lieutenant Sutherland.[13] Once they reached the front they would have little cause to sing as they slugged it out with a fearsome enemy who seemed relentless and determined to stay. Soldiers would have to be quiet at the front, hiding their positions, and leave the music behind.

The mess hall at camp was a place to gather and gossip. Corporal Drew Rankin, newly promoted, often joked about the delivery of the food to the men. It was dished out as one walked down the line. One item was "flung" upon another. The last item was always the ice-cream, which was just plopped on, and then melted over everything.[14] It would come to be remembered with great fondness over in France. Canteens were available on base and one could get a hair cut at the barber shop in the hospital complex. Most men saved money by having a buddy cut their hair.

The 27th Division of New York was one of three divisions formed entirely from a single state National Guard. The other two states who did this were Illinois and Pennsylvania. Major-General John F. O'Ryan was the Camp Wadsworth commander for the New York Division from July 16, 1917, to November 23, 1918. Brigadier-General Charles L. Phillips, commander of the artillery, directed the camp from September 19, 1917, to February 22, 1918, when Major-General O'Ryan went overseas to inspect the front. Brigadier-General Palmer E. Pierce served as commander from June 16, 1918, to November 14, 1918, at which point the division left for France. In France, the chain of command for the 27th Division's infantry came first through the Fourth Army, British Expeditionary Force and later, the II Corps, American Expeditionary Force. Joining the 27th Division at camp were the 69th "Fighting Irish of New York City." They would become part of the 42nd Rainbow Division serving as the 165th Infantry. Douglas MacArthur was an officer in that division. He and Major-General O'Ryan were the youngest commanding generals in the American Army.[15] O'Ryan was not a professional soldier, but was an attorney in New York City. Self-trained, he graduated from the Army's Staff and Command School. He would end up being the only National Guard general to command a division throughout their entire war service.

The town of Spartanburg where Camp Wadsworth was located had been a small city with paved roads and electric lights: much more modern than McAllen, Texas. The town was a 3½–4 mile walk from camp and the sidewalks were often jammed with soldiers. Military vehicles added to traffic problems. The roads leading to the camp were not very good, so the army made some improvements, straightening Snake Road and renaming it Vanderbilt Road. For added social life, the men could visit places such as the Cleveland Hotel or the Hostess House with its screened porches and lounge filled with rocking chairs only half of a mile from camp. In addition, soldiers could attend local dances and listen to bands playing. The Military Police kept a sharp look-out for women of lesser virtue. Many of the men found "nice girls" and got married. Converse College for girls and Wofford College for boys offered lectures and concerts. Across from the Cleveland Hotel, the people of Spartanburg set up a soldiers' club room at the Woodmen of the World Hall where they offered free entertainment. It was open from 4–10 p.m. weekdays and 7–8 p.m. on Saturdays.[16] Everyone was trying to "do their part" in the war effort.

The presence of the camp changed the community in many ways. It provided new jobs, especially in building construction, and the soldiers' purchases contributed to the local economy. The property leased to the government was three miles west of the city proper, nestled in pine woods and cotton fields. The influx of soldiers from other parts of the country changed the demographics of the area, bringing a new mixture of cultures. Since the camp did not have hot running water for showers, the men sought out warm water in town. Even churches offered hot baths to the soldiers.[17] The men appreciated the fact that the town, unlike McAllen, Texas, did not increase their prices and often even offered soldiers a discount.[18]

By the beginning of August 1917, the 27th Division had 764 officers and 24,644 men. After arriving in South Carolina, the 27th Division later traveled back to New York City for a big send-off parade on 5th Avenue on August 30, 1917. It was called a "Farewell Parade." The men were quartered in various places for the event. The 104th Field Artillery Regiment, Squadron "A" Cavalry, and 1st, 10th, and 71st Infantry Regiment returned to Van Cortland Park in the Bronx. The 2nd Field Artillery went to Prospect Park, Brooklyn. The 1st Cavalry was on the Bliss Estate in Bay Ridge, Brooklyn. The 3rd Infantry was at Pelham Bay Park. The Coast Defense Commands of the 8th, 9th, and 13th were protecting the New York harbor. The parade began on 5th Avenue at 160th Street and the men marched towards the Washington Arch at Washington Square. When they returned after the war, this direction would be reversed. The send-off parade was a very patriotic event with thousands jamming the streets, cheering and waving flags and banners, even though the men were not actually leaving the States just yet. The soldiers were given small gifts of gum, candy, fruit, and even cigars and cigarettes for some. The review stand was set up in front of the Union League Club. Various hotels also gave send-off dinners to some 20,000 men. By late afternoon, many of the soldiers boarded trains back to Camp Wadsworth, while others waited in camps and armories in New York for their turn to travel south.

A new style of training was employed at camp based on Major-General O'Ryan's study of European methods. He felt that the British system of physical training had better methods than what the United States had been doing. "So superior seemed the British system of physical training to anything which we had employed in our own army that with slight modifications it was adopted and given over almost wholly to the charge of Major John B. Sharp, the Buffs Regiment, British Army."[19] The Buffs was the nickname of the Royal East Kent Regiment, one of the oldest regiments in the British Army dating back to 1572, based on the fact that at one time they wore buff coats made of soft leather. Their system was designed to create more than muscles in the men. It was designed to "grab their attention" and tighten the relationship "between the mind and muscle, so that the latter would become automatically and instantaneously responsive to the former," and visa versa. This proved to help the men when under the pressure of battle.

Using the new methods, training was set based on particular topics set within a series of schools. A typical day at Camp Wadsworth lasted from *Reveille* at 6:15 a.m. to *Taps* at 11:00 p.m. Calisthenics and tending horses was done in the early morning, and then formal drills began at 7:30 a.m. Drills were repeated at 1:00 p.m. On the Grenade Course men learned the use of both rifle and hand grenade. Taught by Lieutenant Pierre Forestier of the 119th Infantry, French Army, the stance of the grenade toss called for rotating the arm while throwing, very much like a windmill. Grenades were new to the Americans, but the Germans were ahead of the Allies in production and made extensive use of them. The United States initially relied on being provided grenades by the British and French before developing their own. Rifle grenades attached to a rod and were placed down the barrel of a rifle. Cup grenades were also attached to the barrel and both were launched by a blank cartridge, but they were not always accurate. Hand grenades and rifle grenades could either detonate on impact or be set to a time fuse. The British system used a group of men with those launching grenades: two men threw grenades, two men carried them, two men defended those throwing, and two were spare men in case of injury.[20] Fragmenting grenades were used in defensive moves. Nonfragmenting grenades were used in offensive moves, along with phosphorus grenades which screened an infantry move with white smoke, and gas grenades used to clear trenches. The Americans used MK II Defensive Fragmentation, MK III Offensive Blast, MK II Gas, and MK II Phosphorus grenades. The stance for the grenade toss was practiced.

Bayonet Fighting and Physical Training School was led by Captain Cleveland L. Waterbury and Captain Harry Vaughn, along with Major Sharp. The men charged at straw-filled dummies suspended from beams. Bayonet work was new to the Americans. The Springfield Model 1903 rifle, used by the men, used the M1905 bayonet which had a wooden hilt and a nickel steel blade. During training, the men wore a type of fencing mask and kept rifle bayonets sheathed while practicing hand-to-hand combat in trenches. Infantry men later commented that they ended up not ever using the bayonet during the war. A wave attack which they practiced was actually later used at the Hindenburg Line.

Musketry School was led by Major Joseph J. Daly and Major Frederick M. Waterbury. The men practiced with M1903 Springfield bolt-action rifles that the National Guard had used prior to the war. The charging clip could hold 30-06 cartridges and they were considered accurate. The Enfield M1917 rifle was also available. Musketry School focused on marksmanship, and regiments competed for highest score. Automatic Arms School, taught use of the Lewis, Light Browning, and Chauchat guns. The school was led by Captain Charles G. Veyssiere of the French Army Infantry. New to the Americans, the French Chauchat was a light machine gun. It weighed about 20 pounds and was 45 inches long. Unfortunately, it did not always work, but the United States did not have a domestic light machine gun. Captain Veyssiere's instruction focused on the workings of the Chauchat; later, Captain Ernest Schroder and 1st Lieutenant Thomas J. Coursey taught other arms. A rifle range on Snake Road just outside camp limits was used by the Automatic Arms School, Sniper School, and target practice for new recruits.

Machine Gun School was led by Major Edward McLeer, Jr. The machine gun units trained on three types of guns: American Colt, French Benet-Mercier, and British Lewis. The Colt was found to be obsolete. The Benet-Mercier was used strictly to train. The Lewis, unlike the Chauchat, was found to be reliable and would be used by the men of the division in battle. One Pounder School, Cannon was a theory only class, and Stokes Mortar School did not actually have mortars until 60 days prior to the division shipping over seas. The men constructed light three-inch pipe mortars to practice with. The class was taught by Captain A.N. Braithwaite, General List, British Army with Captain Alfred Hall, British Army.[21]

Gas Defense School was led by Captain Harold H. Deans of King's Own Scottish Borderers, British Army. King's Own Scottish Borderers were part of the Scottish Division that dated back to 1689. In this class, men entered a chamber where chlorine and tear gas were released. Outdoor gas clouds were studied as well. In the trenches, lachrymal gas was launched on the men. This very real experience with gas would save many lives later in France. The gas mask had a ten inch square carrying bag with partitions inside. The mask was kept on one side and on the other was a small metal can filled with chemicals that absorbed poisonous material in the air. Air passed through a one inch thick hose cemented to the mask near the mouth. An extension hose went into the mouth and the soldier breathed in the filtered air. Exhaled air was released out the bottom of the mask. A nose clip kept the nose closed. Lenses covering the eyes tended to cloud, but a salve could be rubbed on them to help reduce the fog. The mask was made of rubberized cloth with elastic edges. Two elastic straps at the top held it in place. When the soldier was not in danger, the bag was carried against the body. When he was in danger, the mask was kept close to the face.[22] The French had technically been the first to use gas when they launched tear-gas grenades on the Germans in August 1914, but the Germans developed much more deadly forms of gas and are usually credited with being the first to use it in warfare. Men who became "gas personnel," both officers and non-commissioned officers, had specific training involving wearing their respirators 16 hours a month, including four hours of consecutive wear. Their training continued in France. Of those in the division who did require medical treatment from gas shelling during the war, none of the instances were due to the failure of the respirator.[23]

In Camouflage School, led by Captain A. W. Palmer and 2nd Lieutenant Linwood P. Ames, the men were trained to use both natural and modified camouflage. Camouflage would be imperative for the artillery during the war, with enemy airplanes circling and looking down on them from high places. Camouflage would often be their only defense. Using disrupted patterns of olive and dark green helped to reduce visibility from high places. Sniping, Patrolling and Reconnaissance School was led by Captain H.H. Johnson, M.C, The Welsh Regiment, British Army. Artillery officers did do reconnaissance work at their positions, as would the infantry.

Major William L. Hallahan led the Liaison and Communication School. The telephone was particularly critical for the artillery communication. Many men lost their lives stringing telephone line to try to connect regiments to headquarters. An extensive amount of liaison work was employed between artillery and infantry. The artillery assigned men to advance with the infantry and communicate back to field positions via telephone either the need for artillery fire or the success of a barrage.

Engineer School was led by Captain Ernest F. Robinson with 2nd Lieutenant E. Veyiet and Aspirant Eugene Dalle, 9th Engineer Regiment, French Army. The American engineers in France would have a particularly difficult time as they were often required to repair and build in areas which had suffered years of warfare. They frequently constructed things quickly under enemy machine and shell fire as well as gas.

Transportation School was led by Major James T. Lorre. Because the 27th Division ended up being stationed at the front, the transportation of supplies, food and equipment proved particularly difficult. Using the shell-pocked roads often made one a target for aircraft and artillery. Defensive driving took on a life-or-death importance. Horsemanship was taught at the School of Equitation led by Captain Geoffrey Taylor. Captain Richard B. Wainwright led the School for Teamsters, Horseshoers, and Packers. The army was very dependent upon horses to pull wagons, artillery pieces and to transport material. Horses were better able to move over the muddy terrain than motor vehicles which also tended to break down. On the lighter side was the School for Bands and Field Music led by Captain Henry E. Greene. Francis W. Sutherland of the 104th Field Artillery also directed the divisional band. The quality of music delivered by the military bands was very high and they often performed for the people of Spartanburg.

Officer Training included schools in combat skills and night fighting; telephone usage and wire stringing; the use of buzzers, signaling, and telegraph; lessons in hygiene; map reading and the use of compasses; field sketching and French language. They also underwent training in the trenches. The instructors were Canadian and British officers, as well as non-commissioned officers, and there were lectures by French officers "fresh from the seat of war" who were said to be "practiced in the latest methods of warfare developed in France, including the use of gas, machine guns, grenades, and bayonets." As later noted, "Officers were given the most drastic tests, both physical and professional, and those who were not up to the highest standard were dropped."[24] Sergeants were also drilled extensively.

The division newspaper, *The Rio Grande Rattler*, became the *Wadsworth Gas Attack and Rio Grande Rattler* in South Carolina. They began publication November 23, 1917. The paper carried news on the 27th Division as well as pressing world news. Publication ended on May 4, 1918, when the men left the country. After the first twelve issues, the name was changed to *Gas Attack*. The title was a constant warning and reminder about the new chemical weapons being used at the front. Men were continually ordered to use "box respirators!" The paper ensured the readers knew that British and French officers were at the camp specifically to train officers and non-commissioned men in trench warfare as it was quite different from what they had experienced in Texas. Four French and four British officers were specialists in what was considered modern warfare. Captain Charles Veyssiere trained men in automatic rifle, 1st Lieutenant P. Forestier was an expert in the hand grenade, 1st Lieutenant Bordes was an expert in artillery, and 2nd Lieutenant Veyret was an engineer.[25] The National Guard needed to be trained in ways that prepared them for what they would be up against. The English were closer to the fight, and the men found their instruction to be very helpful. One article mentioned, "If you don't know how to kill with your rifle and with your bayonet, you're a nuisance to your company, to your regiment, and to yourself." It also stated, "You've got to get into your mind the fact that you are going in to fight men who want to kill you; who would rather kill you than feed you as a prisoner, because food is an asset not to be squandered."[26] In addition, one of the men reporting for the *Gas Attack,* W.A.D. of the 107th Infantry Regiment, wrote a frightening account of having seen the enemy "throw petrol on the clothes of wounded men and then touch a match to the poor devils." He continued, "You want to get back to New York!" All of the articles set images forth about the heroes engaged in the war's arena and the cruelty of the heartless enemy.

John H. Eggers, in his 1919 book *The 27th Division,* mentioned that the men were trained to accept that killing and being killed were part of the war. He stated that in their bayonet lessons they focused on meeting their objectives despite the issues of life and death. "The attack was undertaken with a fixed determination to carry it through to success. One can never lose sight of the fact that after the beginning of an attack there is only one thing to do, and that is to go forward."[27] This type of setting of the mind developed a certain level of tenacity in the men.

Camp Wadsworth's trench system was eight miles long. The trenches were angled and curved with a reserve trench. Those trenches were the first training trenches constructed in the United States during the First World War.[28] Most of them were eight to ten feet deep, lined with pine saplings running horizontally with vertical posts placed over them at intervals. The men would be in lines during electrical storms and in wet trenches with washouts. They were trained to jump backwards into the trenches. They would do night fighting and sneak in and out of them, which was called going "over the top." Bunkers 35–40 feet deep were also used. The men spent days and nights in these trenches, including in the rain with no talking or smoking. The instructors were veterans and planned on having their pupils survive. Gas was launched, when the wind was right, for practice in drills. Bells and suspended iron bars were rung, and the men were timed as they hurried to place masks on their faces. The dugouts were not gas-proof, but curtains with chemicals hung over their entrances. Each man tried to reduce the amount of time it took him to get the uncomfortable mask over his head and in place. It would save their lives in France. The artillery would spend most of their time reaching for those masks.

The Glassy Mountain area was used as a gunnery range for both rifle and artillery fire. It was in northern Greenville County near the Glassy and Hogback Mountains, twenty five miles from the town of Spartanburg, in a sparsely inhabited area. Colonel George A. Wingate of 2nd Field Artillery Regiment designed the artillery range at Glassy Rock. Colonel Wingate had been the former adjutant general of the division, becoming a colonel on January 12, 1912. Brigadier-General C.L. Phillips did the initial training of the brigade, but was detached from the division on November 26 by the Regular Army. Colonel Wingate, after being sent to Fort Sam Houston at the end of December for training, returned as a brigadier-general and took command of the 52nd Artillery Brigade for the length of the war. Members of the Regular Army trained the men in the interim.

The Glassy Rock range was set on 30,000 acres of property with woods and small "villages" set up. The huge range, seven miles long and three miles wide,[29] was constructed by the 22nd Engineers on September 24, 1917. It had gun emplacements, trenches, and a complete rifle range. Unfortunately, it was far from camp. Artillery and supply troops were sent by rail or truck, and sometimes hiked. There was a depot at Campobello and Landrum. The officers of the 52nd Field Artillery Brigade were sent for training at the School of Instruction at Fort Sam Houston in San Antonio, Texas, during this time, as

The Officer's Training School at Gun Drill, Camp Wadsworth, South Carolina. The men of the 104th and 105th Field Artillery Regiments used the three-inch gun in the United States and were given the French 75 millimeter guns in Bordeaux, France (courtesy National Archives, photograph no.141B-6).

well as the School of Fire at Fort Sill, Lawton, Oklahoma. Fort Sam Houston dated from 1890, and at the time was the largest army post in the continental United States. It became the center for all medical training. The School of Fire was established in 1911 at Fort Sill, though the fort dates from 1869, and is still used as the United States Army Field Artillery School. Those schools were said to have had courses which were "severe and arduous."[30]

The field artillery fired in "all weather." Their training included battery and battalion problems, focusing on open warfare. Regimental and brigade problems during firing barrages were studied. They drilled in gun pits and dugouts, and practiced the occupation of positions. Barrages were followed by open warfare drills with a tactical problem. Their field training would be completed between March and April of 1918. The brigade had used the three-inch and 4.7-inch guns during the Mexican Punitive Expedition. It was no match for the French 75 millimeter guns and the German 77 millimeter guns. They were considered technological wonders. The regiments would not receive their new weapons while at camp, however. They had to wait until they arrived in France. In South Carolina they still used the same field guns, learning different techniques and studying the mechanisms of the guns they would later use.

The 104th Field Artillery Brigade would use the French 75 millimeter guns in Europe as would the 105th; the 106th would use the 155 millimeter Schneider howitzer. On the range the men were trained in gunnery techniques, took positions, and participated with infantry in maneuvers with blank and live ammunition. The concept of teamwork was drilled into the men as they would often serve in support of infantry. It was important for the artillery regiments to not only fire accurately, but to use good judgment when supporting an infantry advance in order to prevent injury to their own men. Those who had trained on flat terrain in Texas had to learn rolling terrain techniques. This mountain location would be helpful for the terrain they would encounter in France.

Infantrymen from the New York National Guard had been transferred into the artillery to bolster the size. First the army asked for volunteers, and then assigned the remainder. 186 men were transferred from the 12th New York Infantry into the 104th Field Artillery Regiment, which had been the 1st Field Artillery. The final total in that regiment on July 31 was 1,435. 158 men were also transferred from the 14th New York Infantry into the 105th Field Artillery Regiment, which had been the 2nd Field Artillery. 158 men were transferred from each of the 1st, 71st, and 74th New York Infantry Regiments into the 106th Field Artillery Regiment, which had been the 3rd Field Artillery. 128 men were transferred from the 1st New York Cavalry along with their Captain Charles A. Pearson, 1st Lieutenant Harry R. Dilke, and 2nd

Artillery practice firing at Camp Wadsworth, South Carolina. Notice the artillery shells in the caisson to the left of the gun firing. The 104th and 105th Field Artillery Regiments used the three-inch gun at camp, and the 106th Field Artillery Regiment used the 4.7-inch gun in the United States. The 106th would be given the 155 millimeter Schneider Howitzers, in Bordeaux, France (courtesy National Archives, photograph no.141A-21).

Lieutenant Richard F. Cloak, into the 102nd Trench Mortar Battery. There would be no need for cavalry in the Great War.[31] It turned out there would be little need for the Trench Mortar Battery either where they were going.

The discipline was said to be "severe and unrelenting," resulting in a "thoroughly efficient organization."[32] The instructors from Fort Sill School of Fire had told the officers that they would most likely do open warfare, so the men were trained in that style of fighting. The training included gun drills with immediate action; the workings of the mechanisms with stripping and cleaning, and care for guns; gas instruction; instruction in bombing and barrages; signal work; range finding; barrage drills; indirect fire; dismount drills; gun sites; range cards; emplacement digging; and more.

Two infantry ranges were set with 100 targets in the open and opposite trenches. Training included some combined arms exercises at Glassy Rock. The infantry practiced assaults while under artillery barrage fire and shrapnel. Even heavy explosive shells were launched so that men could adjust to their compression. The men charged up the hill while artillery fired over them. At one point, the artillery launched up to 100 rounds of both high explosives and shrapnel. The officers told the men that the enemy was firing from a certain direction, with whatever arms they had decided upon, and that advances were required. Those men designated as "wounded" in the scenario were given a tag with a description of their physical malady based on a situation likely to occur in battle. They were first dressed by regiment medics, then proceeded to a dressing station, and then sent to the field hospital if necessary.

Between September 18 and 19, Major-General O'Ryan departed camp, traveling by ship to France to observe the war conditions. General Phillips of the 52nd Field Artillery Brigade temporarily took over Camp Wadsworth until O'Ryan returned on November 26. Major-General O'Ryan took with him Colonel Harry Hill Bandholtz, 1st Lieutenant Charles P. Franchot, Sergeant Thomas S. Johnson, and Corporal Albert A. Breunig. They met with five other divisional commanders in Paris and then traveled to the Poperinghe Line in Belgium where they were assigned to observe a few British divisions before going to study the French front.[33] The group was actually bombed while observing, so the experience was a realistic picture of the war front.

The New York 27th Division received the best state-side training of any division going into the Great War. Unfortunately, that was noticed by those higher up, creating a situation of great frustration for the commander, and his men. Due to their seasoning from the Mexican conflict, the War Department began raiding the 27th Division as almost soon as they arrived at camp. Officers worried that the division was being completely dismantled and would soon no longer exist. 275 men who spoke French were transferred out. Most were college graduates who largely served as Military Police in France. 532 men were taken as motor mechanics. The 15th Infantry Regiment was renamed the 369th Infantry Regiment and sent to serve with the French 4th Army. The entire 69th Infantry Regiment was sent to the 42nd Division, called the Rainbow Division, as the 165th Infantry Regiment. The 42nd was compiled from National Guard from 26 states and the District of Columbia. That division trained at Camp Mills on Long Island. The 27th Division had to completely rebuild the missing regiment with members from other regiments to balance their 1st Brigade. Then 80 officers were transferred from the 27th Division to command regiments in the United States Army 1st, 3rd, 26th, 28th, 29th, 32nd and 42nd Divisions.[34] The first two were Regular Army. The 1st Division is the oldest division in the army and often called "The Big Red One" after its arm patch with the large number 1. The last five were National Guard units: New England or Yankee Division; Pennsylvania; Wisconsin and Michigan; the 29th was made of New Jersey, Delaware, Maryland, Virginia and the District of Columbia; and the Rainbow Division made of multiple states. Newly promoted Brigadier-General Harry H. Bandholz, who had traveled to France with Major-General O'Ryan, became the commander of the 58th Infantry in the 29th Division. The 58th Infantry Brigade was composed of the 115th Infantry Regiment from Maryland and the 116th Infantry Regiment from Virginia. In addition, 2,500 men from the 27th Division who had important civilian experience were removed to help the War Department. Major-General John O'Ryan commented that it had "great importance in the effect upon morale and efficiency and as well upon the conservation of the combat man power of the country."[35]

Coupled with this was a restriction on recruiting. The National Guard was initially forbidden to recruit while the army draft was in place. Later in the spring, however, they were allowed to recruit non-draft aged men (younger than 21 and older than 31). Twelve hundred men came in fresh; they had no experience, but were welcomed and quickly trained to bring them up to the level of those around them. Redistributing so many men from this one New York National Guard Division throughout various other divisions had an extensive impact. The artillery would also later be detached, serving as divisional artillery for two other divisions, supplementing artillery for nearby sister divisions. All of these divisions would gain the positive effect of the training orchestrated under Major-General O'Ryan. The state of New York sent the largest number of service men into World War I and can be proud of its contribution.

Back at Camp Wadsworth the coming holidays brought celebration and small breaks in training. Thanksgiving Day was celebrated with a turkey dinner. The menu included: cream of celery soup with croutons; olives, pickles and celery; roast turkey with bread and sage dressing and cranberry sauce; baked southern ham; mashed potatoes and fresh peas; mince pie and plum pudding with fruit, raisins and nuts; and coffee and cigarettes. The men were busy reading the November 27, 1917, issue of the *Wadsworth Gas Attack and Rio Grande Rattler* which had re-printed a *New York Times* article by Philip Gibbs, "The Big Tank Drive on the Huns."[36] The correspondent wrote how the British troops, under which the 27th Infantry would come to serve, had assaulted the Hindenburg Line at dawn on November 20. The tanks smashed through the wire and penetrated past trenches and tunnels without the use of artillery. Cutting the wire was a dangerous affair in daylight under artillery shelling. The tanks had been moved over the course of a few nights and hidden below Frequieres Ridge by Havrincourt. The infantry followed the tanks "cheering and shouting." Many German prisoners were taken.

A few weeks later, the South Carolina weather took a drastic dip. On December 10 the thermometer registered 10 degrees. On the 14th it fell to 6 degrees with 8 inches of snow. At Christmas decorated trees were placed about, including a large one in the drill field. A printed Christmas menu was given out at the decorated mess hall with a turkey dinner similar to the one at Thanksgiving with a wider selection of vegetables. Religious services were held. December 29 brought another snow storm, and January 1 the temperature plummeted to minus two degrees.

The nights proved to be very cold in the eight-men pyramidal tents. The tents had rough walls and floors, but the wind blew straight through the structure. There were shortages of blankets and warm weather clothing. Even with two blankets, a poncho and even their half tents over them, the men were freezing. Each man had a tan half-shelter tent which became a whole tent when buttoned to another, or an enlarged tent when joined with three others. Each carried it, wooden pegs, ropes and a pair of folding poles in their tan haversack (backpack). It served as a blanket at camp. The canvas cots also allowed air to flow beneath them.

In the center of the tent sat the little cast iron Sibley stove.[37] It burned wood or coal, but there was a shortage of firewood so scraps of building material were used as well. The inverted funnel-shaped stove sat on the ground. A fire was built under it and a pipe connected to it ran along side the center tent pole to the top of the tent to vent. Tents sometimes caught on fire at the top. The men huddled around the stoves. The water used by the men for bathing froze, needing to be thawed each day prior to use. It would get worse. One man died of exposure in the trench and fourteen were hospitalized. Cases of pneumonia were also linked to the weather.

The men caring for the horses tried to keep them moving to stay warm, but unusually heavy snow fall made it a challenge. The weather in South Carolina became another training element for the 27th Division. The heavy snowfall lasted for two months. This experience, combined with the unbearable heat they had suffered in Texas, helped harden the men to the climate changes that came with living outdoors. The winter of 1917 ended up being the worst one both the United States and France had seen in a long time.[38] Places which usually did not have much cold weather were suddenly suffering from the low wind chill. Sleet storms, snow, and ice seemed to be premonitions of bad things to come.

CHAPTER FOUR

Camp Stuart, Newport News, Virginia (May 1918–June 1918)

The winter of 1917–1918 proved to be very severe, even American southern states experienced record chills with many northern states registered anywhere from minus 14 to minus 40 degrees Fahrenheit. December was one of the coldest months across the United States from Alaska to New York. Sleeping in tents, trenches and dugouts with only little cast iron stoves, the men were exposed to extreme cold. Keeping the American Army in warm clothing was a continual problem that would mount during the coming conflict. Many divisions were only issued one uniform per person, worn day in and day out. The 27th Division newspaper published a complaint about that uniform. It seems that the uniform coat collar of the olive-drab wool tunic was felt to be too high and too small for larger American necks. The coat collar was not only uncomfortable when buttoned, but dangerous to those who felt as though they were being choked. It was deemed by the writer to be "too tight for athletic movement" and difficult to keep clean in the field.[1] In addition to the tunic, service shirt, underwear and wool breeches which laced up the outer calf front, and their blankets, men also slept in their overcoats to keep warm at night.

The paper also mentioned an issue with steel helmets which allowed cold winter winds to blow through. The soldiers found that wearing the Belgian cap as a head-warmer under the helmet helped. "It also serves as a pad, taking up some of the pressure of the steel hat," and was small enough to fit into the pocket when not in use.[2] The soldiers came to call their helmets "Tin hats" or "Tin Lizzies," after the manganese alloy helmets later made by the Ford factory. Initially though, they used the standard British helmet made of steel. Under them, the "dinky caps" kept the soldiers warm. The American Expeditionary

Forces would copy the French Bonnet de Police envelope styled cap, but an assortment of wool overseas hats were worn by the men.[3]

The divisional paper reported that the spiral cloth puttees of the British troops were superior to those being used by the Americans. To wrap the puttee, the wool tape was placed first on the shin and then wrapped over the top of the boot, winding and overlapping it to cover from the boot to the lower pant leg just below the knee. This gave added protection to the shin, calf, and pant leg, and provided another layer of warmth. The wrap was held in place by cotton tape. All the puttees became muddy, but the British version seemed to keep the mud out of the boots better. The canvas leggings, used initially, would not dry and became too stiff. In extremely muddy weather "rubber thigh-boots" might be worn, though for general dampness the soldiers felt that "well oiled boots were nearly water-proof."[4] The army also adopted the sleeveless leather vest from their allies. Department stores like John Wanamaker in New York supplied military clothing for those able to purchase them as advertised in the *Gas Attack*. They carried not only the leather sleeveless vests, but leather puttees which strapped over the calf for those looking for a quicker solution than winding tape.

In the training camps, the American Army struggled with disease control. Men in many divisions contracted diseases such as chicken pox, diarrhea, diphtheria, meningitis, mumps, smallpox, tuberculosis, and typhoid. These common illnesses were responsible for many deaths between 1917 and 1918. Since antibiotics were not yet discovered, controlling sickness became a constant struggle. The New York Division focused on preventative measures such as having the men keep their tent flaps open to circulate the air. Everything was washed with soap and very hot water. The division seemed to do fairly well in this regard. Even so, the paper reported that a thousand enlisted men had been discharged "because of physical defects, and some fifty or sixty officers had met a similar fate." The strict training was focused on a healthy army and Major-General O'Ryan was cited in the paper as saying "that the health record of the division has been remarkable-that it has probably been the best of all the army divisions." This he attributed to the diligence of both the camp officials and the town of Spartanburg, which assisted in "protecting the soldiers from disease."[5] Military police worked crowd control in places like the movie theaters in an attempt to keep contagious diseases in check. Men were also told to use handkerchiefs. Training in hygiene that had begun at the border continued in the mountains.

In the March *Gas Attack* a concern was raised about decorations for the men in the New York National Guard who had served on the border during the Mexican Punitive Expedition. The Secretary of War had authorized a badge and ribbon in December of 1917, but the issue of medals kept surfacing.

It had been decided that medals were only to be given to those who actually engaged Mexican forces, but Honorable William M. Calder of New York introduced a bill in Senate to give bronze medals to those who had served more than four months.[6] That recognition would have to wait until after the war.

Around this time, Major-General O'Ryan sought an emblem for the New York Division, and a contest was set up for design submissions. The selection committee settled on the Orion Patch, a play on words between the commander's name and the constellation. It was adopted as the official symbol of the division in 1918. Orion in Greek mythology was the mighty hunter, which seemed fitting for a commander of well seasoned soldiers. The patch was worn on the shoulder sleeve and featured a red circle surrounding the seven stars (aka "the seven sisters") of the Pleiades. Four outer red stars were positioned north, east, south and west, and three inner stars were nestled in the letters. The red symbol in the center was a combination of the letters N, Y and D, for New York Division. The curved wall of the letter N on the left embraced two red stars and the curved wall of the letter D on the right surrounded another red star. The patch was not actually worn until officially authorized, so it was shipped to France later. Each man was only entitled to wear it if he passed an exam administered by an officer attesting to his character and the carrying out of his duties.[7] It was worn with great pride by the men from New York.

There was much speculation about whether or not the war would end prior to American involvement. The January 9, 1918, issue of the *Gas Attack* reported the hope that war would end by spring.[8] The article rebuked the Germans for trying to "conquer their neighbors," and mentioned how during the Spanish-American War Germany had secretly asked England to join France in stationing naval fleets between Cuba and the United States' fleet. The English Foreign Secretary had replied "no" and said the British fleet, if it took any part in that conflict, would stand between the European fleets and the Americans. The January 26, 1918, issue of the newspaper listed all of the countries engaged in the Great War at that time. Nineteen countries sided with the Allies: Serbia, Russia, France, Belgium, the British Empire, Montenegro, Japan, Italy, San Marino, Portugal, Romania, United States, Cuba, Panama, Greece, Siam, Liberia, China, and Brazil. Eleven other nations broke relations with Germany: Bolivia, Guatemala, Honduras, Nicaragua, Santo Domingo, Haiti, Chile, Costa Rica, Peru, Uruguay, and Ecuador. There were only four countries on the Central powers side: Austria, Germany, Turkey and Bulgaria. Countries declared as neutral included nine in Europe: Andorra, Denmark, Holland, Luxemburg, Monaco, Norway, Spain, Sweden, and Switzerland. In addition, Afghanistan and Persia in Asia, and Abyssinia and Morocco in Africa remained neutral, as did Mexico, Salvador, Argentina, Colombia, Paraguay, and Venezuela.[9]

General Pershing would set up his headquarters in Chaumont, France. The American Army faced a series of challenges. The large numbers of immigrants in the American forces were cause for concern. Eighteen percent of the armed forces were foreign-born, with 70 percent in the United States less than ten years. The ethnic mix of the 27th Division alone included some 26 nationalities. New Yorkers were a little more used to mixing with different groups, although that did not mean they necessarily liked them all. A number of the foreign-born could not speak English and did not understand American customs, making training difficult. Many had come to the United States from countries that were now viewed as the enemy, causing questions about their allegiance. Those men were made to take special oaths. So many Americans were of mixed heritage from countries such as Ireland, Great Britain, Germany and others, that it was difficult to even know what an American really was. Yet the Americans could not afford to restrict enlistment.

While some divisions arrived in France well-prepared, others would arrive with little or no training in the United States. All of the men would need additional training to understand their equipment. Pershing would need to create sister divisions, pairing the better and lesser trained together, and count on new recruits to come up to speed quickly.[10] The American forces would face the German commander of Belgium and northern France, Field Marshal Rupprecht. His full name was Rupprecht Maria Luitpold Ferdinand, Crown Prince of Bavaria (1869–1955). At the point when Americans entered the war arena, the British and French were weary from years of fighting, having given up territory in both 1916 and 1917. Paris was in danger of falling and fresh infantry troops were sorely needed. The Germans were busy consolidating their new positions, appearing to believe so strongly that they would never leave that they built concrete emplacements.

The first group of 27th Division Infantry was ordered to Europe on April 20, 1918. The infantry would fight with the British and American Armies, along side the 30th Infantry Division. The commander of that division was Major-General O'Ryan's close friend, and members of the 30th had served with the 27th in Texas. They would prove to work well together as a team. Initially there was grumbling by the men about serving under the British. The British were still seen as "Red Coats" as taught in the American school systems which focused on the heroic actions of the Revolutionary War patriots. The British had been painted with a dark brush for their actions from Colonial times through the War of 1812, whose centennial had recently past. There was a strong feeling by Americans that their involvement in the Great War was a way to pay back Lafayette and Rochambeau for their help during the War for Independence.[11] The officers of the division worked hard to stress the importance of loyalty to *all* of the Allies. As a highly disciplined division, they were expected to be united in stopping what they saw as Germany's desire for worldwide conquest. Gradually the men adapted.

Major-General John F. O'Ryan and the Advanced Party of the 27th Division left Camp Wadsworth by train on April 29, sailing from Hoboken, New Jersey, May 1 on the U.S.S. *Great Northern*. They landed at Brest, France, on May 10. Back at camp, Brigadier-General Robert E. L. Michie became the temporary commander of the division in O'Ryan's absence. The rest of the division left Camp Wadsworth by train between April 28 and May 6, headed for Newport News, Virginia. The 102nd Engineers, minus Company A and C, went to Camp Humphreys in Virginia. As a temporary training camp, Camp Wadsworth would only last until 1919. The locals would later refurbish many buildings for businesses. Little of it remains today.[12]

The 106th Infantry left from Hoboken on the U.S.S. *President Lincoln* on May 10. Other infantry began sailing for France May 9 to 10 in a convoy consisting of the U.S.S. *Susquehanna*, U.S.S. *Antigone*, and H.M.S. *Kurtz*. The voyage took 7 to 14 days depending upon the speed of the ship, its position in a convoy, and any threat in the water. Most of the men had only light duties on board, giving many of them their first opportunity to rest in a long time.[13] Duties included physical exercises, guard duty, policing quarters, administration, KP, and vigilantly watching for submarines. Observation positions had telephones nearby to raise any alert. At 5:20 p.m. on May 29, the Division Headquarters convoy consisting of the *Calamares, Madawaska, Pocahontas* and *President Grant,* along with smaller ships, was attacked by an enemy sub. The sub was sunk by depth charges set by the destroyers and the U.S. Cruiser *Huntington*. The convoy arrived safely. The same group, minus the *Grant* which disembarked at Brest, was attacked again on May 30 by two subs which were sunk by destroyers and a British airplane. Watching for subs was taken very seriously.

The soldiers on board followed a set schedule. Fresh water was limited so the men learned to shave using salt water, which was unpleasant. On the battle field, they would end up learning to shave with even less. Beards or mustaches were prohibited, because the gas mask had to fit tightly against the face. Any opening could be deadly. Shaving as a daily ritual increased the chance for survival.

On the voyage, some of the division's ships published newspapers: *The Sea Serpent: A Mid-Atlantic Issue of the Gas Attack and Rio Grande Rattler; Mid Ocean Comin' Thru;* and *Rail Splitter*.[14] They contained war news and humor. The men of the division seemed to enjoy reading chatty text; perhaps the diversion lessened the tension. The trip was uncomfortable at best; the ships tended to roll and pitch. Between May 23 and May 31, the infantry ported at Brest and St. Nazaire and by June 5 they were under British training in northern France. The units trained under the 2nd, 3rd, and 4th British Armies in Arques, Buigny, Rue, Gamaches, and St. Valery.[15] Major-General O'Ryan received his orders on May 27. Field Marshall Douglas Haig had chosen both the 27th and 30th National Guard Divisions to serve the British.[16] The two divisions, as part of the 2nd American Corps, would work closely together during the war. Field Marshal Haig was the commander of the British Expeditionary Forces (B.E.F). The American infantry was needed right away.

Those remaining at camp continued with training and military duties. In a typed letter from camp dated May 5, 1918, Corporal Drew Rankin, in the 104th Field Artillery, tried to keep a light heart as he trained, still in the States. He told a funny story with his announcement that he was "studying aviation," and now called "Barney Oldfield." It seems that there was a motorcycle at the Officers Training School at camp with a side car.

> One evening a Captain from another outfit came over looking for the man that ran the motorcycle. Like all orderlies, he could never be found when wanted. So I told the Captain that I used to run one, and asked him if he wanted me to take a chance and run it for him. He said he did. I took it. [However, the brake was broken.] The machine slid gracefully down the hill, and I jammed down on both clutch and brake, in order to make a turn, but she slowed not, and the next thing I knew I was lifted gently off the saddle by a rail fence, and the machine with my foot off the clutch, ran merrily across a field with the Captain. He must of gotten lonesome when he saw I had dismounted without orders, for he started to dismount by the same authority. He must have thought he was home in the bath tub, for he started to climb out backwards. He started to, but did not finish. After spinning around on his neck a few times, he landed with a flop, and the motorcycle kept on going. The blame thing headed for an unfinished building and then got into an argument with a wheel barrow. Result-wheel barrow dented out of shape and one broken handle, which caught in between the rear wheel and mud guard and stalled the engine. The motorcycle got off with a busted tool box, dented oil tank and badly bent rear mud guard.
>
> I got up early the next morning and fixed the rear mud guard so that it did not rub the tire, and fixed the oil tank so that it looks all right, only won't hold any oil, and as I never could see the use of a tool box on the machine, I took it off, and improved the looks very much. The Captain wasn't hurt a bit, except that he stayed in his tent a few days and complained of a headache. But I guess he must be mad at me, cause he hasn't asked me to take him riding since.
>
> I thought my own Captain would stick me in the clink for the episode, but he only laughed when he heard about it, and said that I was the third fellow from the Battery [F] that had dumped that Captain out of that particular side car, and that we had better cut it out, or the Captain would think the Battery did not like him.[17]

Colonel George Albert Wingate of the 105th Field Artillery had been promoted to Brigadier-General on April 12, 1918, and assumed command of the 52nd Field Artillery Brigade. The 52nd Field Artillery Brigade finally left

Camp Wadsworth on May 17–18, 1918, but they were detained at Camp Stuart in Newport News, Virginia, until June 5–6. They watched their division slowly leave without them. The 52nd was detained because the United States was rushing infantry into Europe, and the artillery and trains took up valuable ship space. They were sent later, since the British and Australian regiments had ample artillery to cover the 27th Division's infantry. The infantry from the 27th were designated to serve under the IV British Army and the II Corps of the American Expeditionary Force.

The 52nd Field Artillery Brigade now consisted of Headquarters, the 104th Field Artillery Regiment, 105th Field Artillery Regiment, the 106th Field Artillery Regiment, and the 102nd Trench Mortar Battery. In addition, the brigade included important members of the division's Veterinary Corps that had the daunting job of keeping the horses and mules healthy in adverse conditions under active fire. The 104th Field Artillery Veterinary Corps were led by 2nd Lieutenant Robert A. McAuslin and 2nd Lieutenant August F. Johnson. Second Lieutenant Frank J. Cavency and 2nd Lieutenant John A. Wende led the 105th and 1st Lieutenant George J. Goubeaud and 2nd Lieutenant Charles E. Anderson the 106th.[18] The artillery left their guns and horses behind in the United States. They were assigned new ones in France.[19]

Newport News, Virginia, where the 52nd was sent, was one of two embarkation centers for the American Forces. The other was New York City/Hoboken, New Jersey, where the United States Army used Piers 2–4. Newport News was chosen because of its location in the Chesapeake Bay and rail system connections. From the Newport News piers, men could watch steamers busily chugging on the Chesapeake Bay. The docks served not only as staging areas to transport men, animals and supplies, but also as places to fuel and repair ships and store material. The army had the full cooperation of the United States Navy at Newport News.

Newport News was part of a system of camps which processed soldiers that included Camps Stuart, Alexander, Eustis, Hill and Morrison. Camp Stuart was the largest facility used to process troops. It was named after Confederate General J.E.B. Stuart. Over 115,000 soldiers were processed at this camp, and given overseas examinations. It was located by 16th Street and Roanoke Avenue. The camp covered 800 acres and was run by the Hampton Roads Port of Embarkation on leased land from the Old Dominion Land Company. The camp was in operation from July 1917 to September 1919 and was quickly constructed with rustic wooden buildings spaced apart and parade grounds in the center. The men lived in closely placed tents in the surrounding fields.

The army medical staff at Camp Stuart was kept busy trying to prevent disease. The camp was surrounded by swamps filled with malaria-carrying mosquitoes. Some men succumbed to malaria, a very real threat. Meningitis and tuberculosis were also of concern, along with the first stage of the influenza epidemic. Drainage of the swamps became a top priority. The much marginalized African Americans troops were ordered to do this work. A combination of Mexican crude oil and kerosene was sprayed on waterways in an effort to prevent mosquitoes from breeding. All of the men were encouraged to eat good diets and to be checked for communicable diseases.[20] Sick and wounded from the front were processed at this camp.

Animals were also sent overseas from Newport News, Virginia, and Hoboken, New Jersey. The light artillery used horses classed as "strong active" within the 1,150 to 1,300 pound range. Heavier artillery used the "powerful horses" between 1,400 and 1,700 pounds. Draft mules and pack mules were used to haul supplies. Mules which were attached to the wagons, "wheelers," were over 1,150 pounds. "Leaders," in the front were over 1,000 pounds. A group of animals would be shipped together to the unit camps in France. Since there were between 7,000 and 10,000 horses and mules in corrals near the Virginia piers, there was an abundance of manure and flies. The flies also enjoyed the nearby garbage dumps. The manure was treated with sprays, perishable garbage given to citizens for hogs, and the remaining garbage was burned and used as fill. Care was taken to reduce food waste by making the food more palatable and the proportions more accurate. Tents and buildings had fly paper and traps dangling about. The Army Medical Department not only treated diseases, but also insects like cockroaches and fleas as well as hunted for rodents.

Another problem at camp was a lack of water. The Newport News Water Company could not pump enough to meet servicemen needs and also to fill the ships at port. The solution was to impound water from a reservoir near Lee Hall, Virginia. Water conservation was encouraged, and the lack of water coupled with fear of fire led to careful watch over the terrain.[21]

At nearby Camp Hill on 64th Street, there was a Newport News Hostess House along the James River, were the service men could find recreation during an extended stay. The Hostess House offered lectures, movies and dances with local girls. The Red Cross also sponsored a canteen. While in camp, the men continued with physical exercises, hikes, training, and endless inspections.

CHAPTER FIVE

The School of Fire of Camp de Souge, Bordeaux, France (July 1918–August 1918)

The 52nd Field Artillery Brigade, which had arrived at Newport News, Virginia, on May 16, 1918, finally sailed for France. The brigade members departed on their assigned ships between June 6 and June 30. The men were instructed to wear their life belts at all times and keep their canteens full. The 104th Field Artillery Regiment sailed on the U.S.S. *Calamares*. The soldiers were given a postcard imprinted with "**I HAVE ARRIVED SAFELY OVER SEAS**" in bold capital letters on one side with space for them to sign their name. On the bottom left of the card was printed: "This card will be held until safe arrival of the boat on which I sailed." The postcard would be later sent out by the War Department, and the soldiers could address it to whomever they pleased.[1] In addition, soldiers wrote their own letters during the long voyage across the Atlantic although the division would end up censoring them. The men were not allowed to mail picture postcards home during their stay in France, in case it might divulge their location or assignment.[2]

Each soldier was given a cloth tag meal ticket with the number of his hatch including the letter of his deck, bunker, and raft or life boat in case of evacuation. It was worn at all times and punched at each meal. The soldiers also wore two aluminum dog tags with their name, rank and serial number. The dog tags were attached to a yard of ½ inch wide white cotton tape. The tags were tied in separate descending loops. If killed in action, one tag would be removed and the location of the body recorded. The other stayed on the serviceman for later identification.[3]

The U.S.S. *Calamares* was called a "banana boat" because it was part of the White Fleet Steamships of the United Fruit Company and had refrigerated cargo holds. During peace time, it delivered fruit from Central America to the United States. The ship, identification number 3662, was originally built in 1913 by Workman, Clark and Company in Belfast, Northern Ireland. Frank Workman and George Clark formed the original partnership to build transatlantic ships. The steamer had one smokestack and two masts. It weighed 7,782 gross tons and had a length of 470.4 feet, and breadth of 55.3 feet. It was commissioned by the U.S. Navy in April 1918 and would later also serve the navy in World War II.[4] Waves were painted on the sides as a sort of camouflage to disrupt the silhouette of the ship. The ship made five trips to France transporting troops, and made the trip an additional three times to transport provisions. It usually ported in France at either St. Nazaire or Brest. Between March and August of 1919, it would make five more crossings, bringing troops home.

A small ship, it was fitted with wooden frames out of two-by-four boards to create bunks for the men. Chicken wire was attached to the frames to support straw mattresses, although they tended to sag, leaving those on the bottom tier little room to move with a body practically on top of them. Because the men generally remained below during the day and the windows were always closed, the smell of bananas combined with the body sweat of the men was said to be almost intolerable. Private 1st Class Dudley Hess spoke of "camouflaged air."[5] Since they traveled during summer, there was little air circulation. By the second day at sea many of the men were seasick, increasing the odors and discomfort below deck. Many of the men distracted themselves with playing card games such as poker in the hot, crowded space.

In a July letter to a friend, titled "Somewhere on the ocean, sometime during July with the American Expeditionary Forces," Corporal Drew Rankin, Battery F, asserted facetiously that the trip "to somewhere" was enjoyable and comfortable. They ate on the deck when the weather was good, carrying their food up the ladder, and below deck when it rained.

> The generosity of the men is noticeable. If the boat is rolling the least bit, they invariably share their meal with the next man coming up the ladder. A fellow gave me half a cup of coffee the other morning, and another tried to give me his oatmeal, only I ducked in time.... It's great when the boat gets to pitching. The other morning a chap was coming through with a big pan of scrambled eggs, and another fellow right behind him with a pan of hot water. The boat gave a sudden lurch and the first chap dived head first into his pan of eggs and the other one dived over and washed him off with the pan of hot water, at least he bathed him all over. Folks are not nearly so thoughtful on land.
>
> We have not the slightest idea where we are headed for, and Africa and Japan are about the only places that have not been guessed. But Pat McMurrough insists that we are nearing Ireland, because the water which has heretofore been very blue, is now taking a greenish tint. Pat says that if the first land we sight is green then it is a cinch we are headed for Old Ireland. Never having been this far from home before, I naturally can't contradict him.[6]

Men were outfitted with a rifle, and a respirator which was carried across the chest. A tan cartridge belt was worn with a first aid pouch with twin snap fasteners in which was a tin with dressing and a bandage. They had a canteen with cup, and a mess kit which laced to the haversack containing a dish with a folding handle and a shallow plate. They also had a bacon tin which held an individual's rations, condiment tins with compartments for sugar, coffee, salt and pepper, mess utensils which included two spoons, a short knife and a fork, a wool blanket, a "half" pup tent with its parts, and a rain poncho, all of which had to fit in or attach to the canvas backpack, but only did so when the blanket was folded in one particular way. If everything did not fit, the backpack was said to be a "sad sack" and the soldier had to repack it correctly, presumably to the sergeant's satisfaction. An entrenching tool also was clasped to the top of the haversack.

The men participated in life boat drills in the morning and again at night. They participated responding to the call to "abandon ship." They did physical exercises and had regular duties. Training included target practice over the side of the ship even though the seas were often rough. The *Calamares* was headed for port at St. Nazaire, France, near the mouth of the Loire River. The port had shallow coastal waters surrounding it with a narrow harbor where German U-boats loved to hide. Alarms and bells would warn of the U-boat presence. The residents of St. Nazaire had seen many Americans land already, and seemed to ignore the arrival of more men. The 104th disembarked without fanfare between June 18 and 27, along with the 106th Field Artillery. The rest of the 52nd Field Artillery Brigade landed at Brest.

At St. Nazaire, the American soldiers stayed at the French "rest camp" close to the estuary of the Loire River, west of the city. The camp consisted of Adrian huts which were leaky, narrow, floorless wooden buildings covered in tar paper. William Clarke, who had arrived at that camp earlier with the infantry, called it a "miserable French army camp." The men slept on damp ground or used their pup-tent. There were bed sacks for some but they needed to be filled with hay to make a mattress. They had hoped to be able to wash clothes, but there was insufficient water for this even though Napoleon had built a small reservoir for the area.[7] It was still light at 9:30 p.m. making the day seem longer. There was a Y.M.C.A. canteen and a rail station at St. Nazire; within 24 hours the artillery was packed into small railroad cars and sent south.

The men of the 27th Division would become known as O'Ryan's Roughnecks. Major-General O'Ryan had sent out a memo to his officers on July 29, 1918, which may or may not be the cause of the nickname. The memo said, "Go to it 'rough'-with the bayonet-remember that the enemy's occupation is the authoritative signal for the launching of the counter-attack and that no counter-attacks so delivered have ever failed."[8] Rough and bayonet seemed to be linked. The infantry of the 27th would serve under the British and Americans, using British and Australian artillery for cover. After additional training in France, they were stationed at the East Poperinghe Line in Belgium from July 9 to August 20, 1918. The 27th infantry participated in the Battle of Dickebush Lake at the Dickebush Sector from August 21–30, and the Battle of Vierstratt Ridge by Mont Kemmel at the Scherpenberg Sector in Belgium August 31–September 2. The 27th Division Infantry defended the East Poperinghe Line under heavy attack by the Germans who occupied Mont Kemmel. They had relieved the British divisions, and proceeded to construct and occupy a secondary position opposite the mountain. There they were subject to artillery fire day and night with daily casualties. Within the month they merged into the Ypres-Lys Action of August 19–September 3.

It was in August 1918 that the Allies began the "Hundred Days Offensive," or Somme Offensive, which lasted from August 8 to November 11. The push was against the Hindenburg Line on the Western Front in France. The 27th Division Infantry joined this attack at the Knoll, Guillemont Farm, and Quennemont Farm on September 27. Stationed at the Hindenburg Line near Bony, France, they fought on September 29–30. Bony and Bellicourt were heavily fortified by the enemy as were Guillemont and Quennemont Farms. The 3rd British Corps were on their left with the Australian Corps, 9th British Corps and two other British troops. The 27th was in the II American Corps with the 30th Division. The 30th was to their right, along with the 10th French Army. The St. Quentin Canal Tunnel ran parallel to the Hindenburg Line at their location. The 6,000 yard long tunnel had been built by Napoleon in 1811 and once fortified by the Germans was considered to be impenetrable.[9] The infantry assaulted the tunnel and won an outstanding victory. On October 17, 1918, the infantry fought the Germans at the La Selle River by St. Souplet, France, using the river as a defensive line. The next day they defended the Jonc De Mer Ridge by L'Arbre de Guise and attacked at St. Maurice River by Catillon on October 19–20. They stopped fighting only with the Armistice. The American 30th Division had served on their left and the 34th British Division on their right as part of the II American Corps and 4th British Army.[10]

So called "Sunny France" was almost constantly rainy and damp throughout the war, with mud encrusting everything. Many American soldiers found the local conditions generally unsanitary. Most villages were collections of farms with animals sharing a roof with the family. There were heaps of manure in front of houses, considered a sign of French wealth. The 27th Division had rules about their own animals' manure. It was to be heaped ten feet square and five feet high and sprayed each day with a 5 percent mixture of Cresol in water. Cresol, a compound made from coal tar and wood tar, was used as a disinfectant. The pile was then covered with six inches of soil and a new pile started. The towns did not have open toilets available either. The few that existed were locked. The locals generally used the streets.[11] A number of divisions found it impossible to bathe at the front, while lice invaded their clothing seams and rats climbed around in their dugouts. Since many divisions had sent their men into the war with only a single uniform, the lack of cleaning combined with the rigors of trench warfare, resulted in dirty and torn clothing.

Major-General O'Ryan, however, gave strict warnings to his men about "keeping themselves fit," so the infantry set up places to bathe. He stressed the importance of trying to get sleep before an attack and even told his company and platoon commanders that if they had to, they should "literally put their men to bed as nothing makes greater drain upon physical fitness than lack of sleep." He also stressed the importance of good food and encouraged every effort to deliver hot food to those at the front,[12] though that was not always possible. A number of the food servers would earn citations for completing their tasks under the difficult conditions at the front.

The prohibition against alcohol that had been a central focus of the Mexican Punitive Expedition was relaxed in France and the servicemen were allowed to drink wine. The army worried endlessly about the large number of available unattached French women and the annual venereal report. They emphasized to the men the need to use protection. The army provided prophylactics and warned that with any sign of venereal disease, the soldier must seek medical immediately. Failure to do so, or to not be cured, could lead to punishment and possible court martial. Pershing held the unit commanders personally responsible for the venereal rates in their units. In turn, the A.E.F. tried to provide alternative recreation, supporting various organizations who offered "safe" activities for soldiers on leave. The Y.M.C.A. set up centers in the towns, provided soldiers with magazines and newspapers, and set up stores where soldiers could buy articles of interest. The prices were often higher than those in the commissary, since that their material had to be shipped in at a cost. The commissary had their material shipped for free, which factored in the price.[13]

The American artillery was trained at a number of sites in France, including camps at Coëtquidan, de Souge, Hunt, and Le Courneau. Retraining was needed whether or not the men had been trained stateside, because few of them had had access to American artillery pieces and none had used the French artillery pieces. Some regiments had only trained using logs.[14] The more experienced soldiers learned quickly. Non-experienced regiments spent most of the time in training, and did not encounter action at the front.

The 52nd Field Artillery Brigade did not spend their service in training. Nor would they serve alongside their divisional infantry. In fact, they would not see their division again until after the Armistice. First they were sent to the School of Fire of Camp de Souge near Bordeaux. The six-thousand healthy men of the 104th, 105th, 106th, and the 102nd Ammunition Train were eager to serve. They traveled south by train in uncomfortable Pullman cars that each carried 40 hommes (i.e., men) and 8 chevaux (i.e., horses). Each car was supposedly designed to fit those numbers, but it could never carry them comfortably and the ventilation within the small space was very bad. Soldiers often had to shovel out manure and add clean straw before they could sit. The cars actually only fit 20 to 30 men, and being squeezed together resulted in a lot of bruises. There were no bathrooms on the train. As they traveled, the American forces were surprised that most of the villages they passed contained only old men and children. The young French men were either in the army or dead. The women dressed in black were out on the farms, carrying on the work.[15]

At Bordeaux, the main train station was located in the center of the town. The old location is now called the Gare de Bordeaux-Saint-Jean or the Bordeaux-Midi. The rail stop was at the southern end of the Paris-Bordeaux railway and the western end of the Chemin de fer du Midi to Toulouse line. The Bordeaux station had opened in 1898. Trains were important arteries connecting regions and now served to transport troops. The station nearest the camp to which the men were headed was the Bonneau Station.[16] Camp militaire de Souge was about 20 kilometers west of Bordeaux in the municipality of Martignas-sur-Jalle in the department of Gironde. Still in use today, it now consists of 2,855 acres and is home to the French Army's 13th Régiment de Dragons Parachutistes and a flight test center with firing ranges and training grounds.

The 52nd Field Artillery Brigade trained at the School of Fire of Camp de Souge for six weeks from July 12 to August 30, 1918. From August 6 to September 1, Lieutenant-Colonel John T. Delaney commanded the brigade. Camp de Souge had been a large French artillery school, established in 1900, prior to the arrival of the Americans. Soldiers entered the camp under a wooden archway with the name of the camp overhead. Inside the gate ran a long street with double wooden barracks on either side. The barracks had concrete floors and electric lights. The wooden bunks had straw-filled mattresses. There were pine trees and some scrub trees by the men's quarters. The officer's quarters, mess hall and hospital were nearest the gate, along with the quarters of the brigade commander. At the far end of the road were the Y.M.C.A. hut, school buildings, and the camp commander's office. The schools for soldiers, however, were far from these buildings. Private Hess mentioned that when they arrived, "we hit the training camp and the camp hit us. Sand, flu, all around." The men arrived in very good condition, already hardened, and ended up experiencing little sickness during their entire tour of duty, a small miracle considering the conditions they would suffer.[17]

There were little rows of cafes and stands around the camp which soldiers frequented during their free time. The new soldiers seemed to be always hungry, and many of the French profited from it until their resources dwindled. The Americans quickly ate up all the food supplies in the region causing prices to rise rapidly. This must have been a particular hardship for the French soldiers who were literally paid in pennies. The soldiers from the States seemed oblivious to this. French bread, cheese, jam, chocolate, and milk were much more interesting than army "slum" (stew) and "canned Willy" (corned beef). Private Hess wrote about how the men used their Sunday passes to visit Bordeaux. Bordeaux was a bustling large city offering all of the adventure a soldier could want: restaurants, shopping, and the cinema. There was a Y.M.C.A. post there as well. Hess called the lorries transporting them "the Bordeaux Church Special," commenting that few of the men went to actually attend church.[18] The women in the city seemed to be more attractive than what they had seen so far, but the enlisted men did not get overnight leave.

Training at the camp consisted of a very difficult and tightly packed curriculum divided into schools. The 104th and 105th Field Artillery Regiments finally received their French 75-millimeter guns. The men learned to handle their guns in teams: 1,435 men under Colonel Merritt H. Smith, and 1,401 men under Colonel Dewitt C. Weld, Jr. The 106th Field Artillery Regiment also received their 155-millimeter howitzers. The 1,472 men of that regiment served under Major Lewis H. Eller. There were 4 guns to a battery, 24 guns to a regiment, and 72 in the brigade. The equipment came complete with horses. In addition, the 102nd Trench Mortar Battery received their twelve six-inch Newton Mortars.[19] Two hundred and twenty-eight men served in that battery under Captain Charles Pearson, Jr.

First came lectures and then the men went out to the field where the lessons were applied. There were gun drills on sighting, loading and firing for cannoneers. The mechanism of the gun was studied, previously a tightly held French secret. The gun did not require tools to assemble and disassemble. Range work included drills and tests for the cannoneers overseen by officers in observation towers with field glasses and telephones. The field, sandy with pine trees, was set up with white panels to represent houses and a church, or to mark trenches. The men practiced problem solving and strategic firing at specific points. Correcting the elevation and calculating distance to the target were part of the work. Orders were received via telephone and instructors evaluated and criticized the men's actions. Batteries took turns with all officers having an opportunity to fire on a problem. While one battery was on the range, the others practiced loading field pieces to acquire speed and accuracy. Then the guns were shifted and the sightings adjusted.

There were classes in transmitting messages via wireless telegraph and signaling to airplanes. Repairing telephones, laying wire, and setting up switch boards and exchanges would prove vital to the artillery. Draftsmen learned about topography, map-making and field sketches. Mechanics learned gun repair. Every battery sent representatives to the machine gun school to learn how to protect ammunition from enemy airplanes. Non-commissioned officers were given updated training on gas attacks that they passed on to their troops. The drivers and cannoneers were taught to handle the horses and guns on the dusty roads during long hikes. Six to eight horses pulled each gun on the limber, and the men had to know how to quickly bring the guns into action.

Officers were on the range from 7:30 a.m. until noon, spending afternoons studying regimental positions on maps and reviewing firing data. They learned about camouflage, liaison work, and construction of gun emplacements. In the evening, officers gathered around blackboards and were critiqued.[20] The Americans needed to learn many French words: a "côte" was a hill, slope or coast; a "bois" was a wood; a "forges" was a forge; a "ferme" was a farm; a "forêt" was a forest, but a "foret" was a drill bit or place of drilling; a "salient" was a battlefield feature which projected into enemy territory exposing three sides to danger. A salient was vulnerable, and a deep salient could lead to a pincer move by the enemy around the flanks of those caught there. The Allies were often fighting in salients in France, and knowing those geographic words helped them understand their terrain. The Americans often served under the French Army, and phrases like "garde à vous" (attention), "repos" (at ease), "halte" (halt), "qui vive?" (who goes there), and "avance à l'ordre" (advance with the password), were crucial. The words "vin blanc" and "vin rouge" were easier for the men to learn: white wine and red wine.

Nicknames prevailed for many groups. The Americans called the French "Frenchies" or "Froggies." The French called the Germans "Boches" for beast, which Americans picked up. The Americans would also call the Germans "Jerry," "Fritz," "Huns," "Teuton" for Teutonic, and "Bolonie." The French and Germans called the British soldiers "Tommies," which was a generic term used for a British soldier, based on the name Thomas Atkins. Australians were called "Diggers." The English called the Americans "Sammy" for Uncle Sam or "Yanks" for Yankees. At home Americans called their boys, "Doughboys." The certainty of its origin is largely unknown. Some lean towards it being a negative term given to infantry at first by the cavalry. The infantry, being closer to the ground during a march, were often covered in dust while the cavalry rode by looking down on them. Dust resembled being sprinkled with flour. However it began, the word became an affectionate term used for Americans serving in the Great War, forever connected to that period, even though it had started prior.

At camp, information on gas attacks was an important part of the training. The 52nd Field Artillery Brigade had previously trained under both gas and live fire, giving them an advantage. The Germans used many different kinds of gas at the front: some caused tearing and sneezing, but others were more deadly. Both men and animals were vulnerable to these attacks. If a gas alert sounded, the men were instructed to quickly place the masks carefully over their face and then the face of their horses. The rubberized cloth with elastic edges had two elastic straps that fit over the head. The bottom fit snug to the chin, but the eye pieces often grew foggy, and saliva dribbled from the rubber tube in the mouth. When worn for an extended period of time men would sweat and itch, and bits of gas that made it past the elastic would cause the eyes to water and the nose to run. Any facial hair might have broken the seal and let the poison in.[21] Chlorine blistered the lungs, causing death by suffocation. Mustard gas was the most feared. It caused red patches on the body that burned the flesh; the burns could spread, too, eating the flesh to the bone. Men were given sag paste to smear on potentially exposed skin which trapped in heat, and could become contaminated by exposure to mustard gas. Three categories of gas were used by the enemy:

1. Asphyxiants which hit the respiratory organs, causing irritation, heavy spasms and sometimes causing the small blood vessels in the lungs to fill with fluid leading to pneumonia and death, such as phosgene, chlorine, and nitrous fumes.
2. Paralysants which paralyzed the respiratory system, such as cyanogens and prussic acid.
3. Lachrymators or irritants which produced tears and affected the tissues of the eyes, such as benzyl bromide, ethyliodoacetate, chloropicrin, dichlorethyl sulphide (mustard gas) and others.[22]

By introducing lethal chemicals into the war, the Central powers opened the door for it to be used against them. The Allies did use some of these mixtures, resulting in more horrific deaths as waterways and forests became contaminated. Despite the fear of gas, the Allies had far more casualties from conventional shells. By the end of the war, 70 percent of the casualties were from artillery shells.[23]

The 52nd Artillery Brigade would end up being sent into a very dangerous area covered by enemy artillery in better fortifications at higher elevations. The German artillery was considered the best in the world at this time. Unfortunately for the Americans, the Germans had had four years to set up sophisticated defensive systems made of concrete and sandbags surrounded by barbed wire. The enemy artillery used field pieces like the 340's, 220's, 155's, and 105's to mention just a few. German heavies, the 210 millimeter naval guns loaded on rail cars, would send shells towards American lines. The Allies were subjected to the Minenwerfer or "Minnie" German heavy trench mortar high explosive, or "H.E." shells, which made a huge explosion from the 50 pound shell.[24] The Minniewerfer were also called the "Iron Mermaid" because they had a fish-like tail which helped stabilize them in flight. The Allies would also be under fire from the Austrian 77 millimeter high speed shells, called "Whiz-Bangs," which seemed to travel faster than sound by some accounts. There were nicknames for many of the shells: "Jack Johnson," "Archies," and "G.I. Cans."

Soldiers were warned to never speak about their military engagements, and to simply respond "I do not know" to questions asked them by outsiders. Mentioning locations was particularly dangerous as many of the Germans could speak English quite well and, when dressed in a captured American uniform, sometimes would blend into mess lines with the Americans. No maps or notes with any information about offensives were to be carried to the front, lest they fall into enemy hands.[25]

All out going mail was censored. Colonel Drew Rankin, 104th Field Artillery, always typed his letters home and in one, he jokingly censored himself with the letter "x."

> When we disembarked from the S.S. xxxxx we landed at xxxxx and from there went to xxxx where we stayed xxxx and then left for xxxx and went into action the first time at xxxxx where we stayed xxxxx days and then after a rest went back into action at xxxxxx where we still are located. You see I am learning so much about censorship that I can fool the censor every shot and he can't find anything to censor. By the time one leaves out all he is told to leave out, about all he can say is that he is getting plenty to eat, and likes it fine.[26]

Soldiers were trained in ciphering codes at the camp. "Every message, every unit, station, central, name of everything and in fact every word sent over the telephone had to be sent in code. Codes were arranged and changed every so often and from this time on until the Armistice was signed; every word sent over the phone was ciphered."[27] Men were trained to set up and use the wireless and telephone. The phone lines and wires which were strung would prove to be vital to the success of the artillery. The telephone system enabled the 52nd Field Artillery Brigade to respond quickly to changing needs on the ground with the help of the infantry liaison to direct the fire. In addition, teams practiced using blinker lights and signaling with flags. Lectures and field work included training in trenches that were set up in various configurations: diagonal, triangular and square. The men had to pass exams in each area to prove proficiency. They were classed in trench digging and dug-out construction. Rifle and pistol target practice was done.

The 104th and 105th Field Artillery Regiments would use French 75-millimeter guns, which became the favorite field gun of the Americans due to its revolutionary technology. The gun was invented in 1897 and its construction was a carefully guarded French secret. Its formal name was the Canon de 75 Modèle 1897, but it was called the French 75mm, the "75," or the Soixante-Quinze, which is French for 60–15 (60 plus 15 equaling 75). It had a hydropneumatic recoil system considered very advanced at the time, that used both glycerin and air. The glycerin oil was stored in a cylinder underneath the gun. When fired, the barrel slid back on rollers and the action of the piston being pulled back pushed the oil through a small opening into a second cylinder under compressed air. The oil absorbed the recoil, and the pressure of the compressed air returned the barrel to its original position. The entire process only took two seconds. The aim did not need to be re-adjusted after the gun was fired either. It fired rapidly and accurately with a range of about 5–5½ miles. At the camp the cannoneers were trained to be experts in this firing process. The crews learned direct and indirect firing, studying the proper shell and fuse for different targets and simulating problems on the field.[28]

When the war had begun, the French had about 4,000 of the 75 Modèle 1897. By the end of the war they had 12,000. Eventually the New York National Guard started training with them and the gun would later be used in World War II as well. In 1918, the French gave the American Expeditionary Forces about 2,000 of these guns. The Field Artillery Brigades became quite attached to their painted olive drab guns, often sleeping under them with their tents pitched under the carriages. Sometimes the soldiers named their guns after women or perceived personality traits. The guns were treated with great respect as the men learned to place sandbags around them, camouflage them under netting strung from poles, hide them in trenches, hitch them to horses, pull them with ropes, position them towards the enemy, and clean them endlessly. The guns were drawn by six to eight horses with the drivers mounted on the "near" horse on the left side. Packs and baggage were lashed onto the "off" horses. Due to the mud and hilly terrain, the men often helped the horses by pushing the wheels and pulling on lines.

In contrast to the other two regiments, the 106th Field Artillery Regiment was assigned to use the heavy 155 millimeter Schneider howitzers. These pieces had a range of almost 7 miles. The Model 1917 was very good at a high angle elevation, used for curved fire or indirect shooting, and could hit targets that the flat 75-millimeter guns could not. The howitzers also gave very little trouble to the cannoneers. They could be placed in a deep sheltered valley, or thicket.[29] The howitzer was originally designed by M. Schneider of the French firm Schneider et Cie. The 1915 model was designed for ammunition with a brass cartridge case, but the November 1917 model was fitted to use a propelling charge contained in cloth bags.

The 102nd Trench Mortar Regiment trained on a different field at camp.

They used the British Stokes Mortar. It was effective at direct fire, lobbing high explosive shells into enemy trenches. By 1918 the French front consisted of a long series of endless mud trenches. The mortar brigade became familiar with those trenches as they were only effective when close to the enemy.

It is a common misperception that artillery is safe behind the front lines during war. Once the guns fired, they became the primary target of enemy artillery and airplanes. The distinctive light and smoke, particularly when firing at night, made their position obvious, and the artillerymen often had to deal with counter battery fire while trying to protect their own infantry. In order to find enemy artillery brigades, the army used Flash Rangers and later Sound Rangers. The Flash Rangers were usually placed at two or three high points to observe the flash or puff of smoke coming from an enemy gun. The time was recorded between sight of fire and impact and then reported to headquarters where the distance was gridded on maps. By careful coordination between two rangers placed at different points, with a third used to authenticate accuracy, the enemy gun could be located, often within ten yards. Later, sound ranging was used with stopwatches clocking the time of sound. In order to increase accuracy, the Allies used five gallon gas cans fitted with microphones to record the difference in time between the fired ordinance and its arrival (sound travels about 1,100 feet per second). Again the distances were plotted on a map. The rangers also recorded Allied launches, helping them become more accurate in meeting their targets. Any observed troop movements were reported.[30]

The artillery range at Camp de Souge was flat and sandy. In the center of it was an old stone building used as a target for volleys. There was a dense pine forest nearby which had a tendency to catch fire when the shells burst. Shells were greased before loading, causing them to spin out towards their targets. The artillery weapon system was set up for a surface-to-surface long range indirect fire. Artillery was used to suppress and destroy enemy cannon and rockets.

The artillery had different defensive and offensive uses for the guns. Examples of defensive uses are deployed defense, position defense, and zone defense. A deployed defense was dependent upon a particular tactical plan. Tactical plans included observed fire on targets, organized fire for emergencies (which usually required course correction after receiving proper data), and counter-attack against another battery. A position defense was either based on observed fire or specifically requested by infantry. A zone defense was much like a position defense, but it could be shallow, average or deep. Either concentrations or a standing barrage might be used as well. Offensive moves were usually part of a direct attack and might use either organized fire or specific concentrations on a visible enemy.[31]

Different types of fire were also required from the 75s. Harassing fire was used when the artillery intended to do something. Concentrations were set on a target using fewer guns to avoid waste. A general barrage created a curtain of fire and flying metal, laid down in front of friendly infantry before an offensive or defensive move. It would take out obstructions in the way of the advancing infantry. There were different types of barrages as well: a normal defensive barrage was used to protect infantry from an enemy attack; a rolling barrage was used as an offensive move that progressed in front of infantry as they advanced. Rolling barrages were useful in trench warfare to break a deadlock, but required sufficient density to be effective. The goal was to make it impossible for the enemy to fire on the moving infantry and to obscure the advance under smoke and flying dirt. Each battery could lay a path of fire about 200 meters wide a certain distance in front of the advancing infantry, the area known as the danger zone. Barrages lasted for 3–10 minutes, then lifted and were repeated on an area farther out. The recommended number of guns for a rolling barrage was one battery per hundred yards of frontage, using two rounds per gun per minute. A protective barrage sent forth the maximum fire on an enemy stronghold using heavy artillery. A counter-preparation barrage could be used against an enemy trench. For offensive maneuvers, a box barrage was deadly. It created a wall of bursting shells in the shape of a box which could encircle a battery or an entire village. The box was then raked inside, combined with high explosives and sometimes gas. No one caught in a box lived.[32]

According to one artilleryman, the preparation for fire included a number of sights and sounds. Men were trained to speak in low voices, so they were only heard by those nearest them. Then came "the click of shells against shells as ammunition was cleaned and greased," the "snap of the breech closing," the "crash of guns as they shook dugouts and sent gravel down the walls of trenches," and the "clanging of empty shell cases being tossed out of the way." There were bright flashes of light when a gun fired. Sometimes shells also sparked and smoked.[33] After firing from a position, if there was no return fire, the men would canvas the area and remove or bury any spent material so as to not reveal the position to the enemy. There were assigned ammunition dumps where drivers unloaded material. Horses, when not pulling guns, pulled loads of ammunition and spent shell casings to the dumps.

At the training camp, everyone went to school, but the officers of the 52nd Field Artillery Brigade were so well trained that many of them served as instructors. In general, officers learned more complex forms of barrages, and had to perform sightings and calculations based upon variables such as distance, barometric pressure, and wind. They observed from different positions to learn first hand the results of a different offensive tactic. Each type of fire was assigned a number of rounds per piece per minute. After a certain length of time, the guns needed to cool for a few minutes before returning to fire. All of these things needed to be carefully calculated. Precise details were recorded in firing diaries.[34]

The care of horses was also taught. Time was spent harnessing and maneuvering teams. Many of the units entering France had previously practiced using tractors to pull their artillery pieces. They soon found that tractors were unable to handle the wet, pocked terrain, breaking down frequently without access to the materials needed to repair them. Fortunately for the 52nd Brigade, they had served with horses already. The demand for horses and mules was a continual problem at the front. There were never enough and many of the animals contracted mange and influenza. Horses had arrived sick at the ports or became sick while being transported by train in poorly ventilated cars. The climate in France was rainy and cold and the animals often stood in the mud for long periods of time, an unsanitary situation. Some of the horses the army had procured were untamed. While the cannoneers learned the art of firing, the drivers became experts in handling the horses and carriages through harrowing conditions such as shell fire, deep mud, and unstable roads.

The fields in France had been churned up by the shells and there was little forage at the front line. Feed for the horses had to be rationed and drivers were constantly on the search for something extra to give the hungry horses. Men often chipped in to buy hay out of their own earnings. There were not enough veterinarians to care for the animals either. At Camp de Souge, 543 animals died in just three months, mostly from influenza. At Camp Coëtquidan, 1,151 died over four months. At the front, 3 to 4 horses died per battery per day.[35] Keeping the artillery in horses was nearly impossible. Horses became valued more than men, and they were fed first before the soldiers; careful rub downs were mandatory.

The drivers of the horses put in long days. In addition to feeding, grooming, watering, and harnessing the animals, they also had to endure "falls, bumps, kicks, and bites" from the animals.[36] Horses initially let a gas mask be placed over the head, thinking it a feed bag, but after that they resisted. They did not understand that under a gas attack it could save their life. The mask had to be placed over the head within the shortest time possible for survival. It was a challenge. Drivers had to encourage weary animals to haul ammunition and powder, and pull guns through the muddy terrain. There were forced marches at night, and the cold French rain which never seemed to stop. The cleaning, feeding, watering, harnessing, mounting, and riding of horses became central to the artillery. Water would be a particular problem for horses, as well for men, because many of the rivers and streams were polluted by gas and dead bodies. The soldiers developed great affection for the horses in their brigades and it was not unusual to see a man cry over the suffering of a horse. Fred

McKenna of the 103rd Field Artillery referred to the horses as "trying, willing and suffering" wearing heavy packs for hours as they waited and shivered with "sweat, mud, hunger, and thirst." At the front, the roads were filled with the dead carcasses of the animals which just could not make it.[37]

An added contribution to the horse shortage was the raiding of field artillery horses by other divisions. A ruling came forth stating that it was forbidden for horses to be taken from a regiment without the proper authorization, being considered "equivalent to breaking up the unit concerned." The relationship between the animals and men caring for them was taken very seriously and must be maintained.[38]

Camp de Souge also served as a prisoner of war camp. They were guarded by soldiers from the French territories and Asians worked on the grounds, giving the camp an international flavor. The French soldiers in their blue uniforms guarded the Germans in their gray-green uniforms. The Allies learned a great deal from their prisoners: confiscating notes they carried, which helped the Allies understand the type of interrogation their own men might encounter. If the Germans were warning their soldiers against being plied with fine food and alcohol by their captors in order to get information, then it was likely American soldiers would have the same tactic used against them. Confiscated documents also revealed information about enemy artillery. German artillerymen had been instructed to use brief concentrated fire instead of long barrages because the long barrage gave the Allies time to take cover. They would be able to kill more men with short concentrated bursts in Allied territory.[39] The Germans used this tactic extensively.

The 52nd Field Artillery Brigade trained for six weeks at the School of Fire, from July 12 to August 30, 1918. Discipline was kept very high under the intensive training and the French School Commandant called them "the best Artillery Brigade that had attended the camp." On September 1, the men were sent by rail to Longeville near Bar-le-Duc, department of Meuse, region of Lorraine. To reach this area, they had to travel diagonally across France from the south west to the north east, riding the famous French 40 and 8. Bar-le-Duc is directly south of Verdun. When they arrived, they were attached to the 33rd Division to serve as its artillery.[40] The artillery of the 33rd Division, the 58th Field Artillery Brigade, had not had sufficient training in the United States, due largely to not having guns, so their artillery spent a large amount of time in France training, initially at Le Valdahon and Ornans. The infantry brigades of the division included the 65th Infantry Brigade with the 129th and the 130th Infantry Regiments and the 66th Infantry Brigade with the 131st and 132nd Infantry Regiments. The 52nd Field Artillery Brigade from the 27th Division was well disciplined and well trained. They would serve the 33rd Division well in their upcoming battles.

CHAPTER SIX

St. Mihiel Salient Offensive (September 12, 1918)

On July 24, 1918, while the 52nd Field Artillery Brigade was in training, General Pershing was in conference with the commanders of the Allied forces in Bombon, France, planning the first all American offensive. There was tension between Marshal Ferdinand Foch (1851–1919) and General Pershing. French General Marshal Ferdinand Foch was the Generalissimo (Commander-in-Chief) of the Allied Armies. He also commanded the French forces. Foch wanted to break apart the American units and use them in support of a British offensive in the north. Pershing was outraged. He wanted an American offensive at St. Mihiel. A compromise was reached with a second offensive to follow the first in the Meuse-Argonne region. The 1st American Army was organized on August 10, and on August 30 it assumed command of a front from Port-sur-Seille, east of the Moselle River, to Watronville, 11 kilometers southeast of Verdun. General Pershing had a second meeting on September 2 at Marshal Ferdinand Foch's headquarters with Foch, and General Henri Philippe Benoni Omer Joseph Pétain (1856–1951); that is when the war plans were formalized according to Pershing's liking. General Pétain was a national hero in France and following the Battle of Verdun was nicknamed the Lion of Verdun. This was going to be Pershing's first offensive showing what the Americans could do.

The mission of the offensive was the reduction of the St. Mihiel salient. Located southeast of Verdun, the Germans had held the area since September 1914. There was a bulge of about 200 square miles near the village of St. Mihiel creating the salient with the Allies to the south and the Germans to the north. The area between the two sides was known as "no man's land." The salient was loosely shaped like a triangle with St. Mihiel in the west corner, or at the "nose." The strongest defenses of the enemy were in the two wings. At the salient's eastern front the Germans were located on high ground with a clear observational advantage. The western face ran along the rugged and heavily wooded heights of the Meuse River. The southern face followed the heights of the Meuse and crossed into the plain of the Woëvre where the Germans maintained additional observation points. For four years the Germans had held that ground, building strong defensive works with miles of barbed wire. The Allies had smaller hills in the area from which to observe their targets. In 1915, the French had made several unsuccessful attempts to straighten the line and dissolve the salient. The stalemate had led to fairly quiet conditions prior to the arrival of the Americans. The plan was to push the Germans back from their positions to the Vigneulles-Thiaucourt-Regniéville line, hold them with a small force, and then move the battlefront to the east later in September. A win here would bolster the Allies' morale while lowering the confidence of the enemy. The French doubted the objective could be accomplished before winter. They considered that the only way to win this battle was to accept the cost of a large number of casualties. Pershing chose to use the American soldiers to draw out the enemy before destroying them.[1]

The main problem for the French in this area was that the German artillery harassed the Paris-Nancy Railroad line which ran north through St. Mihiel to Verdun. The taking of the St. Mihiel salient would free the railway line, along with a number of villages which had been held captive since 1914.[2] The offensive also had an objective to eliminate the threat on the flank of the Verdun fortifications. Pershing wanted to press all the way to Metz by the Moselle and Seille Rivers. Metz was the capital of the Lorraine region. The Germans expected he might do that by attacking east of the river, and they reenforced that area in anticipation. The French commander Marshall Foch decided against that action. Pershing and Foch disliked each other, often causing conflict between them in pressure situations. Pershing preferred an independent American Army, but recognized he was in France and needed to work with Foch.

The St. Mihiel area was also vital to the Germans because of the coverage it gave them of two primary interests: the Mézières-Sedan-Metz Railroad and the Briey Iron Basin. The railroad lines running into France from the north and northeast were used to transport troops and material into the area, and to move coal and iron ore out of northern France and Belgium. The iron mines of Lorraine were heavily guarded by the enemy. The iron basin in Briey produced 4/5th of the iron ore in continental Europe, used to make steel and flux for smelting. Steel was used for weapons and equipment. The French had exported ore to Germany in 1913.[3] The train lines provided rapid deployment of both men and product, and the Germans had no intention of leaving. This offensive would lead into a much larger offensive planned by the Allies.

Since the region by St. Mihiel tended to become swampy during the fall rains, the plan was to begin the first offensive early in September, between the 12th and 16th. Roads were constructed to assist in supplying of the troops. Brigadier-General Pershing placed his headquarters at Ligny-en-Barrois, 40 kilometers south of St. Mihiel. 300,000 men would be involved, including 70,000 French. The 2nd, 5th, 82nd and 90th American Divisions would form I Corps led by Lieutenant-General Hunter Liggett (1857–1935). Liggett was a 39-year veteran of the army, an ardent student of tactics with experience and training. I Corps would press north and take the right portion of the salient. IV Corps would be led by Major-General Joseph T. Dickman (1857–1927) and consist of the 1st, 42nd, and 89th American Divisions. Dickman was a seasoned veteran of war. The 1st and 42nd Divisions included officers originally from the 27th Division. IV Corps would also press north, making the main attack on the southern portion of the salient and continue on towards Vigneulles. V Corps included the 4th and 26th American Divisions, along with and the 15th French Colonial Division and would be led by Major-General George H. Cameron (1861–1944). In November Cameron would lose his only son, 1st Lieutenant Douglas Tilford Cameron, who had served in the 7th Field Artillery of the 1st Division. Douglas had served in the 27th Division in the Divisional Headquarters Company and as an adjutant prior to serving in the 1st Division. The 27th Division contributed officers to the 26th Division as well. V Corps would press east, making a secondary attack along the western portion of the salient and then link up with the IV Corps. The II French Colonial Corps would be placed at the nose of the salient in the center.

In support of this overall plan, General Pershing ordered the 52nd Field Artillery of the 27th Division to attach to the 33rd Division. The orders came via Special Order No. 121 dated September 3, 1918. The 33rd Division was commanded by Major-General George Bell, Jr. The division was from Illinois and was dubbed the "Prairie Division." The 33rd would often be paired with the 29th Division. Nicknamed the "Blue & Gray Division," a throw back to the Civil War era, the soldiers came from New Jersey's 113th and 114th, representing the blue of the North, and the 115th from Maryland and Delaware along with the 116th from Virginia representing the Southern gray. Brigadier-General Harry H. Bandholz formerly with the 27th Division commanded the 58th Infantry Brigade within the 29th Division.

The 33rd Division and the men from the 52nd Field Artillery Brigade marched over two days from Longeville to Nixéville, France, in the beginning of September. Nixéville is southwest of Verdun. From September 8 to 25 the 33rd Division was assigned to the French XVII Corps, under Major General Henri Claudel, to relieve French units, and the American 93rd Division, from the Meuse River west to Haucourt. They were stationed at the front line in the Verdun-Fromeréville Sector to support the XVII French Corps, under the

2nd French Army. Their part of the line ran from the Meuse River, west to the village of Haucourt. Haucourt had been destroyed by the Central powers in 1916. The French Corps were composed of a number of French divisions. As the Americans trudged through the mud along the rolling hills the rain poured down. The artillerymen had to work hard to steady the wheels of the caissons, sometimes using line to help pull the horses up the steeper inclines. The men traveled at night and tried to rest during the day, but the threat of German planes overhead made rest very difficult.[4] The Americans, in general, were placed in what had been quiet sectors in France. They were to relieve British and French divisions who then moved to active areas. Things changed rapidly, however, with the arrival of the Americans, and quiet areas suddenly came alive with active shelling.

As the 52nd Field Artillery Brigade prepared for battle, the influenza epidemic was at its peak. This round in the fall was the second, more deadly, version of the virus that became pandemic. A mild form of influenza had surfaced in the late spring and summer of 1918. This second round was more severe, and a third form would follow it in the spring of 1919. Between 1918 and 1919 an estimated 21.5 million people would die world-wide. Camp Wadsworth reported 600 cases of the flu with 409 men dying in October of 1918, their deadliest month. The 27th Division had left camp when the flu was still mild. It was named the "Spanish flu" because the Spanish were the only ones reporting it in their newspapers. Censors throughout the rest of Europe blocked reports due to the war; no one wanted to appear weak. The virus hit young adults the hardest, reportedly because it over-stimulated the body's immune system and younger systems tended to react with greater strength. It caused the lungs to flood, leading to pneumonia. 360,000 A.E.F. soldiers contracted the illness and 25,000 of them died. In France, many victims sat along roadways, unable to move, waiting to be evacuated by the ambulances. Some, who recovered, would later contract pneumonia in the freezing rain of France and die.[5]

The region of Lorraine is bordered Belgium, Germany and Luxembourg, making it a culturally diverse area. The eastern section had actually been annexed to the German Empire following the Franco-Prussian War (1870–1871) that helped unite Germany. Because Napoleon had looted the Prussians, they in turn looted France during that war. The Great War was fought in a region with a long history of conflict between Germany and France. The Lorraine region had also been the birthplace of Joan of Arc (Jeanne d'Arc), patron saint of the French. It was a region steeped in military history.

This particular sector by Verdun was important to the Central powers because it was close to the railroad lines running into France from the north and northeast. The city of Verdun, on the banks of the Meuse River, was founded by the Gauls long before the Romans arrived. The city became a part of the Holy Roman Empire in 843 under the Treaty of Verdun. The 1648 Peace of Westphalia awarded the area to France. The name Verdun, in Latin Verodunum, means strong fort and for centuries it had made use of its natural setting for protection. Major-General John F. O'Ryan, in his account of the activities of his division, mentioned that the forts of Vaux and Tavannes were located on the right side of the river, and the left bank was home to the forts of DeMarre and Choissel, among others. The hilly terrain offered cover for artillery and he considered it to have been made for battle.[6] The Germans took full advantage of many of the French forts that circled the city, as well as the thick forests and the mountain tops. Verdun had a number of hills surrounding it and a number of stone forts with draw bridges circling it; Douaumont was the largest one. The Meuse River runs generally north and south there, but twists and turns near Verdun. The German command was at Dun-sur-Meuse and Stenay. The French commanded the Citadel of Verdun, Rampont and Souilly. The enemy line was uncomfortably close to Verdun, and the French were having trouble maintaining the line, because the enemy was well placed with keen observation posts.

Back in 1916 the Central powers had used the greatest group of artillery ever previously assembled against Verdun. General Sir Douglas Haig, Commander of the British Expeditionary Force, along with French forces had focused an attack on the Germans in Picardy near the Somme River in an attempt to take pressure off of the city of Verdun, but it failed and the Germans opened the Battle of Verdun which was a devastating loss.

The Battle of Verdun, begun on February 21, 1916, to the end of that year, had been brutal with great loss of life. The Germans still hoped to gain Verdun, and the French were fighting valiantly to protect it. Many of the smaller towns in the vicinity had been completely destroyed during the earlier battle. Verdun was a city in ruins, having suffered greatly from four years of fighting. The French were holding the line, but were weary. The enemy, on the other hand, had four years to build entrenchments with concrete bunkers, and lay miles of barbed wire. Their pill boxes were sunk into the ground, and vegetation had grown over them, making them very difficult to see. The well trained German artillery commanded the heights, obscured by woods on the eastern side. They were well protected. The heights of the Meuse River on the right bank near Verdun had a high ridge with wooded ravines, backed by the eastern plains of the Woëvre leading to Germany. The left bank of the river also had high hills. The Germans had observation posts throughout the region. The front line at the Verdun- Fromeréville Sector in Lorraine, at the 33rd's arrival, ran in the following manner: the French held the line from Avoucourt eastward through Haucourt, the valley by Forges Brook. It followed the brook and passed south of the village of Béthincourt and north of Le Mort Homme as it traveled due east. The Germans held the north side of the ravine while the French held the south side. As one crossed the Meuse River to the east of Forges, the front line ran between Samogneux and Brabant-sur-Meuse and then turned southeast; Bezongaux and Vaux were in the hands of the French.[7]

During the nights of September 7 and 8, 1918, the 33rd Division began to move infantry regiments into the Verdun- Fromeréville Sector in Lorraine. First headquartered in Blercourt on September 7, the 33rd moved to Fomeréville directly northwest of Verdun to relieve units of the 157th French Division and the 120th French Division. The 33rd was the first American division to hold a portion of the front at the Meuse River, their sector running from the Meuse opposite Samogneux to the ruins of Haucourt. The French 18th Division of the French XVII Corps was to their right and the French 157th Division of the same corps was to their left. They would work extensively with the French in this area.

On September 8 and 9, the 104th Field Artillery Regiment and the 1st Battalion of the 105th Field Artillery Regiment moved southwest of Verdun to the vicinity of Nixéville to relieve the French 53rd Regiment, A.C. (artillery). The 2nd Battalion of the 105th Field Artillery Regiment relieved the French 53rd Regulars in the section to the right of the 33rd Division. Batteries A, C and D of the 106th Field Artillery Regiment, now commanded by Major Guido F. Verbeck, were sent to relieve the French heavy artillery units. Some members of the 105th and 106th Regiments of the 52nd Field Artillery Brigade followed, driven in trucks. The American 8th Division was then stationed to the left of the 33rd Division with the French on their right.

While the 104th Field Artillery Regiment was moving towards their assignment, they were ordered to take over the positions of the French 157th and 120th, located by Le Mort Homme—Côte 304 Sector farther north. The French at these locations, well known to their enemy, were being moved elsewhere on the front. Côte/Hill 304 was west of Le Mort Homme (the dead man) and there were two shallow trenches by the two hills in front of Béthincourt. Le Mort Homme also had a dugout and tunnels. The northern end of a tunnel had been destroyed by artillery fire in August of 1917. A narrow gauge railroad or trench railroad was there, used to supply troops. In this region of France, most of the hills were either named or numbered, and positions gridded on field maps used assigned code numbers if an area name was not specific enough. These numbers were then used in communications to the cannoneers. Soldiers manning field telescopes plotted distances that they relayed to increase fire accuracy. The high ground gave the 75-mm guns a better vantage point.

There had once been a small village at Le Mort Homme but earlier in the war it was destroyed by enemy artillery fire from the direction of Béthincourt during the battle of Verdun. The Germans, and later the French, had taken that particular hill, and debris from those battles was still evident on the ground. The peak of the hill had been damaged by thousands of exploding grenades. The French had held the hill since August 20, 1917, a little more than a year. They had driven the Germans stationed on that hill to a line from Avocourt to the Meuse River by Forges. The exposure at Le Mort Homme to enemy fire was very great and some 10,000 Frenchmen had died there with their bodies initially decomposing as it was impossible to remove them while under the attack. Some Frenchmen were buried alive by bursting shells. Even today fragments of bones can be found in the surrounding woods. Côte 304 had also been a place of barrages as the Germans tried to take out French artillery located there. It was actually lowered by seven meters during the bombing. These events were of no comfort to the arriving Americans. Beginning your service in a foreign country on Dead Man's Hill in an area which had seen much bloodshed would challenge anyone's nerves.

One of the problems facing artillery in getting to desolate places like Le Mort Homme was the fact that many of the roads listed on their military maps were impassable. Many of the roads, which fell between the lines of what was called "no man's land," had suffered from repeated bombing and as a result were filled with craters. Le Mort Homme had three roads leading towards it from the south. The first one, leading to the eastern slope, was not negotiable. The second one that led to the western slope had continuous shell holes 2–5 feet deep and 4–10 feet in diameter. An individual might be able to carefully traverse it, but not artillery pulled by horses. The way was also hampered by rusted barbed wire and two old trenches. The third road from the ruins of Esnes going north had been repaired by the engineers. The 104th Field Artillery Regiment traveled to this location at night in complete darkness in order to avoid detection. The only sources of light allowed at the front were tallow candles and the occasional kerosene lamp, which were forbidden out in the open. There was no smoking permitted on the march either.[8] The artillery would do much of its work in the pitch dark under cloudy skies.

The position of the 104th Field Artillery Regiment was now north of Cumières on high ground west of the Meuse River. Cumières had been destroyed earlier, and the land made uninhabitable. It is considered a village that died for France. Placing artillery on high ground was a challenge when using heavy equipment pulled by horses on slippery terrain. From Le Mort Homme, and the Bois (woods) des Corbeaux, the regiments had a clear view of the enemy on the other side of the front. The woods of Corbeaux had been destroyed by shell fire in 1916, so the enemy could see them as well. Familiar with the ground they had once occupied, the enemy was nestled into the high places of Montfaucon, the right (east) bank of the Meuse River, and the Bois de Forges.⁹ Initially, the right bank had been held largely by Austro-Hungarian troops with second-rate troops at the centers of resistance, but that would change when the Germans arrived. The 104th Field Artillery Regiment, along with the rest of their brigade, would take part in what became known as the St. Mihiel Offensive.

In the evening of September 11 and 12, the rest of the 52nd Field Artillery Brigade moved into the Bois des Sartelles, which was just south of Fromeréville. The artillery would first be firing from the left bank of the Meuse, and then in later weeks take the right. Things had been quiet there, largely due to the fact that both the French and the Austro-Hungarian troops were basically exhausted. With the arrival of the Americans, came a change in activity. The Central powers eventually replaced the weak Austro-Hungarians with top notch German troops.

The division would establish their salvage dump in the Bois des Sartelles the following week. Field hospitals for the 33rd Division were set up in buildings at Fromeréville and Sivry-la-Perche, with triage and a hospital at the French barracks at Glorieux by Verdun. Fromeréville had good roads intact making the work of ambulances easier. The 52nd Field Artillery Brigade would end up doing all of their fighting within a 20 mile radius of the city of Verdun, and dressing stations would move with the men, however the use of tents would be a problem due to aerial bombing, and they would be forced to use brush and trees for shelter. The walking wounded would go to Marre.¹⁰ Fort Marre had been built between 1875 and 1877 but was badly damaged by a German barrage in 1916. It was a typical French fort made of stone blocks with a moat.

The 52nd Field Artillery Brigade headquarters, along with the commander of the 33rd Division, was then set up at La Hutte in the Bois Bourrus southeast of Le Claire.¹¹ The stone fort in the Bois Bourrus had been built in 1881 and could fit about 290 men. The 52nd, under the command of Brigadier-General George Albert Wingate, was enlarged to include not only the American 104th, 105th, and 106th Field Artillery Regiments and the 102nd Ammunition Train of the 27th Division, but also the French 212th R.A.C. (a regiment of field artillery using the 75mm guns), and the 2nd Battalion of the French 308th R.L.C. (a regiment of field artillery using the 155mm howitzers). The two French regiments would stay with the 52nd for a number of days. This now enlarged Field Artillery Brigade would take part in the St. Mihiel Offensive with demonstration fire, while the 1st American Army sought to reduce the St. Mihiel salient. The artillery was assigned to open the way for the 1st American Army drive.

The 52nd Field Artillery Brigade began demonstration firing at 1 a.m. on September 12, opening part of the Allied front as a diversion to cover the

American attack at St. Mihiel. The fire continued until 6 p.m, the maximum capacity for the guns. They were firing south at a great range, focused on an area north of Verdun. Because of the distance, the 104th Field Artillery Regiment had to use the "D" shell.[12] They were using the high ground south of Chattancourt. The E and F Batteries of the 105th Field Artillery Regiment were west of Marre, with the rest of their regiment firing from the high ground on the southern slopes of Le Mort Homme, southwest of Cumières. The 106th fired from the high ground 900 meters southeast of Le Mort Homme. The brigade's participation, however, was purely for demonstration. The 33rd Division did not execute an attack with the 1st Army. In addition to the 52nd Field Artillery Brigade, army guns and the XVII French Corps guns all fired together. "The reverberation and volume of sound was so great that it made the whole earth jar."[13] It was intended to intimidate and break the morale of the Central powers. One member of the 80th Division described the "lesser guns" as sounding like "the barking of many dogs." The shock of the combined assault was effective but only for a brief time, "and then the machine guns began to pop and rattle and sputter, and the whole world was filled as if with the noise of great machinery grinding out death."[14]

The enemy returned shells which "burst within 15 or 20 yards of the guns and showered splinters all around them." Gas shells also burst near the guns. The danger lay not only in the men being hit or gassed, but in ammunition igniting and exploding. The fire at Marre was so heavy that the artillery had to change their position. The smaller group from the 105th Field Artillery Regiment was moved to Le Mort Homme, where they continued nightly fire.

The guns of the 52nd were often asked to fire outside of their sector while stationed near Verdun. "This was much harder than it sounds, as a gun well placed in its pit is only expected to fire through an arc 1600 mils or 45 degrees."[15] On the east they were exposed to the heights and once they fired were subjected to being shelled. Any movements also exposed them to being fired upon. Batteries B, E and F of the 106th Field Artillery (howitzer) were held in reserve, since their guns could not reach the same distance. From September 7 through the 25th the 104th Field Artillery Brigade would suffer four wounded men from German counter attacks. One member of the 105th was killed and five members of the 106th were wounded. The 1st American Army was successful, however, in reducing the St. Mihiel salient.

On September 13 to 16 the 79th American Division was placed on the west side of the 33rd Infantry Division, relieving part of the 157th French Division. The 52nd Field Artillery Brigade would attach to that American division later in October. At noon on September 14 both the 33rd and 79th Divisions were transferred from the XVII French Corps to the III American Corps under Major-General Robert L. Bullard. The 33rd Division modified

St. Mihiel Salient Offensive 117

This photograph of an unknown member of the 104th Field Artillery Regiment sleeping in his bunk was taken on September 15, 1918, by C.R. Jackson of the Signal Corps at Le Claire, Meuse, France. The cat was a stray. Notice the ammunition and high explosives surrounding the resting duo. This followed the attack on the St. Mihiel salient, right before the Meuse-Argonne Offensive during the time the members of the 104th Field Artillery Regiment were under heavy enemy fire and gas (courtesy Jonathan K. Brooke, Spartanburg County Historical Association. Subject 23548, number E).

their positions September 15 to 17, setting up camouflage for protection. Their new role was to be part of the defense of the Verdun Sector. Two of the batteries of the 105th returned from east of the Meuse River in the 18th French Division's territory, and moved to Bois de Sartelles during the nights of September 16 and 17. For security, they moved in the dark over the slippery, pitted roads, the horses pulling caissons loaded with artillery. The only sounds were horses clomping, caissons rumbling, and the quiet footsteps of the men, marching in silence.

The heroic actions of three members of Battery B, 104th Field Artillery Regiment displayed the dedication of those soldiers. On September 14, Herbert M. Brink, mechanic and Privates 1st Class William J. Nette and Ralph B.

Sullivan were in Montzéville. That area had suffered from repeated enemy bombardment. On that day the shelling caused the camouflage over the large ammunition dump to catch fire. Nine of the 75mm shells exploded and the three men left their protected area to put out the fire. Their actions not only saved the ammunition but prevented detection of the dump by the enemy. The ammunition was vital to the next operation of the brigade.[16]

The men of the brigade spent a great deal of their time trying to keep the artillery concealed from aerial observation. It was a constant area of concern. The Germans had both airplanes and observation balloons, as well as observation stations high in the hills. The enemy planes would drop flares to signal where the columns were, so that their artillery could position their guns on the assigned target. For the Allies, hiding became a continual activity, broken up only by the constant rain. One strategy was to set up overhead camouflage at a new position, then quickly fire at the old position before moving rapidly into the new position to hide. In that way, the return volley would hit where the men used to be, rather than where they actually were.[17] This concealment was all part of preparations for the major offensive to come. The men seldom just sat and rested; there was always something for them to do. The guns required constant attention between firings, and ordinances had to be carefully greased and stacked. Training also continued. The 33rd Division opened a Divisional Infantry School located at the Bois de Nixéville, South. Most of the sergeants attended officer training, but then opted out of accepting commissions to stay with their men.

On September 20 to 21, the 1st American Army and the French 4th Army officially opened the Meuse-Argonne Offensive. 600,000 men were moved rapidly into place for the offensive. The artillery was assigned to do preparatory fire to clear the way for the infantry. The offensive was set against the German lateral line of supply using the Carigan-Sedan-Mézières Railroad. The objective in the Argonne Forest was to reduce it by out flanking it from the west. It was expected to be a costly initiative, if it even could succeed, as the Germans were heavily entrenched in that area in a well-concealed position. The 52nd Field Artillery Brigade would be particularly vulnerable to enemy attack from the east once the flash of their guns recorded their position. Their right flank was completely exposed.

Two battalions of the 33rd Division were relieved by units from the American 4th Division and one battalion from the American 80th Division on the second night of action. On September 22, the 33rd Division was officially transferred from the French to the 1st American Army. On September 23 liaison agents were sent to adjoining divisions and brigades to help coordinate actions. This would contribute greatly to the 33rd Division's effectiveness in carrying out their assignments.

CHAPTER SEVEN

The Meuse-Argonne Offensive (September 26–October 6, 1918)

The Meuse-Argonne Offensive is considered an epic battle which essentially ended World War I. The Allies made a heroic assault on the strongholds of the Central powers along the Hindenburg Line near the Meuse River and into the Argonne Forest. The United States engaged 1.2 million soldiers to this one battle, resulting in about 12,000 wounded and 26,277 dead. It was the bloodiest battle the United States had ever known up to that point.[1] It also involved 100,000 animals. The action directly followed the St. Mihiel salient attack, designed as a "one-two punch" which required every bit of "guts" the Doughboys could muster. The French saw it as vital to pivoting the enemy northward out of France.

Three separate offensives were planned to happen simultaneously against the larger German line. The French and Americans planned an attack on September 26 in the south between Reims and Verdun along the Meuse River and through the Argonne Forest. The British would renew the Somme Offensive on September 27, attacking the center of the line between Cabrai and St. Quentin. A combined Allied attack east of Ypres in the north would begin on September 28.

The American 27th Infantry Division took part in the third attack serving under the British. The 52nd Field Artillery Brigade of the 27th Division would take part in the Meuse River Offensive under the French and Americans. Through its infantry and artillery, the 27th would support the fight on two fronts. General John Pershing led the American Army in the Meuse River region with General Henri Joseph Etienne Gourand (1867–1946) of the French IV Army. Gourand was nicknamed the Lion of Champagne. Prior to the war he had served in French Sudan and Morocco. He had broken two legs and lost an arm in 1915 when struck by fragments of an exploding shell. Within six months he was back in command. The 15th Infantry Regiment of the 27th

Division (now called the 369th) was serving in the French IV Army. The American Army line in this area ran east to west from Forges on the Meuse River, northwest of Verdun, to the center of the Argonne Forest. The French IV Army, to the west of the American Army, covered the rest of the Argonne Forest westward to the east of Reims.

The Germans' best defensive lines were located in this third area of the Meuse-Argonne Offensive. Their lines were close to 12 miles deep. At the Argonne Forest they were trying to create a salient to the west of Verdun towards the heights of St. Menehould. Had the Meuse-Argonne Offensive not taken place, the Germans would most likely have pressed forward towards their goal and cut off Verdun. The German Army Group Von Gallwitz, under General Max Karl Wilhelm von Gallwitz (1852–1937), controlled the entire area from the city of Metz, capital of the Lorraine region, to the Meuse-Argonne sector. Von Gallwitz had been the commander of the German Fifth Army from 1916 to September 27, 1918, until General der Kavallerie Georg von der Marwitz (1856–1929) took command of the Fifth Army. Between the two, they held the Meuse-Argonne sector, with five divisions totaling 70,000 men in the front lines and another eight divisions in reserve.[2] The reserve was considered relatively weak, although the line was an important part of their defensive system. The Germans intended to defend it with every piece of artillery they had, including a host of strategically placed machine gun nests. The two most powerful enemy positions between the Argonne Forest on the west and the Meuse River on the east were Montfaucon and the Bois de Forges, both of which were considered impregnable. From Montfaucon, the enemy could see the entire battle area.

The Hindenburg Line, called the Siegfriedstellung by the Germans, stretched from Arras to Laffaux. It had been constructed as a fortified line the winter of 1916 to 1917, requiring fewer men to defend it. Near Verdun, the Germans called the line Kriemhildestellung or Kriemhilde Stellung. It was heavily fortified as a last defense between Verdun and the north-south railway, used to supply the German western armies. It was vital to their cause.[3] The Central powers had four lines of fortification running east to west between the Meuse River and the Argonne Forest placed along a series of ridges and valleys running the same direction. The first three lines were well organized and had intermediate positions between them. The first line, called the Haupt Stellung, ran between Regneville and Vienne-le-Château, close to the front line. The second line, called the Giselher Stellung, was five kilometers behind the first line. The Giselher was anchored around the hill of Montfaucon and went through the Argonne south of Apremont. Kriemhilde Stellung, part of the Hindenburg Line, was the third line. It was six kilometers north of the Giselher and ran from the Bois de Forêt across the heights of Cunel and

Romagne, and included the high ground north of Grandpré. The fourth line eight kilometers out was a less developed defensive line called the Freya Stellung.[4] It included the heights of Barricourt, and extended west to Buzancy and Thénorgues. The Kriemhilde Stellung (Hindenburg Line), Hagen Stellung, and Giselher Stellung were principle lines of concrete and barbed wire. A series of local lines also ran west to east throughout the area. Some had less installations in place like the Volker Stellung and Freya Stellung. All of the lines made good use of the natural heights and the woods for additional protection.

The word "stellung" means position. The Germans named a number of the positions along the Hindenburg Line after Wilhelm Richard Wagner's (1813–1883) mythological old Norse characters and gods in his operas; Kriemhilde, Siegfried, and Wotan to name a few. Most are found in *The Ring of the Nibelung* which has a mortal obtaining a ring granting world domination. It did not end well for the characters in the operas. The French and their allies viewed the war as a battle between civilization and the barbarians or the beast (French "boche"). The Allies often called the Germans "Huns" as a reference to their ancient history. Here at the line, the name Kriemhilde became symbolic of the "pagan hordes." Many Allied soldiers felt they were fighting evil itself. The line was considered impregnable, full of concrete trenches, forts, dugouts, machine gun nests, and miles of barbed wire. Enemy observatories ran along a central north-south ridge at Montfaucon, Cunel, Romagne, and the Bois de Barricourt. The Allies would have to move in the exposed channels below them. Only a "ceaseless slamming night and day"[5] would win the war here.

The American and French plan was to slowly bend the left side of their line, like a triangle's arm, north and then east, pushing the enemy back towards Belgium and Germany. On the right side of the line by the Meuse River, the line "swung in this sector as a gate does upon its hinges."[6] It was believed that if the line was pushed the enemy would be forced to leave. It would end the war. The initial plan was to make a 16 kilometer advance, penetrate the German third defensive line and force an evacuation of the Argonne Forest. A further advance would follow. As part of this, the heights east of the Meuse River were to be cleared as far as the Bois de la Grande Montagne. The 52nd Field Artillery Brigade was placed at the very point of the hinge, along with the 33rd Division. It was understood that as the larger Hindenburg Line was under attack, the Germans would most likely retreat to this point and protect it. On the left side of the line, the task was to reduce the enemy presence in the Argonne Forest by outflanking them from the west. A frontal attack would have been suicide, considering how well entrenched the enemy was, protected by the thick forest. The Argonne Forest contained a combination of beech, ash and oak trees with low shrubs that formed a thicket. Trails and footpaths wound around numerous streams, springs and pools. The clay soil tended to stay wet. The forest also was filled with multiple enemy machine gun nests.[7] It was a dangerous place for the Allies. The line projected forward in its middle, forming a salient with the forest on the left and the heights of the Meuse River on the right. The valleys between the high places had steep sides.

On September 26 the line extended east to west from the Forges Brook through Béthincourt and then west. Béthincourt was in ruins. The line crossed the Meuse River by Samogneux and Brabant. The Allies were located on the southern slope of the Forges Ravine, and the Germans were on the northern slope near Forges Wood. The Central powers' locations were heavily fortified, but the Austro-Hungarian troops, protecting this formerly quiet sector were considered less than first-rate.[8] Two railroad centers supplied the German Army with a railway parallel to this front from Vosges to Lille. Destroying the German Army in this area would sever the ability to move equipment. The heights at the Meuse River, called the Maas River by the Germans and Dutch, were the last stronghold of the Central powers and the last line of defense west of the Rhine. A win here would free northern France and southern Belgium by crippling the enemy and forcing a retreat.

Directly following the St. Mihiel Offensive, General Pershing placed ten American divisions between the Meuse River and the western edge of the Argonne Forest. The positions of the ten divisions, west to east, were I Corps with the 92nd under the French and the 77th, 28th and 35th Divisions under Major General Liggett; V Corps in the center with the 91st, 37th, and 79th Divisions under Major-General Cameron; and III Corps with the 4th, 80th, and 33rd Divisions under Major-General Bullard. Officers of the 27th Division also were serving in the 28th Division from Pennsylvania. The III Corps held the 3rd Division in reserve, also with officers from the 27th Division. The 52nd Field Artillery Brigade was still attached to the 33rd Division. The American plan was to break both the Giselher and Kreimhilde positions and to drive the enemy from the Argonne Forest. It would prove very costly. Five of the American divisions had not yet seen combat. With little experience, they were facing an enemy in well prepared defensive positions with a height advantage overlooking them. To counter this, the divisions with less and more experience were mixed together in the hopes that the less experienced would rise to the level of their comrades.

The III Corps, with the 33rd Division, was assigned to break the enemy positions between the Ruisseau de Forges (stream or brook of Forges) and the Bois de Forêt (woods of the forest), and then move north to the villages of Buzancy and Stonne. They were to organize the west bank of the Meuse for defense. Three divisions were in the front line of the III Corps: the 33rd Division was to the east with its right on the left bank of the Meuse River; the 80th Division was in the center; the 4th Regular Division was to the west. The 4th Division was expected to liaison with the 79th Division to their left which was the right division of the V Corps, while the 33rd Division was assigned to liaison with the 18th French Division to their right which was left of the XVII French Army Corps and east of the Meuse River.[9] This liaison process between corps on the line proved to be very beneficial. The objectives of the 33rd Division were the enemy's second position of the Hagon Stellung-Nord, and the main American Army objective of the Voker Stellung. The Hagen Stellung-Nord was also called the Etzel Stellung. It ran between the Bois d'en Bois and Bois Sachet, south of the Bois Jurè and crossed the Meuse River running due east. The Volker Stellung connected to the Etzel on the east side of the Meuse and ran south of that line heading east.

The 1st American Army began moving men into the Verdun area during the nights of September 5 and 6 causing traffic jams on the insufficient and shell pocked road. The engineers did a great deal of work in these areas, in some cases constructing roads and bridges for the first time, and in other areas repairing roads scarred by years of warfare that left huge holes and piles of debris. The ruins from a number of towns would be used as road fill. The engineers often worked under the watchful eyes of the enemy, receiving direct fire and gas. Despite the difficulties, the 52nd Field Artillery Brigade moved 4,614 men into this cramped area.

The 1st American Army officially began the Meuse-Argonne Offensive on September 20, supported by the French 4th Army. Phase one occurred between September 25 and October 3, 1918. On September 25, the batteries of the 104 Field Artillery Regiment were clustered on the Le Claire-Esnes Road about 500 meters west of Le Claire. There were 1,447 men in the regiment. The engineers had repaired the road but transport to here had been difficult. It had taken six to ten horses to pull each 75mm gun to that place, with other horses carrying ammunition and supplies on additional limbers and caissons (a given battery might have 160 horses). Moving a large field artillery regiment through drying mud at night in complete darkness on unstable roads in rolling countryside was a major project for the crews of men who worked each gun under an individual officer. Once they reached their location, the horses needed to be sheltered. The direction of fire for the guns was northward towards Béthincourt and Forges where the Germans had outposts and bombing posts along the brook.[10] Both towns had been completely destroyed during the Battle of Verdun, but the woods were thick and well defended. The Cumières-Béthincourt Road near the Mort Homme into Béthincourt was in the "no man's land" which ran between the Central powers and Allied lines. "The whole landscape was a barren waste with hardly a sprig of living stuff and not a living soul in sight. Wherever you looked the ground was pockmarked with shell holes."[11] Visibility on September 25 was poor. During the day, Corporal Leland B. Hall of Battery F, 104th Field Artillery Regiment, was in Germonville guarding the ammunition dump. A German airplane flew by the dump and he brought it down with his machine gun. He would later receive a Divisional Citation after being wounded.[12]

Colonel Merritt H. Smith was still in command of the entire 104th Field Artillery Regiment and established his headquarters in the Bois Bourrus, 300 meters southeast of Le Claire. There was a stone fort nestled in the thick woods of the Bois Bourrus with dugouts and shelters which could accommodate several thousand men. The fort had been constructed in 1881 with tunnels and a moat. Corporals Richard M. Cott and Albert Liptax of Headquarters Company were assigned to make the regimental field maps under difficult circumstances for the duration of the Meuse-Argonne Offensive. Second Lieutenant Sidney N. Riggs was in the Bois de Chaume near Consenvoye acting as a liaison officer with the front line infantry. He maintained the telephone link back to Division Headquarters and the artillerymen to help direct fire needed for the advance. Riggs would end up needing to be evacuated after suffering under heavy shell fire on the 26th, as well as being severely gassed.[13] The regiment was going to be firing at long range, again using the "D" shells. They made their preparations in the dark. They were part of the full brigade support for the 129th, 130th, 131st, and 132nd Infantry Regiments of the 33rd American Division.[14] The headquarters of the 52nd Field Artillery Brigade and the 33rd Division were moved to a dugout in the Bois Bourrus called La Hutte.[15] The dugouts were lined with piled sandbags.

The 75mm guns were good at using high explosives to cut through areas. The guns were used to break through heavy barbed wire defenses in front of the advancing infantry, but were not particularly good at attacking a trench or destroying fortified positions that had cement bunkers. The 155mm Schneider howitzers, mortars, or even just grenades were better at those types of bombardments. The high explosive (called H.E.) shells of the 75mm weighed 12 pounds (5.3 kilograms) and were filled with melinite (picric acid) and fitted with a delay fuse. When these shells hit their target, they made a huge explosion; the compression was said to go right through any nearby person's chest to rattle them. 75s also fired 16 pound (7.24 kilograms) time-fused shrapnel shells. Each shell contained 290 lead balls designed to burst over a battalion and then shower down multiple balls, an action that earned them the nickname of the "flying bullet." Each shell had a brass case which was ejected upon firing and needed to be cleared away from the gun. They would be transported to the salvage dump.

This first phase of the offensive used 2,700 Allied guns along with 189 small tanks and 821 airplanes to support the infantry. The French added a combination of guns which ranged from the 75mm to huge naval guns mounted on railway cars. At 11:30 p.m. on September 25, the long-range guns of the army and corps artillery were aimed towards the rear of the German Army. The sound of the shelling was said to be "terrible." The guns blasted away until 5:30 a.m. so no one slept. At 2:30 a.m. three corps of army artillery joined them intensifying the barrage. The preparatory fire moved into a rolling barrage. Witnesses to the beginning of this offensive stated that the "effect was of an intense electric storm accompanied by continued thunder claps. The horizon in the rear was clearly outlined by a quivering glow reaching up into the sky."[16] The heavy artillery fire by the army and corps artillery was intended to do as much damage as possible to the heavily fortified lines.[17] It was also meant to intimidate the enemy.

The artillery commander's diary for the 52nd Field Artillery Brigade, and the individual regimental diaries, recorded the orders for fire, but their accounts focused on recording simple facts. When coupled with divisional reports and comments recorded by artillerymen, the daily events of that offensive emerge more clearly. On a rainy September 26 at 5:30 a.m. following the heavy artillery fire of the army's big guns, the 52nd Field Artillery Brigade with their attachments began their own preparatory fire ahead of their assigned infantry. Their objectives were clearly defined. Two battalions of the French 212th R.A.C. (75mm guns) attached to the 52nd Field Artillery Brigade were to offer a standing and then rolling barrage in front of the 131st Infantry of the 33rd Division. Two battalions of the 131st were in line, with one in support. To their right was the 66th Infantry Brigade with Company A and the 1st Gas and Flame Regiment. The 131st Infantry in the 66th Infantry Brigade were ordered to attack and press on to the ground northeast of Drillancourt, Gercourt et Drillancourt, the Tranchée (trench) du Bois Juré, the Tranchée du Bois Rond, and the northern edge of the Bois de Forges. One group of French guns was on either side of the American 104th and 105th Field Artillery Regiments.[18] The early morning standing barrage by the 75mm guns along the Forges-Béthincourt Road lasted for 25 minutes to cover the crossing of the infantry over the Forges Brook and swamp. This was a difficult crossing for the infantry as the stream had marshes on either side. It required advancing down deep slopes and around the enemy-filled Bois de Forges, and then proceeding towards the Meuse River. Duckboards were thrown over enemy wires; the men waded through the marshes under direct fire. The French artillery sent out a 20-minute rolling barrage 300 meters further in front of them so that the infantry could set up along the road. The barrage in front of the 131st Infantry was 800 meters wide. In all, six batteries of 212th R.A.C. fired for five hours and 15 minutes.

At the same time the French battalions were firing, the 104th and 105th Field Artillery Regiments sent forth a standing and then rolling barrage in front of the 132nd Infantry of the 33rd Division, on the other side of the 66th as they made a right turning movement. Two of the 132nd Battalions were in line with one in support. The 132nd Infantry in the same brigade had as their mission to advance through the Bois de Forges and organize a defensive line on the west bank of the Meuse River from the Côte de l'Oie to the road fork 400 meters north of the corner of the Bois de Forges, avoiding a frontal attack on the Forges woods. The town of Forges had been destroyed during the Battle of Verdun but the woods were thick and filled with enemy forces. The 104th was instructed to send a barrage "straight forward to the north" and then turn to the right ahead of the men, stopping along the Meuse River by the railroad track. The barrage required a "narrow lane."[19] The turning motion to the east placed the infantry near the Meuse River across from Brabant. The barrage sent by the 104th and 105th Field Artillery Regiments in front of the 132nd Infantry was 1,300 meters in width; each regiment covered half the width. Their field diary records that they first fired for three hours and 15 minutes. The barrage then progressed 100 meters every four minutes for one hour and 20 minutes. Finally, the barrage covered 100 meters every five minutes for one hour and 50 minutes.

The 104th Field Artillery fired from the high ground about 1,700 meters south and east of Chattancourt, another city completely destroyed during the Battle of Verdun. The place set for this fight to the finish was surrounded by dead villages. They were determined to win. Northward from Verdun the Meuse River swung in a serpentine manner to the east where the 104th was located, then to the west by Chattancourt, and swung east again after Cumières (also destroyed earlier). Batteries E and F of the 105th Field Artillery Regiment were still west of Marne, to the east of the 104th. The rest of the 105th fired from high ground 1,200 meters southwest of Cumières on the southern slopes of Le Mort Homme. The 105th was commanded by Colonel DeWitt C. Weld. During the battle, the firing was carefully communicated via telephones using strung wires. The position of the guns at Le Claire was considered too far from the front to support, as they were now south of the other artillery regiments. Batteries C, D, and E were therefore moved to the ravine north of Moulin (Mill) de Raffecourt, and the post command of the battalion moved northeast of Le Claire to the Tranchée (trench) de Misery southwest corner of the Bois de Forges. The congested roads slowed their movements.

The 106th Field Artillery Regiment (155mm howitzer) and the 2nd Battery of the French 308th R.L.C. (155mm howitzer) serving under them, were instructed to concentrate fire on specified points in the sector as the attack progressed. The howitzers were good at taking out things requiring curved fire, such as trenches. The 106th Field Artillery Regiment was located on high ground 900 meters southeast of Le Mort Homme. They would later support the left side of the attack. The 106th had been commanded by Colonel John D. Howland until the regiment reached Camp de Souge. At that point, the command passed first to Lieutenant Colonel John T. Delaney and then, on September 1, to Colonel Emery T. Smith.[20] The night prior to the action, the 102nd Ammunition Train of the 27th Division supplied all of the ammunition, working until midnight even as the big guns began firing. A shell was usually carried over each shoulder from the wagons to the ammunition dump area. Members of individual regiments then carried shells carefully up muddy paths to the gun emplacements in the complete dark. Keeping the batteries stocked became increasingly dangerous as they carried ammunition to the front over unstable roads while under fire. The 102nd Trench Mortar Battery was held in reserve, since the range was too far for their mortars.

The work of the 52nd Field Artillery Brigade was meant to enable the 132nd Infantry to advance in this section by avoiding a frontal attack at the Bois de Forges, which was heavily fortified by the enemy, and instead go around it.[21] First, the 3rd Battery of the French 212 R.A.C. sent out a limited standing, and then a rolling barrage from the right flank of the 132nd Infantry to the remains of the village of Forges. This was done purely as a deception to confuse the enemy about the exact front of the attack. After the barrage lifted, the infantry was supposed to take the flank and rear trench, clearing out any remaining enemy soldiers. To the right of the 132nd Infantry the deceptive barrage covered 1,500 meters in width, progressing 100 meters in four minutes and lasting for one hour and 17 minutes.[22] The infantry had cut lanes through the wire south of Ruisseau (brook) de Forge and taped them for the troops to follow in the dark.[23] The 132nd Infantry moved forward from Forge Brook to the line along the railroad tracks.[24]

Meanwhile, the 33rd Divisional Infantry, with the III Corps, attacked northwest of Verdun from Passerelle du Don, 800 meters east of Béthincourt, all the way to the Meuse River. The left flank of the division reached their assigned area north of Drillancourt, east of the village of Gercourt-et-Drillancourt, and the Tranchée du Bois Juré. They then assisted the center of the division in capturing the Bois de Forges. They held the line from Côte de l'Oie on the south to the outskirts of the town of Dannevoux on the north,[25] then moved to the right to make room for other American III Corps divisions to come through. As a rule, the infantry had little use for rifles in this area: they mostly used machine guns and automatic rifles with hand grenades. The reason was that "the Germans used machine guns extensively."[26]

After the initial assault, the German Army harassed the Allies by firing on the roads, as well as at the front lines. Three members of the 104th Field

Artillery Regiment were wounded the first day as the Americans began the attack at the Meuse River and Argonne Forest. One of those severely wounded by machine gun fire in the initial assault was the commander of Battery C, Captain Charles Gray Blakeslee. The 105th had two wounded men and the 106th had six wounded; one man died from his wounds. The 132nd Infantry of the 33rd Division advanced through the Bois de Forges and organized a defensive line on the west bank of the Meuse from Côte de l'Oie to the corner of the Bois de Forges. The 131st Infantry reached the ground northeast of Drillancourt, Gercourt-et-Drillancourt, and the Tranchée du Bois Juré, from where they assisted the 132nd Infantry in reducing the Bois de Forges and capturing Drillancourt, Gercourt-et-Drillancourt, the Tranchée du Bois Juré, and the Tranchée du Bois Rond. They organized a line of defense on the west bank of the Meuse. Members of the 33rd Division crossed the Forges Brook and met their objective with the "help of good artillery support and an overhead machine gun barrage."[27] The 33rd Division ended up being the only American division to reach their objective within the projected time frame.

The guns of the forward group of the 104th were then pointed north against the enemy in the Bois de Châtillon and the area of Vilosnes to assist elements on the left group of the 105th Field Artillery Regiment who were turning towards the left to help the infantry. At one point the 104th Field Artillery members were spread over a wide front, from Brabant southeast to the Bois de Châtillon on the northwest.[28] Throughout the offensive they were continually moved forward as ground was taken, in order to stay within range of their targets. Because they were at the hinge of the 1st Army movement, they would always be within the 20 mile radius of Verdun. Divisions closer to the left arm of the line covered more kilometers as they pushed that arm northward against the pivot point in the east.

The barrage in front of the 132nd Infantry was 1,300 meters wide. The 104th and 105th each had fired over one half of that section. Infantry often advanced through the smoldering ruins caused by their artillery. "The infantry regiments reported that the standing barrage and concentrations mentioned so effectively covered the crossing of the Forges Brook and swamp that they suffered few losses during that period." The barrage was "accurate and effective." The 132nd Infantry that advanced through the woods felt they had to "run to keep up" with the artillery fire. The 131st Infantry, on the other hand, reported that since they were on open ground, the barrage covered by the French 212th R.A.C. "retarded their advance." Nevertheless, both objectives were met "without interruption."[29]

The result of the barrage was very effective, enabling the crossing of the Forges Brook and swamp with few losses. The accuracy of the artillery saved the lives of the infantrymen to whom they had been assigned.[30] The infantry made use of the artillery barrage's thick smoke screen under a layer of fog, but bullets were popping left and right from the many enemy machine gun nests. The infantry had crossed the marsh at Forges Brook on foot bridges built by the engineers who had also been under fire. Engineers scurried to build and repair roads to assist with supplying the troops. Participation in the battle engagements of the Meuse-Argonne Offensive from September 26 to November 11 would eventually earn the 104th, 105th, and 106th Field Artillery Regiments the right to have silver bands on their regimental color staffs.[31]

The American III Corps was able to break the enemy positions between Ruisseau de Forges and the Bois de Forêt, and then move north to Buzancy and Stonne. There they organized the west bank of the Meuse River for defense with the III Corps in the front line. During the section of the offensive to follow, the 33rd Division was located on the right of the American Army nearest the Meuse River. The division pivoted and swung around in a half circle to a front along the west bank of the Meuse River and held the line from Forges to Laiterie de Belhaine.

The objectives now for the 33rd Division with its attached artillery were first to attack the enemy's second position at the Hagen Stellung-Nord (North) and then to follow the American Army objective of the Volker Stellung. Both of these would be done on a scheduled day simply called "D-Day." The 33rd Division, with the III Corps, attacked the German positions from the Meuse westward to the Passarelle du Don. They were subject to fire from both the front and the flank, yet they met their missions one by one.[32] Despite being under constant fire, the 52nd Field Artillery Brigade held the right flank of the 1st American Army along the west bank of the Meuse River from Forges to the westerly edge of the Bois, de la Côte Lemont.[33]

The 33rd Division captured 1,500 prisoners, and collected 42 pieces of artillery and 161 machine guns at the beginning of the offensive. "Prisoners taken in this action said that they could not withstand the artillery preparation and barrage."[34] The prisoners were handed over to the Military Police and held in a "divisional cage" or detention area until they could be evacuated. At Gercourt, Captain George Toomey of the 106th Field Artillery manned some of the captured enemy 77mm guns.[35]

The 33rd Division held its position until October 2 when the lines were extended west as the division took over the former sector held by 80th Division that extended to the western edge of the Bois de la Côte Lemont. This front was 14,000 yards in length. The 52nd Field Artillery Brigade had to send barrages in two directions, forming a right angle. They were under continual observation by an enemy artillery that held higher, more protected ground on the east bank of the Meuse River. They were also observed by enemy airplanes.

After recovering from the shock of this opening to the offensive, the German 5th Army brought six reserve divisions to the front line slowing the Allied advance. The week of September 26, the few area roads were filled with traffic jams bottlenecking at Fromeréville, as the Allies tried to prepare for their next move. There were not enough roads for the massive movements of troops, and those that existed were shell-pocked. They quickly filled with trucks, trailers, wounded soldiers, regiments moving, horses, and a steady stream of artillery that moved from 8:30 p.m. to 6 a.m.[36] The engineers were kept busy nonstop. That week culminated with bad weather, seeming to follow the troops and settle over them continuously. The clouds and rain helped protect the troops from aerial observation, but the men's raincoats were soon soaked through.

The 33rd Division defended the Meuse Sector between September 27 and October 7, 1918. The division largely patrolled and organized its lines. The Meuse River was covered by divisional sentry outposts at strong points, defended by machine guns. They experienced constant artillery fire and gas coming from both banks of the curving Meuse River. The 33rd Division had the distinction of having been the most gassed division in the A.E.F. during the entire war. The German Army had been particularly ordered to destroy Allied artillery moving in the area and to use gas "whenever possible." Their gas shells were "frequently mixed with H.E. and shrapnel."[37] The American government report on the 33rd Division and the use of chemical weapons during World War I noted that although the 33rd Divisional artillery "had large stocks of gas munitions on hand," they were generally not used for retaliation against the enemy even with the nightly gassing by the enemy.[38] The Austro-Hungarian units opposite the division on the east side of the river were replaced by first-rate Germans, although they were tired and under strength. The weather remained cool and overcast for the entire week, with the on-and-off rain and mist making it miserable and raw. The mist and fog also tended to keep the gas low to the ground, increasing danger for everyone. Men mentioned the nights being the worst with sleep interrupted by the cold, shelling and gas alerts. Fortunately, the weather alternated between fair and rainy days, so they experienced occasional relief.

On September 27, the 33rd Division moved south of Gercourt-et-Drillancourt and began a 9:00 a.m. advance via Esnes and Béthencourt to the valley south of Hill 281. They had two days of nice weather in which to do it. The army used numbered grid maps so that the field telescopes could site locations and give the coordinates to canoneers. Unnamed hills were numbered; vague areas were given coordinate numbers when a wood's name or town was not specific enough and the codes were recorded. The 105th Field Artillery Regiment had had all batteries firing into the heavy fog, since 5:30 a.m. covering the 132nd Infantry advance. They were firing blind, so the only way they knew they were successful was through updates from the liaison they had stationed with the infantry along with four runners.[39] Between September 26 and October 3, the 105th lost one man and 13 men were wounded. The injured had to remain at the front until the ambulances could reach them. Not even food wagons could reach the front.

During the advance, the 52nd Field Artillery Brigade moved one battalion of heavy artillery from the French 308th R.L.C. to the Ravin des Caurettes, west of Cumières. There they joined the 106th Field Artillery Regiment howitzers.[40] At 11:00 a.m. the 106th Field Artillery Regiment sent details to operate German guns captured near Drillancourt. The 106th was also ordered to fire on three enemy batteries on the east side of the river in the Bois de Chaume at 3:50 p.m. as well as near Consenvoye. At 5:40 p.m. they fired again near Consenvoye, and at 10:00 p.m. fired on another enemy battery located on the roads north and east of Consenvoye. A request also came for the 106th to assist the 80th Division with cover fire, but they were out of range, so the request was resent to the corps. At the end of September, the 102nd Trench Mortar Battery moved two platoons into the Bois de Forges.[41]

Meanwhile, the 104th Field Artillery Batteries C, D, and E had begun at 10:30 a.m. to take positions near the ravine north of the Moulin (Mill) de Raffecourt. Their command post was in the Tranchée (Trench) de Misery at the southwest corner of the Bois de Forges on the west side of the river. The roads there had protective camouflage over them. The 104th were protected during the move by another battery. At this point, the other divisions were still trying to complete their objectives. At 7:30 p.m. the 1st Battery of the 104th Field Artillery moved from Le Claire to a new position near the southwestern corner of the Bois de Forges, the location of their command center near another bend in the river. Movement was done at night and the placements had to be secured and sometimes re-built to be ready for firing by daylight, so the men often functioned on little sleep. What little sleep they did get was often disrupted by the sounds of the artillery barrages from either side.

At 1:30 a.m. on the 28th, the 106th Field Artillery Regiment fired with one battery on the village of Brabant-sur-Meuse, where enemy movement had been detected. With another battery they also fired on the Brabant-Malbrouck Road. Brabant was on the east side of the Meuse River, across from Forges. The enemy recovered from the initial bombardment and sent harassing fire back across the river. The Central powers also moved in three new divisions to stop the Allied advance down the Aire Valley. The Allies, though stalled, were pressing farther and farther northeast as the 33rd Division rotated the hinge. The 105th Field Artillery Regiment added to the firing on the village of Brabant at 3:45 p.m. and the 106th was ordered to fire again on it at 4:30 p.m. as the 105th moved their position beginning at 5 p.m. Because of the hilly terrain, the 75mm guns had to consistently raise the angle of sight during the barrages.[42]

The 1st Battalion of the 105th, after attempting to move forward towards the Moulin de Raffecourt, was turned back by American Military Police. They repeated the attempt the following day and this time reached the mill.[43] The 104th Field Artillery Regiment, in the southwestern corner of the Forges woods, had to seek shelter from enemy shelling and gas. Between the 27 and October 7, they would have four wounded and two of those died. The German artillery in the heights was said to be "awful."[44]

Some members of the 33rd Division Infantry relieved the 80th Division the evening of the 28th. The 80th Division had requested supportive fire from the 52nd Field Artillery Brigade, but their guns were out of reach so the request was again forwarded to the corps' guns. To their right were the 129th Infantry and Company B, along with elements of the 123rd Machine Gun Company. To their left were the 130th, Company C, and other elements of the 123rd Machine Gun Company. Company A and D, and still other elements of the 123rd Machine Gun Battery, were in the reserve of the 65th Brigade. By the evening, the Allies had advanced 11 kilometers and captured Baulny, Épinonville, Septsarges, and Dannevoux.

Between September 28 and October 3, a gun crew from Battery A, 104th Field Artillery Regiment, comprising Sergeant Stephen W. Halton, Corporal John Daly, and Privates Raymond Bates, Matthew Solinski, and James P. Brow, were busy in the Bois de Forges. They repaired and then operated recently captured 77mm guns, firing them against the enemy.[45] On September 28, Private Charles L. Crovat of the 104th Field Artillery Headquarters Company took his own heroic action in the Forges woods. Accompanying the 132nd Infantry on their assault, he established wire communications with the regiment while being shelled and subjected to machine gun fire.[46]

Sunday morning, September 29, amidst the rain squalls and drizzle, the enemy artillery and gas shells were heavy. German shells were often described as shrieking before exploding. The H.E. shells were called "whiz bangs" by the Allies because of the whizzing, whistling, sound they made before letting off a huge bang. When a high explosive shell exploded overhead, it was described by one man as "a great swishing scream, a smash-bang, and it seems to tear everything loose from you. The intensity of it simply enters your heart and brain and tears every nerve to pieces."[47] The air concussion from the shell was enough to knock a man down. The 350 shells "screamed and rumbled in the air for an almost interminable length of time before they fell."[48] The thermite shells had "flares of fire"; star-shells that "burst and showered stars" were largely used at night so their "bluish-white light" could reveal Allied movements.[49] The Germans used a large number of both heavy and light guns with a variety of shells, and sometimes infantry would be semi-buried under the dirt that flew up following a shell's explosion. Shrapnel would leave messy wounds, unlike those from machine gun fire which tended to be cleaner.

Firing from a fixed position was very dangerous for gun crews because it drew the attention of the enemy guns. Once they fired, the men had to scramble to jump into dugouts or trenches to protect themselves from return fire. The worst shell was the dud which failed to explode. Everyone just waited and watched, unsure if it would stay dormant or go off. Edward Sirois, an artilleryman from the Yankee Division, mentioned that when you were in the midst of firing, you did not notice the enemy fire, and did not get time to see what was happening. "Fragments flying and falling around your gun-pit tried the nerves."[50] The men of the 52nd were under constant fire their entire time at the front.

According to the offense plan, the Kriemhilde Stellung was supposed to have been breached by September 26. Instead, the 26th dawned with the Kriemhilde Stellung still intact and held by the enemy with six new divisions at the line. The 52nd Field Artillery Brigade had been quiet in the morning, after little or no sleep, but in the afternoon they barraged Brabant-sur-Meuse and the road to Malbrouck on the east bank of the Meuse. Heavy fire came back. The heavens also sent down more rain and drizzle. The 1st Battery of the 105th Field Artillery Regiment moved to a position near the Tranchée de la Roue. The 108th Engineers worked on repairing the roads, building bridges in the forward area and new roads through "no man's land" under frequent enemy artillery fire.

The 52nd Field Artillery Brigade fired on enemy batteries and filled requests by the corps in the field for counter-battery work to suppress heavy shelling. The 106th Field Artillery sent harassing fire across the river on enemy batteries in the Bois de Chaume and on the roads northeast of Brabant-sur-Meuse and Consenvoye. From their elevated positions, the brigade noticed enemy movement southward to the Haraumont-Écurey Road, and they notified the corps artillery.[51] At this point in the offensive, the 104th Field Artillery Regiment had 1,447 men, the 105th had 1,395 men, the 106th had 1,470 men, and the 102nd Trench Mortar had 235 men.

On the far left of the 33rd Division, intense enemy fire and gas shelling occurred at intervals throughout the nights of the 29th and 30th.[52] The French 212th R.A.C. fired on observable batteries between the left flank front of their sector to Consenvoye. Members of the 104th Field Artillery in the Bois de Forge had the difficult assignment of entering a recently evacuated enemy dugout which had been mined. Sergeant Peter F. Kelly and Private, 1st class, Alfred McGinness of Battery E had volunteered to clean it out. Unfortunately, the mine exploded. Kelly was seriously wounded and later died; McGinness was also wounded.⁵³ At 6:00 p.m. on September 29 the Batteries C, D, and E of the 104th were ordered to support the front of the 65th Infantry Brigade. During the night, the 65th relieved the 80th Division, retaining the artillery for the 4th Division. The 33rd Division also expanded its front so that the 1st Army's front now extended from Bois de la Côte Lemont through Nantillois and Apremont southwest to the Argonne.

On Monday, September 30, the rain continued with mist and a cold wind. The artillery suffered an attack of gas concentrations and did counter battery work to defend the position, all the while breathing through the uncomfortable masks. Shelling was heavy on the Cumières Road and the Bois de Forges. The 106th fired back high explosive shells and gas. The artillery brigade assisted the 65th Infantry Brigade's front in the morning by firing on trench mortar batteries, and fired again on enemy batteries in the afternoon. The French 212th R.A.C. fired on batteries at the front from their left position to Consenvoye. The 212th also responded to requests for fire from the 131st Infantry.⁵⁴ The trench mortar and the field guns were beyond range for some of the requests being made, so those were forwarded some of them to the corps artillery.

As the battle extended into the first week of October a new chancellor was named in Germany. Chancellor Georg von Hertling had resigned. The new chancellor, Prince Max of Baden, initiated peace talks with Woodrow Wilson.⁵⁵ The men at the front heard rumors about an end to the war, but were ordered not to circulate them. During October, men continued to get wounded and die as negotiations took place in secret places.

Tuesday, October 1, began relatively quietly for the artillery under cold dripping skies. At 8:00 a.m. the French 212th R.A.C. was relieved from the brigade and moved to the Bois de Nixéville-Nord at 5:00 p.m. The 18th French Division planned an attack on the east bank of the Meuse River for 4:30 a.m. the next morning. At 11:40 a.m. the 106th Field Artillery Regiment moved three battalions to the Tranchée Anatolie and Tranchée de Balis near the Moulin de Raffecourt to support an advance being made by the 8th French Division. The regiment also fired 80 rounds of high explosives and 15 rounds of gas east of the river. The 52nd Field Artillery Brigade often supported the divisions surrounding them, serving their part of a network collaborating in the larger offensive. At 7 P.M the enemy artillery in the area of Sivry-sur-Meuse sent gas near the 130th Infantry Division, while the corps artillery fired on an enemy battery.⁵⁶ The 130th Infantry were in the Bois (woods) de la Côte Lemont. The 129th Infantry Division of the 33rd Division was in the Bois de Dannevoux.

The absence of clean water was an ever present problem, despite the fact that it was continually falling from the clouds. The men at the front line were not able to bath often, and everything was covered in the sticky French mud. Men used the quart of water in their canteen to drink, wash themselves, and clean their mess kits. To save on water, they often scoured the mess kit with mud instead. Most of the men just ate out of a can anyway, since it was difficult for hot food trucks to deliver to certain areas of the front from the kitchens set up in safe areas to the rear. Gas shelling contaminated the food, and the regular shelling on roads placed the transportation crews in danger of injury or death. The men at the front largely lived on canned corned beef, dubbed "corned Willy," along with hard tack, a large cracker, and canned beans. Two days "iron rations" consisted of two cans of corned beef and six boxes of crackers.[57] Some units had canned roast beef, called "monkey meat," or salmon, called "goldfish." A number of divisions would live almost entirely on "goldfish." The men at the front often just ate one meal a day, usually around 6:00 p.m. Hunger was ever-present, as was the dampness and constant shell fire. Many of the men suffered from dysentery caused by the gas. Some of the men kept mixtures of water and bicarbonate of soda in their canteens for just such emergencies. Since the men needed to be clean-shaven for the gas masks to fit snuggly, they would often drink half of their cup of coffee and shave with the rest. It was unpleasant, but could save their lives.

    The lack of washing led to the men's clothing becoming infected with lice, called "cooties" by the British. The Americans quickly picked up that lingo. Some of the men from New York called them "seam squirrels." The lice laid eggs in the seams of clothing and their bites caused itching and sores. Men tried to kill them by running lit candles or lighters quickly over the seams and many of them took delight in simply squeezing the insects between the thumb nail and index finger.[58] Clothing could be placed in liquid naphthalene to kill the lice, but there was no laundry at the front and the men only bathed two or three times a month. Even if the clothing was cleaned, the eggs would then hatch and the lice would continue the misery. The insects also spread trench fever, a painful illness characterized by a high fever. Recovery took a full month and relapse was common. Little was known about how such diseases were transmitted at the time. William Clarke's comment was, "The devil himself must have conceived this torturous punishment to inflict upon the human body."[59]

    The American soldiers complained constantly about the sticky mud, which caked onto their shoes and leggings. It seemed to build up layer upon layer, and there was no place to wash. The mud in the fields often reached up to their knees. The horses and caissons often stuck in the mud. Horses' faces were covered in it as they tried to find drinking water. The infantry in the trenches slipped on mud and slept in it. Mud was everywhere and on everything, making everything heavier and more difficult. Unable to wash themselves or their clothes, the men were perpetually coated in the dusty colored muck.

On Wednesday, October 2, the enemy barraged from 5:15 a.m. to 6:00 a.m. sending over twelve mustard gas shells near Company B's machine gun emplacements. At 6:30 a.m. the first battalion of the 104th Field Artillery Regiment fired to silence the enemy batteries at the request of the commander of the 65th Infantry Brigade.[60] After that, the enemy artillery was relatively quiet for the morning, taking shelter from the weather, but during the day they increased shelling on the Gercourt-Drillancourt Road, the Bois de Forges, and the village of Forges, sending members of the 104th scrambling. Enemy aircraft were active as their own troops moved near Vilosnes-sur-Meuse. During the night, the Central powers fired upon the village of Forge, along with Cumières. At 3:00 p.m. the 105th Field Artillery sent their 1st Battalion from the Moulin de Raffecourt forward to the Bois de Sachet.[61] At 5:30 p.m. the 106th Field Artillery (howitzers) did counter battery work against enemy guns on the east bank of the Meuse, the Bois de Consenvoye, and the numbered location H.19.11. By 8:15 p.m. the 106th took a new position east of Béthincourt, but the road to Cumières was blocked, stopping them from their advance and forcing them to camouflage their guns and bring their horses back. The 104th Field Artillery Regiment was ordered to use one battery to send neutralizing fire north in the area of Vilosnes where the river turns west, and then to use another battery to attack the enemy batteries east of the Meuse. Between 9:30 p.m. and 10:15 p.m. Company B of the 33rd Division fired, and threw sneezing gas on Hill 294. The gas was an irritant to nasal passages. At 11 p.m. the enemy retaliated with a heavy bombardment of gas and artillery at the front of the 129th Infantry. Over the course of the war, 72,807 Americans succumb to the gas, resulting in 1,462 deaths. The gas mask only protected the lungs and face. Injuries also occurred on the skin.

In the first two days of October, three officers of the 52nd Field Artillery Brigade were wounded, two enlisted men were killed and 17 enlisted men wounded. On October 2 there was heavy enemy shell fire in many locations, particularly in the Bois de Forge, making it difficult to supply rations to the front. Many of the men on the supply train would be wounded and earn divisional citations for their perseverance.[62] All of the men were trying to "do their bit" in the war effort. Cooks tried to establish kitchens close to their regiments, placing them in increased danger. One kitchen took a direct hit later in October; although destroyed, the cooks re-established it and continued serving meals.[63] Some elements used a trench to cook. While supervising the distribution of rations in the Bois de Forges on October 2, Lieutenant George E. Wolfe of the 104th Field Artillery Regiment remained at his post under heavy shell fire until he was severely wounded.[64]

On October 3, the enemy sent over harassing fire and the 52nd fired back. Constant volleying was part of daily life for the soldiers by now. The Americans kept the pressure on despite the fierce resistance. At 4:10 a.m. the 106th Field Artillery Regiment began firing on machine gun nests. Their guns were very good at attacking batteries, dugouts and trenches because they could reach high angles and provide curved fire. One private from the 106th was slightly wounded during the volley. At 12:45 p.m. the 52nd Field Artillery fired on Central power batteries. The rain had stopped in the early hours, so the 105th Field Artillery Regiment moved its 1st Battalion into the northwestern edge of the Bois de la Côte Lemont where they were concealed. They were ordered to neutralize hostile fire and break up any counter-attacks between the Bois de Brieulles, the Bois de Forêt, and Brieulles-sur-Meuse. These were all important enemy strongholds, with the one in Brieulles having prevented an advance of the 80th Division for several days. The enemy would often leave the city during the day only to return at night and fire on the Allies. They would also sneak into the woods with machine guns and attempt to fire on the backs of those at the line.

The 105th Field Artillery Regiment completed their movement by 5:00 a.m. having had little or no sleep. From their new position they protected the right flank of the 4th Division, as they attacked under the III Army Corps. During this attack two enlisted men of the 105th Field Artillery Regiment were killed, while the wounded included three officers and 17 enlisted men.[65] The army set up first aid stations and dressing stations in the rear. Tents and farm houses often served as temporary dressing stations. The evening of October 3 ended with the 106th firing on an enemy battery at 7:35 p.m.

While these attacks were happening near the river, to the west the Lost Battalion of the 77th Division was surrounded by the enemy and fighting for their lives. Those men were mostly from New York City and had trained at Camp Upton. The American divisions were moving according to General Pershing's orders, but the battalion was deep in enemy territory and many men were dying. The line from the west had I Corps with the 77th, 28th and 1st Divisions. In the center was the V Corps with the 32nd and 3rd Divisions. In the east was III Corps with the 4th, 80th and 33rd Divisions. Each area had its own risk.

Members of the 102nd Ammunition Train in the 52nd Field Artillery Brigade had the daunting task of delivering dangerous material in this area while under fire. The individual regiments would then send men to pick up material for their locations. Private William Moran of Company G, 102nd Ammunition Train, was driving a limber on the Béthincourt-Forges Road containing grenades when some exploded. Moran removed unexploded grenades from the road so that others could pass safely and returned to duty.[66]

Colonel Drew Rankin of the 104th Field Artillery Regiment described some of his surroundings in a letter typed on October 3, without listing where he was or mentioning the horror he had seen at the front. He commented on the many "aeroplane" duels witnessed while anti-aircraft guns continually fired. From the guns elevated positions, the gunners must have had a perfect view. The anti-aircraft guns were often 75s mounted on trucks, although three-inch guns and the Hotchkiss AA were also used. The 75s proved very versatile due to their unique recoil system. They did not move out of place when fired, and so did not need to be adjusted after each shot. This, coupled with their rapid fire which could range from 15 to 30 rounds per minute at least for a short duration, made them the heroes of the war. During this battle the Germans had aircraft, balloons, and three Zeppelins in the air.

Colonel Rankin described duels in the sky:

> One day two German planes sneaked over the line in the midst of a cloud and swooped down on an observation balloon sending it down in flames while the observer had to jump out in a parachute. They repeated the performance further down the line and then beat back before the allied planes could come up. After a bit the allied planes made a rush on the German lines and dropped two German balloons in like manner, making the score 2–2 for the day.
>
> Another day an allied plane and a German plane were having a little tussle about five thousand feet up and I guess the Frenchman was shooting a little too straight to suit the Bolonie, for the German plane turned turtle and then started to fall end over end towards the earth. We all thought he was done for, and even the anti-aircraft guns stopped firing and just when we were picking out the spot for him to land on, he straightened out his plane within three hundred feet of the ground and skimmed over the hill towards the German lines. I understand, however, that the dough-boys got him with a machine gun when he crossed the front line trenches.

Rankin stated he felt the bombings were "lessening," which he may have said to protect his mother, the letter's recipient, from knowing the fullness of the danger he was in. He did sense a lessening of the German artillery's strength. He complained about the large French guns which had been fitted on flat railway cars as they shook everything off the walls of the barracks when they fired. Later he had found out that the French had been "shelling a town in the German lines about fifteen or twenty miles away." He also mentioned a German scouting plane which flew over his camp, meeting an Allied plane.

> They brought him down in flames although he was not hurt outside of a few scratches. I understand that when he landed the aviator who brought him down ran up to the German. [The German] surrendered and handed over all his medals to his Allied captor, and then shook hands in a very sportsmanlike manner. His machine was burned beyond recovery and one of the boys brought part

of a wing in to camp from which I have cut a little piece of the veneer for you as a souvenir. It consists of three paper thin layers of wood glued together in such a way that they are as strong as metal, and yet light as wood.[67]

On the afternoon of the 3rd, the 102nd Ammunition Train was ordered to load all trucks with ammunition and travel at night to the 4th Division at Cuisy. The 1st Battalion of the 105th Field Artillery moved forward along the northeastern edge of the Bois de la Côte Lemont, but they were heavily shelled and gassed. There was live machine gun and rifle fire as well. Between October 3 and 4, the 33rd Division made their advance.

The second phase of the Meuse-Argonne Offensive took place from October 4 to 6, 1918, during which the 1st American Army would attack across its entire front. The heights of the Meuse and the Argonne Forest were still the objective. The Allies had 16 divisions placed from Fresnesen-en-Woëvre to the Argonne Forest, but there were three enemy strongholds facing the 1st American Army: The Madeleine Farm and the Bois de Fays, north of Montfaucon beyond the Bois des Ogons, and the heights of Cunel.[68] The I Corps with the 1st, 28th and 77th Divisions were ordered to clear the Argonne. To the right of them, the V Corps with the 3rd and 32nd Divisions were focused on the central heights of Romagne. To the right of them, III Corp with the 33rd, 4th and 80th Divisions continued to advance on the heights of the Meuse River as they had been doing from the opening of the offensive. The 33rd Division was set to protect the east flank of the 4th Division, which was in the center of their grouping. The 52nd Field Artillery Brigade was ordered to give support in this protection of the flank, and to neutralize the enemy artillery in the Bois de Châtillon, the Bois de Sartelle, and in two ravines east of Liny-devant-Dun. Brieulles, the ravine north, and the trenches northwest of the city were also to be fired upon.

On Friday, October 4, at 3:00 a.m. the corps began the second phase of the Meuse-Argonne Offensive by continuing attacks on the west of the Meuse River. These late night barrages were intended to exhaust the enemy, but they also exhausted the Allied infantry and artillery. Because of the twisting nature of the Meuse River and the various hills and high places along its banks, firing seemed to vacillate between the east and the west as the troops pushed northward. The 33rd Division pivoted into a position next to the river, placing them again at the right of the corps and protecting the east flank of the 4th Division. At 5:25 a.m. they attacked with the 4th Division in the center and the 80th Division on the left. The 52nd Field Artillery Brigade provided supporting cover to protect the flank of the 33rd and neutralize the enemy as planned, and then performed counter attack in response to enemy fire coming back.

The mission of the 106th Field Artillery Regiment was to neutralize the enemy artillery in the Bois de Châtillon, the Bois de Sartelle, the two ravines east of Liny-devant-Dun, and the east of the Meuse River with their heavy artillery. Battery C, D and E of the 106th were south of Le Mort Homes. The remainder of the 106th fired 3,000 meters west of the village ruins of Forges. Batteries A and C of the 1st Battalion of the 105th moved to the high point of the Bois de la Côte Lemont, but experienced heavy shelling and sneezing gas as well as fire from enemy aircraft. They were also subjected to heavy machine gun and rifle fire, being close to the infantry front lines. Battery B was being held in reserve. They did not fire in this exposed position, but were ready. Instead, at dusk they were ordered back to the Bois de Sachet. Batteries E and F of the 105th Field Artillery Regiment remained in place, but the 1st Battalion moved to the Bois Juré, south of Dannevoux, and fired north of Vilosnes to assist the 4th Division. At 1:40 p.m. the 2nd Battalion fired east of the river on enemy batteries at Brabant and Consenvoyes.[69] The 104th Field Artillery Regiment neutralized fire coming from the enemy stronghold in the Vilosnes area using one battery, and attacked enemy batteries east of the Meuse with another. The group near Forges was under heavy fire from the enemy.

During the night of October 4 and 5, the 65th Infantry Brigade sent patrols to see if Hill 263 was held by the enemy. It was not, but the infantry did not occupy it. In the afternoon and evening of October 5, the 52nd Field Artillery Brigade was ordered to fire on Haraumont, Liny-devant-Dun, Brielles and Tranchèe (trench) de Teton. Brielles was a traditional French village with a church. Unfortunately, artillery often aimed specifically at church steeples as well as any tall buildings, since they served as lookout points for the enemy. The 33rd Division was instructed to take the trench so that their machine guns and automatic weapons could fire on Brieulles and the ridge northwest of it. The mission proved impossible. At 12:50 p.m. the 106th Field Artillery Regiment fired on Haraumont and Liny-devant-Dun.[70] The sun peeked out for the 5th and 6th as they also did counter battery work against the German guns on both banks of the Meuse. The 105th Field Artillery Regiment participated in launching harassing fire at the enemy, including in the Bois de Sartelles and on Brieulles-Haraumont and the Tranchèe de Teton. The enemy fired throughout the day and night on the woods. On October 6, 20 Allied planes bombed Brieulles, setting the town on fire. The 80th Division also launched gas and high explosive shells for 30 minutes.[71]

By 6:15 p.m. the 2nd Battery of the 308th French Regular Heavy Artillery had moved to the Bois des Sartelles. It had been a very long day, but the front was now from the Bois de la Côte Lemont, the Bois du Fays, Gesnes to Hill 240, Fleville, Chehery, and then southwest through the Argonne Forest. Since the St. Mihiel line was stable, some of those divisions were now focused on the Meuse-Argonne attack on the east bank of the river. The left arm of the Allied forces was gradually creeping north and east through very hard fighting. Amidst the battle, at midnight on the 5th the clocks were systematically set back one hour in a civilized manner signaling the end of daylight savings time.

The German artillery on the right side of the Meuse River held the heights overlooking the right flank of the 33rd Division, where they were well covered by woods and a strong defensive system. Their harassing fire made it difficult for the Allied advance, so taking them out was paramount for success. On Sunday, October 6, amidst fog with poor visibility, the enemy again sent over shells, mustard gas and sneezing gas. The Allied artillery was very active back as all available guns of III Corps were targeted on the Bois de Châtillon. The 52nd Field Artillery Brigade aimed their 75mm guns at the Tranchèe de Teton and on Brielles. The Bois de Forêt was now burning.

The A, B and F Batteries of the 104th Field Artillery Brigade moved north to join other batteries in the Moulin (mill) de Raffecourt who were firing on the enemy line. The 2nd Battalion of the 104th Field Artillery also moved from Le Claire to the Moulin de Raffecourt, near the 1st Battalion of the same regiment. The 1st Battalion of the 105th Field Artillery Regiment remained at the Bois de la Côte Lemont with the 123rd and 124th Machine Gun Regiments, supporting the artillery with harassing fire on Brieulles, the ridge to the northwest, and the Tranchèe de Teton. They neutralized the area with machine gun fire, artillery shells, and an infantry raid. The 106th fired on the Tranchèe de Teton as well.

On October 6, the 33rd Division and the 52nd Field Artillery Brigade were transferred back to the XVII French Army Corps under Major-General Henri Claudel to attack the enemy heights on the east bank of the Meuse in preparation for the third phase of the offensive.[72] The 33rd Division used one battery of the 132nd Infantry, supported by a machine gun battery and the artillery of the 104th Field Artillery Regiment. The 2nd Battery of the 105th and 2nd Battery of the 106th, under Colonel Emery T. Smith, engaged in an attack on the enemy heights on the east bank of the Meuse River. The overall mission was to drive the enemy back as far as the Bois de la Grande Montagne. They began a rolling barrage parallel to the direction of the river north of Consenvoye. Near the river, more concentrated fire crept up to the wooded heights. The rest of the field artillery, under the artillery brigade commander, provided additional artillery support with the mission of taking out the well-placed enemy artillery. The American 33rd and 29th Divisions were adjacent to the French 18th and 26th Divisions. The objective of the 33rd Infantry was to advance to a line from the south of the Bois de Chaume on the right, then south and west to the northern outskirts of Consenvoye. The woods on the high ground were extremely difficult for the 33rd, but their attacks were successful, even under constant fire with active enemy aircraft.[73] Between September 27 and October 7, the 104th Field Artillery Regiment had suffered four wounded men with two dying from their wounds. The 105th had fourteen wounded men with one death, while three men from the 106th had been wounded and four were killed. By the end of the second phase of the offensive, the Argonne Forest was finally in the hands of the 1st Army.

CHAPTER EIGHT

The Meuse-Argonne Offensive (October 7–November 11, 1918)

The third phase of the Meuse-Argonne Offensive lasted from October 7 to October 11, 1918. The center of the Allied line was one kilometer south of the menacing Kriemhilde Stellung. The Allied plan was to encircle Romagne and pierce the Kriemhilde. Tactical control of the 33rd Division passed to the French XVII Corps east of the Meuse River on October 7. Three battalions of the 33rd's infantry assembled in the Bois de Forge and prepared to cross the river. The joint attack was scheduled for October 8when two battalions of the 132nd Infantry would cross the Meuse at Brabant-sur-Meuse. Focusing on the heights of the Meuse, they would move north-northwest in contact with the French 18th Division. The advanced line extended south of the Bois de Chaume southwest to the northern outskirts of Consenvoye. The 33rd Division was given three objectives: the normal Allied objective of point 352 to point 243-Consenvoye Road, the first Allied exploitation objective of the east to west line along the northern edge of the Bois Plat Chêne and the Bois de Chaume, and the second Allied exploitation objective of the line along the Villeneuve Ferme-Sivry-sur-Meuse Road.[1]

Monday, October 7, the town of Brieulles was bombed again by the divisional artillery. The weather was cloudy, helping to block aerial observation. The brigade artillery was relatively quiet during the rest of the day with only periodic fire. Heavy shelling came on from the Central powers during the day, with both mustard gas and sneezing gas thrown into the Bois de Dannevoux and the Bois des Moriaux. The enemy also shelled the area of Forges with gas from 10 p.m. until 12 a.m. For the Allies gas masks and safety trenches were the main determination between life and death. The 106th Field Artillery Regiment sent back harassing fire.

The 52nd Field Artillery Brigade was relatively quiet, preparing for the attack which would take place the following day. The 1st and 2nd Batteries of the 104th Field Artillery Regiment had moved back to the southwestern portion of the Bois de Forges, near the shelling. The 2nd Battalion of the 105th Field Artillery Regiment moved over night from the Bois de la Côte Lemont to the southern slopes of the Côte de l'Oie. Companies A and D, and the 124th Machine Gun Company, moved to the Bois de Forges at 9:00 p.m. The 123rd Machine Gun Company of the 33rd Division remained in the Bois de la Côte Lemont with the 1st Battalion of the 130th Infantry. The 2nd Battalion of the 106th Field Artillery Regiment (howitzers) moved near Chattancourt. This position formed a salient by the Bois de Maulamont with well entrenched enemy on both flanks.[2] They were able to maintain this dangerous position through October 8, the first day of the scheduled attack.

Meanwhile to the west, the I Corps executed a flank attack, reinforced by the 82nd Division to relieve the "Lost Battalion," which was pinned down by the enemy. Members of the 308th Infantry of the 77th Division had become isolated between the Bois d'Apremont and Charlevaux. Out of 650 men, 450 were killed. The rescue was successful; the weary survivors finally left their positions. The men returned to active duty and many of them would later receive medals for their bravery under fire. During the rescue, the now famous Sergeant York of the 82nd Division wiped out 35 enemy machine guns and took 132 German prisoners.

October 8 had been designated "D-Day" for the 1st American Army with the objective of gaining the high ground of the Meuse opposite the Giselher Stellung. Unfortunately, after three days of sunshine, the weather turned not only to rain but to hail. The night of October 7, the 52nd Field Artillery Brigade had detached and moved the 2nd Battalion of the 105th, and the entire 104th Field Artillery Regiment which would now serve under Colonel E.T. Smith. The detached group had then attached to the XVII French Corps temporarily for their operation. The assault was to be on the east bank of the Meuse to the slopes of the Côte de l'Oie the next day. The group was to assist the French in their assault. They were in an area within direct view of the enemy, with rising ground which was open. The group had not fired on the 7th. On the 8th they would receive severe shelling and gas.[3] The 106th was placed under Colonel Davis of the 132nd Infantry. Following the French advance, the members of the 33rd Division were to attack.

At 5 a.m. on October 8, without preparatory artillery fire, the French advanced under heavy enemy shelling and gas. It was estimated that 90 enemy shells were launched per hour from the many enemy guns in a desperate attempt to stop that advance. At 5:30 a.m. the XVII French Army Corp with the 18th French Division on the west and 26th French Division on the east (each with two Senegalese battalions), along with the 58th Brigade of the 29th American Division, seized the observatories of Haumont, Ormont, and the ridge of Malbrouck. The 104th Field Artillery Regiment laid down a rolling barrage to cover the 132nd Regiment of the 33rd Division. The line of fire moved along a line parallel to the river, north of Consenvoye, finishing near the river and becoming more concentrated as the ground ascended to the wooded heights.[4] The 33rd Division then followed the French assault with the 132nd Infantry Regiment. They crossed the river by the bridges at Samogneaux and Brabant, and moved through open country near the river to the ridge of the Bois de Chaume. The joint attack advanced the line south of the Bois de Caumeron on the right to the northern outskirts of Consenvoye. The XVII French Army Corp was now astride the Meuse.

From 8:40 a.m. until 3 p.m. the 1st Battalion of the 106th Field Artillery Regiment (howitzers) sent harassing fire against the Bois de Chaume. The 2nd Battery of the 105th Field Artillery Regiment joined the French guns in a barrage, ceasing their fire by noon. At 4:00 p.m. the 33rd Division advanced under a rolling and standing barrage which was laid down on the east bank of the Meuse for two hours by the 75mm guns, with fire by the heavy artillery for one and one half hours. The enemy pounded the Bois de Forge with both 75s and 155s from 1:30 to 4:00 p.m. but their artillery was noted to be weakening. They seemed to be moving some of their material back, although that did not make it any less dangerous for the Allies. The 33rd Division was successful in meeting its objectives that day. The remaining 52nd Field Artillery Brigade supported the 66th Infantry of the 33rd Division, which relieved the 65th Infantry. The infantry of the 33rd had reached the Giselher Stellung on the 8th and on two successive days, but each time was ordered to retire to make contact with the 29th Division on its right. The 29th Division had not been able to overcome the enemy in the Bois de Consenvoye, the Bois de la Grande Montagne and the Bois d'Ormont.[5]

The XVII French Army Corps used 600 guns for the advance. The enemy counter barrage began with harassing fire in the afternoon. Enemy aircraft was active over the Bois de Moriaux with light concentrations of gas launched in the Bois de Dannevoux. The enemy sent continuous fire by heavy and long-range guns throughout the night of October 8. The American forces, with the French, were able to push the Germans back along the river. Over 5,000 enemy prisoners were captured by the XVII French Army Corps.[6]

In the midst of the activity, at the farm at Le Claire horses pulling a limber filled with ammunition became frightened and ran. Two cases of hand grenades belonging to the 104th Field Artillery Regiment dropped from the runaway limber and exploded, causing twelve casualties. 2nd Lieutenant Ralph Regan Finney, Corporal John Bush, and Private, 1st Class, Robert McCauley, from Battery A rushed to aid the wounded and direct their removal from danger. Since material was usually pulled by horses or mules, when they spooked under fire, it became very dangerous. Often times the men had to hand deliver boxes of ordinance because the passage was just too difficult for normal transportation.[7]

On October 8 and 9, Sergeant William H. Roach, Corporal William L. B. Farrell, and Corporal Frank Reilly of the 104th Field Artillery Headquarters Company set up a forward observation post in the Bois de Forges. They had to set up in a tree and maintained the position throughout the night under heavy shell fire and gas. Their purpose was to observe barrage signals and report their accuracy by telephone to the Battery Headquarters. In another heroic act, Captain Francis P. Gallagher of the 104th Field Artillery repaired and put into action a captured German Battery of 77mm guns while under heavy shelling, firing them effectively against the enemy.[8]

III Corps ordered the left boundary of the French XVII Corps and of the 33rd Division changed for tactical reasons to a line from Béthincourt to the northern corner of the Bois de la Côte Lemont ending two kilometers west of Viosnes-sur-Meuse at midnight. The normal objective had been met with the capture of the Tranchée de Heraclée (Trench of Heracles) and Consenvoye, and the first exploitation objective line was held by the Bois de Chaume and Bois Plat Chêne. Patrols advanced to the 2nd exploitation objective by the Sivry-sur-Meuse Road. The 1st Battalion had reached within a few hundred meters of that road, but the counter attacks were very heavy and members were forced to withdraw in the afternoon to the Bois de Chaume and Bois Plat Chêne line. The Bois de Chaume and the Bois Plat Chêne were "reeking with gas."[9]

After a night of cold rain followed by morning fog, at 6:00 a.m. on Wednesday, October 9, under Colonel Smith, the artillery laid down a standing barrage in front of the 33rd Division Infantry, rolling forward at 6:40 a.m. Creeping barrages were developed to place a curtain of artillery fire in front of an advancing infantry as they slowly moved forward, usually advancing 50 meters per minute. The action required careful coordination between infantry and artillery. Despite heavy enemy artillery and machine gun fire, the attack resumed at 8:30 a.m. Although fatigued, the men pressed on.

Six battalions of the 33rd Division crossed the Meuse River under fog over a bridge that had been built by the engineers at Consenvoye. The water was 16 feet deep here and the bridge needed to be 156 feet long. The men had worked under full view of the enemy for the five and one half hours it took to build the bridge. They wore gas masks as profuse enemy shells were launched against them. The troops successfully crossed the bridges, and dug in at the southern edge of the Bois de Chaumes. By 11 a.m. the 33rd Division had met their objectives. At the close of the day, the XVII French Army Corps had a front 500 miles from south of Sivry-sur-Meuse along the north edge of Bois de Chaume through Bois Boussois, the Bois de Molleville, the Ferme (farm) D'Ormont, the northern edge of the Bois d'Haumont, and the northwestern edge of the Bois de Caures, along the Bois de Champneuville through the Dauphin work, the Bonnet work in LaWavrille and Côte 351, to the northeastern corner of the Bois des Fosses beyond Baumont. There the Germans had stopped the French advance. The 29th Division Infantry was also driven back. That forced the left side, held by the 33rd Division, to "retire."[10] The enemy artillery fire on the Bois de Consenvoye was so heavy that it completely cleaned out the underbrush, leaving a clear sight through the woods.

On October 10, the 33rd Division shifted focus to taking the Bois de Chaume. The woods were filled with enemy machine gun nests. At 6:05 a.m. the divisional artillery began a heavy barrage, and gas was returned by the enemy. Colonel Smith's small group of artillery supported the troops east of the Meuse with western barrages and fire. The enemy pounded the Bois de Chaume from 1:00 p.m. to 5:30 p.m. with high explosives. They also did light shelling in the Bois de Dannevoux, Bois de la Côte Lemont and the Bois des Moriaux throughout the day. At 8:00 P.M the Germans shelled the Bois de Forges.

The command center of the 104th Field Artillery Regiment was located in the northwest corner of the Bois de Forges, and suffering heavy shelling. Batteries C, D and E of the 104th Field Artillery had crossed the river via a bridge at Consenvoye and took position south of the village near what had been the German trench system running east and west.[11] The infantry of the 33rd by the Bois de Chaume had such difficulty with enemy artillery that it was forced to withdraw. They could not maintain their position at Haraumont. The 132nd Infantry Regiment called for support from the artillery and Batteries C, D and E responded immediately. The Argonne Forest to the west had been cleared and was now in the possession of the Allies. The eastern section of the line, however, was still a problem.

On October 10, the Batteries A, B and F of the 104th Field Artillery Regiment were considered too far from the enemy lines to be effective, so they were moved to the southwest edge of the Bois Juré, south of Dannevoux. The woods there were filled with well organized enemy defenses with numerous machine gun units. The regiment marched north and west from Verdun, where the river turned to the west. It was an exposed position for them and rather than risk attack by firing, they concentrated on trying to conceal their guns from enemy observation using poles and overhead netting. The woods in this region of France held the smell of death. Since high explosive shells tended to evaporate anyone they hit, little particles of flesh were often nestled under the wet foliage. The dank odors of decay, coupled with remnants of gas, made many of the artillery locations very unpleasant. The men needed the protection of woods, yet the woods were a reminder of how many men had already died.

The Central powers kept up a constant barrage on the regiment from the north and east. It was difficult to get rations to the men with roads and bridges continually under fire. The Forges Wood was gassed, as were the artillery positions on the right side of the river. Any food that could get delivered in these areas would be ruined. During this phase of the operation, Colonel Smith, commander of the 104th Field Artillery Regiment, became seriously ill and while he continued to perform his duties for a long time, was ultimately sent to get medical attention. Lieutenant-Colonel John T. Delaney would later take his command. The rain had stopped temporarily, but they would be in for a week of more.[12] From 11 p.m. to 1 a.m. on October 11, the sound of enemy 105mm shells at Dannevoux kept the 130th Infantry awake.

On October 11, the 4th Division extended its lines to the right and took the northwestern edge of the Bois de la Côte Lemont. The enemy counterattacked with bombs from airplanes, and the infantry called for the assistance of the anti-aircraft guns. The planes, with their large black cross, were said to have looked like birds of prey in the sky. They circled, giving out their distinctive engine whirl. They would also drop propaganda from time to time which looked "something like snow, with light playing on it" as it fell.[13] Major-General O'Ryan mentioned in his book that only 150 injuries of the total A.E.F. were due to aerial bombing. While their bombs were not very effective, they served to locate troops and report back to enemy artillery which then inflicted much suffering on the Allies.[14]

During the night, some of the 75s of the 104th moved closer to the troops east of the Meuse to more effectively send out barrages. The enemy continued to shell the Bois de Chaume, and in the early evening shelled the Bois de Forges. The 52nd Field Artillery Brigade responded to calls from infantry for support, doing counter battery work.

Between October 11 and 12, the 1st Battalion of the 104th Field Artillery Brigade moved to the Tranchée de Heraclée, southeast of Consenvoye, getting closer and closer to the Kriemhilde Stellung. The second battalion of the 104th Field Artillery Regiment was commanded by Commander Major James E. Austin. They were the first American artillery group to cross the Meuse River north of Verdon.[15] Major Austin had first personally crossed the river while under heavy fire to scout the position for his battalion. As each area was conquered by the Allies, the line moved north, along with the artillery. The 106th Field Artillery Regiment progressed their fire to the region of Haraumont. The 2nd Battery of the 105th Field Artillery Brigade moved from the Bois de Forges to the southwestern edge of the Bois Juré. Between the 12th and 13th of October the defense line of the 33rd Division was organized along the front line east of the river. Each move closer to the enemy placed the soldiers in greater danger. The shelling, machine gun fire, and gassing continued day and night. From midnight on October 11 to 7 p.m. October 12 the east bank was under machine gun fire. A counter attack began at 2:15 a.m. while hostile airplanes were circling in the air.[16]

The fourth phase of the Meuse-Argonne Offensive lasted from October 12 to 15. General Pershing reorganized his forces once again. The newly created 2nd American Army was given the task of reducing the St. Mihiel salient and making a thrust against Metz, capitol of the Lorraine region. General Hunter Liggett was given charge of the 1st American Army allowing General Pershing to orchestrate the combined forces. A new front line was designated for the divisions to take the next day. The Germans still held the Kriemhilde Stellung. At dusk on Saturday, October 12, the 52nd Field Artillery Brigade and a battalion of the 105th moved to a new position on the southern edge of the Bois de Juré near Gercourt. The regimental commander moved his headquarters east of the two battalions, north of Consenvoye on the west bank of the Meuse and defensive systems were organized. One of the men wounded on the 12th refused medical treatment. After being wounded in the Bois de Forges, Sergeant John F. Byrnes of the 104th Supply Company went on to conduct a detachment to Cumières to secure rations for the men and forage for the animals. He returned to the gun positions near Chattancourt while under heavy enemy shelling.[17]

On Sunday, October 13, the 33rd Division was in position at the Bois de Chaume and Plat-Chêne. The weather was so foggy that Allied airplanes could not ascend until noon, though Brieulles was fairly clear.[18] Units of infantry bivouacked in trenches just south of Consenvoye, near the Consenvoye-Brabant road. There was increased artillery fire by both the Allies and Central powers, but the 52nd Field Artillery Brigade was relatively quiet. 2nd Battalion of the 105th, and the 106th, fired on Sivry-sur-Meuse to cover the construction of emplacements across the river on the west bank being made by the 102nd Trench Mortar Battery across from Sivry-sur-Meuse. The Trench Mortar Battery had been kept in reserve through much of the battle due to their shorter range. The infantry had now advanced close enough for use of the mortars. American soldiers such as Private Matthew J. Stotthard of Battery D, 104th Field Artillery Regiment were busy transporting the battery kitchen across the Consenvoye bridge while under enemy shelling and gas, even while rumors quietly circulated about Germany accepting the United States president's terms.[19] Fearing it was largely German propaganda, the men were ordered not to repeat it.

On October 11 and 12 the 2nd Battery of the 105th Field Artillery Regiment had moved its 75s forward to Gercourt-et-Drillancourt, and the night of October 13–14 the 3rd Battalion of the 106th Field Artillery Regiment followed under heavy shelling. On October 14–15, the 33rd relieved the 65th and 66th Brigades under a cold drizzle. The 33rd Division and three batteries of the 104th Field Artillery Regiment huddled in the wet trenches near Consenvoye Those that could draped their tents over one wall of the trench to stay as dry as they could. The 52nd Field Artillery Brigade was mostly silent during the morning. The exception was from 7:20 a.m. to 8 a.m. when the 75s of the 105th and the 155mm howitzers of the 106th supported the 29th Division in their attack east of the 34th meridian, particularly the heights of the Grande Montagne. At 9:30 a.m. they adjusted fire and continued until 2 p.m. Later in the afternoon, the 2nd Battalion of the 105th set a counter battery attack against enemy guns near Villeneuve Ferme. The 1st Battalion took over the mission of covering the construction being done by the trench mortar emplacements, firing until 10:20 p.m. Throughout the night, the enemy continued light shelling and light concentrations of gas aimed at Consenvoye.

Between the 9th and 15th, the artillery was under constant heavy artillery fire, machine gun fire, gas, airplane bombing, and fire from snipers. Despite all that, the 52nd Field Artillery Brigade successfully supported an attack by the 29th Division on the heights of the Grande Montagne, as well as the positions held by the 33rd Infantry Division. The Germans in the area were now in mixed units from various divisions, making it difficult for the Allies to determine their numbers or to identify individual units. The Central powers' forces were a combination of German and Austro-Hungarians.[20] Previously, the Germans had replaced a division when it lost 2,000 men, but now they were working with whatever they had in a desperate attempt to hold the line.

The men of the 52nd, suffering from lack of sleep and hunger combined with lice, filth, and the constant rain, had not had a break from direct, intense fire since their arrival at the front. Mustard gas hung around them in the woods like a lurking shadow of death. They had also been lifting and firing shells weighing 12–16 pounds each for hours at a time. Now the men of the 52nd faced units of the Austro-Hungarian and German last stronghold and their front of 17 divisions, with six in reserve. Still a formidable foe, the Central powers were considered "under strength and weary."[21] The 33rd Division, along with the 52nd Field Artillery Brigade, was still under General Claudel of the XVII French Army Corps. They were not about to give up.

On October 14, the entire Allied front attacked the Central powers. Côte Dame Marie was captured and the Hindenburg Line was broken. Cunel and Romagne–sous-Montfaucon were in the hands of the Allies. The line advanced two kilometers north of Sommerance. As the Germans withdrew from the far reaches of the western front, they collected in the area in front of the 33rd Division. They showed no apparent intention of leaving. In an attempt to keep communications open, Private, 1st Class, Aaron J. Cuffee voluntarily swam the Meuse River at Consenvoye with a phone cable while under heavy fire and gas shelling assisted by Sergeant Charles Levy from the Headquarters Company of the 104th Field Artillery Regiment.[22]

The Volker Stellung extended east from just south of Consenvoye across the Brabant Wood and to the south edge of the Bois de Moirey.[23] On October 15, the 3rd Battery of the 104th Field Artillery Regiment moved into the muddy Tranchée de Heraclée southeast of Consenvoye. From 6 a.m. to 11 a.m. the enemy artillery countered by shelling the area surrounding Consenvoye. During the afternoon and into the night the 77s and 155mm howitzers focused on the Bois de Chaume and the Consenvoye-Étraye Road. The road was gassed until 7:30 p.m. Within the trenches the men would often dig themselves into a wall while they tried to rest and stay warm. A carved out wall spot was a safer location, as the shells tended to explode upward and out at angles and the body was smaller when curled up and surrounded by earth. The Allied artillery did counter battery work and sent over harassing fire, but the 52nd was largely quiet, trying to rest amidst the noise.

The 33rd Division attacked the German line accompanied by the 29th Division, to their right. Between October 15 and 16 the 2nd Battery of the 104th Field Artillery Regiment moved forward from the southeastern corner of the Bois de Forges to the wood between the Bois Juré and the Bois de Septsarges, north of Ruisseau de Menomme. These areas had been battered by Allied artillery just weeks prior. The 1st Battalion of the 106th, Batteries A, B, and F, moved west of Gercourt. Other members of the 106th Field Artillery Regiment moved from the northern edge of the Forges-Béthincourt Road to the southwestern edge of the Bois Sachet.[24]

The Americans now entered the fifth phase of the Meuse-Argonne Offensive, lasting from October 16 to 31. The XVII French Army Corps planned an attack at Molleville Ferme for Wednesday, October 16, as they pushed left and forward. The artillery group under Colonel Smith supported them. The 52nd Field Artillery Brigade located near Consenvoye was basically placed in a triangle with the northern tip near the Bois Juré on the left and the Bois de Septsarges on the right; the base of the triangle was the Cuisy-Gercourt-et-Drillancourt Road from the Bois d'en Dela on the west to Drillancourt on the east.

The command of the 1st Army had been given to Lt.-General Hunter Liggett who, after reviewing the soldiers at the front, decided the constant hammering in bad weather with no rest needed to change. He began his planning. Pershing had reorganized the A.E.F. and also created the 2nd Army under General Robert L. Bullard, while he stepped back to direct the entire campaign. Between the 16th and 17th of October, the 33rd Division finally received hot meals, as opposed to the "canned Willy" enjoyed by so few. The warm food worked wonders against the cold rain. The men also received blankets and exchanges for the unwashed, lice infested uniforms, many of which were shredded. These new uniforms would be worn daily by the members of the 52nd Field Artillery Brigade for the next five weeks of desperate fighting. The men's spirits were lifted, despite the scattered enemy shelling and circling airplanes.

On the 17th, the 52nd Field Artillery Brigade was assigned to cover the advance of the 29th Division. Again they faced heavy enemy shelling, machine gun fire, and hostile airplanes. Despite the 105th Field Artillery Regiment's harassing and neutralization fire, by the afternoon and evening there was an increase in enemy activity. The Germans shelled the entire area surrounding the Bois Sachet, the Bois Juré, Drillancourt, Consenvoye and Gercourt-et Drillancourt using high explosives, shrapnel and mustard gas. Sergeant John D. Murphy of Battery D, 105th Field Artillery Regiment, ran into trouble delivering supplies to his battery between Gercourt and Brabant-sur-Meuse. The animals of his transport were all killed by shell fragments.[25]

Starting October 17, General Liggett reorganized the divisions under him for an assault aimed at creating a new American front in a straight line from Grandpré in the west to the east bank of the Meuse River. Friday, October 18 through the 19, the 1st Battalion of the 104th Field Artillery Regiment sat quietly in the wet trench southeast of Consenvoye. Colonel Merritt H. Smith had been in command of the battery but was very sick, so on the 18th of October Lieutenant Colonel John T. Delaney formally took his place. Colonel Smith was moved to the rear.

Meanwhile, the 52nd Field Artillery Brigade was restoring its normal organization by dissolving the supporting groups operating independently since the initial attack east of the Meuse River on October 8 and returning those regiments to the brigade. Then the artillery brigade commander moved his headquarters forward to the northwestern edge of the Bois de Forges. The 102nd Trench Mortar Battery fired seventy-five rounds into Vilosnes. This was their sole opportunity to take part in the offensive since most of the work had been at distances beyond their reach.[26] The brigade continued to assist the 33rd Division, holding their position despite being rattled by heavy artillery fire day and night. Between the 18th and 21st, the 33rd Division was relieved by the French 15th Colonial Division. The 105th continued to fire on the Central powers.

October 18 and 19 proved difficult days for the 104th Field Artillery Regiment. Privates, 1st Class, John Noland and William Sieven of Battery E were delivering ammunition to their battery near Consenvoye when they were severely wounded. Noland required the amputation of a limb and Sieven died of his wounds. Privates, 1st Class, Walter McAvinne and Francis A. Pearce of Battery F were wounded and evacuated. Private Schuyler R. Smith of Battery A was killed at an exposed observation post at Dannevoux. Private Martin Schneider of the Headquarters Company died at his observation post overnight under an improvised protection. Captain Arthur W. Hofmann was wounded and knocked out by an exploding shell, although he was able to return to duty following medical treatment.[27]

Sunday, October 20, was another chilly autumn day with a downpour. The rain had become a constant figure with a personality all its own, greeting the men in drips and splashes each day. The men of the 52nd Field Artillery Brigade generally slept next to their guns or in holes dug two feet deep with their pup tents over them. According to one source, "They thought nothing of being soaked from the waist down and to lie down on the wet ground to sleep-and it did not affect their health to do so."[28] Their good health was attributed to the fine conditioning they had received. At dawn, troops began to relieve the west bank of the Meuse, quietly moving on into the night.

On October 21, the 52nd Field Artillery Brigade was relieved by the French 15th Colonial Infantry Division. The brigade was ordered to march to Dieue-sur-Meuse, south of Verdun, to rest in billets. From then through the end of the month, the sun came out as though celebrating with them this break from the fighting. Members of the 52nd had begun marching the previous night, and between the nights of October 20 and 21, the brigade was stretched out from Dieue-sur-Meuse to Bois la Ville. The 104th Field Artillery Regiment was assigned to billet at Bois de Cinq Frères. Both the 105th and 106th were assigned to the Bois la Ville and Fauberg Pave, Verdun. The 102nd Ammunition Train, and the Trench Mortar Brigades were assigned to Fauberg, Verdun. This would be an encampment with no luxuries. While the men of the 52nd were marching, the American forces captured Cunel and broke the Khiemhilde Stellung. The III and V Corps secured the Bois de Forêt and the Bois des Rappes, and pushed to the northwestern edge of the Bois de Bantheville. As the line closed east, the 1st American Army prepared for a final assault on Sedan to the north. Most of those at the front were kept in the dark about things, although newspapers were dropped from time to time by Allied airplanes.

The previous rule for divisional movements had been to only move at night, but on October 22 the rule was enlarged to also include misty or dark weather. That change allowed troops to move from 3:30 p.m. until 9:00 a.m. The 52nd, minus the 105th Regiment at Gercourt which moved the following day, started moving south at midnight on the 21st for the Bois la Ville, the Bois de Nixéville, and the Bois Claude. The 1st Battalion of the 104th Field Artillery Regiment at Tranchée de Heraclée formed an independent column, rejoining the rest of the regiment at Bois Juré until the staging area south of the Verdun-Dombasle Road. On the 22nd, the 33rd Division also moved along the Meuse River headed for an area between Dieue and Tilly during the day and night. They had been assigned to the French II Colonial Corps.

On October 23, the 33rd Division reached their destination and relieved the 79th Division. That marked the end of the 33rd Division's stay adjacent to the Meuse River north of Verdun. The 52nd Field Artillery Brigade of the 27th Division had served the 33rd Division for seven weeks of hard fighting, while its own infantry fought at the western front in Flanders. The 33rd Division had the unhappy distinction of being the most gassed division in World War I with 2,000 of its men suffering from the effects. The 52nd had suffered with them. During the battle between October 8 and 23, the 104th Field Artillery Regiment had 12 wounded, two died of wounds, and two were killed.

As the 33rd parted, Major-General Bell, Jr., penned a letter to the 52nd Field Artillery Brigade which they received a few days later. In it he stated his thanks for their work. "Every request of ours you have met in a uniform, earnest and efficient manner, and your cooperation has contributed in a great measure to our success in the recent operations. Please express to your officers and men my appreciation and sincere regret that the exigencies of the field service necessitate your separation from us at this time."[29]

The men in the artillery regiments intended to use the assigned rest time cleaning men and equipment, but due to the scarcity of horses needed to pull artillery pieces for the 79th Division, the 2nd Army took the 52nd Field Artillery Brigade so recently detached from the 33rd Division, and attached them to the 79th Division. The 33rd Division took the 55th Field Artillery Brigade of the 79th Division with them instead as they moved into the Troyon Sector between Wadonville-en-Woëvre and Fresnes-en-Woëvre. On October 25, while en route to billets for rest, the 52nd Field Artillery Brigade was ordered to immediately return to the line to serve the 79th Division who were preparing for the next phase of the Meuse-Argone Offensive. They were to have no rest.[30] They were to return to the intense shelling.

The enemy still held the commanding heights with its well-placed observation places, maintaining control over the Meuse River and its bridges, along with the protective marshes. By October 23, the 104th Field Artillery Regiment of the 52nd Field Artillery Brigade had lost six men, two outright and four from wounds, and 23 men had been wounded. The 105th Field Artillery had lost two men, one from wounds with 25 men wounded. The 106th had four men killed in action, and another died from his wounds, while 20 men had been wounded. As of October 25 they were attached to the 79th Division. The 79th was composed of guardsmen from Pennsylvania, Maryland and Washington, D.C. The diverse division included 15 nationalities with four religious expressions: Protestant, Roman Catholic, Greek Orthodox and Jewish. Major-General Joseph E. Kuhn was the commander. The artillery would now work with the 157th and 158th Infantry Brigades of that division. The 157th Infantry Brigade included the 313th and 314th Infantry Regiments, while the 158th Infantry Brigade included the 315th and 316th Infantry Regiments.

Between October 25 and October 26, the 79th Division came under the 1st American Army. While influenza raged in France, along side artillery fire and gas, miraculously, the 79th Division had not suffered much from the flu. Even though most of the evacuations were cases of influenza or bronchitis, the figures were relatively low. Nevertheless, the division commanders were strictly instructed to "inspect each man at least once a day."[31] Any illness had to be reported and those afflicted were evacuated. Threats to health also came from the huge rats and millions of fleas and flies. Dead bodies of men and animals were everywhere drawing both rats and flies. Rats also nibbled on the empty ration cans left by the soldiers. In flooded trenches the rats tormented soldiers, growing ever larger. It was crucial for quarters to be kept clean.

The 52nd Brigade, now part of the 79th Division, left Baleycourt and passed through Thiéville to Charney where they crossed the river to Bras. Then they traveled through Gamagneaux to the hill east of town and to the Grande Montagne sector on the east bank of the Meuse River. Between October 27 and 29, the 79th Division relieved the 29th American Division in the sector of Grande Montagne, northeast of Brabant-sur-Meuse. The 52nd Field Artillery Brigade relieved the 158th Field Artillery Brigade of the 29th Division between October 28 and 30. The entire 79th Division then became part of the XVII French Corps. Those French lessons back at Camp Wadsworth had proved very handy to the 52nd Field Artillery Brigade. The headquarters of the 79th and 52nd Field Artillery Brigade was established at Vacherauville, which was little more than a pile of rubble. The new position of the artillery would be on the left, or to the west, of the 79th Division from Baleycourt through Thiéville to Charney, and across the river to Bras and through Gamagneaux to the hill east of the town. The relieved 158th Field Artillery Regiment had only been in that position for a week, but was glad to leave due to the "terrible" heavy shelling. To the members of the 52nd it was just more of the same as they tried to clean their billets, men, and material, and to condition their horses.[32] The 104th Regimental Headquarters and the headquarters for the 1st Battalion, Batteries A and B moved to the Bois de la Ville with the Supply Company at Côte Talou.[33]

The next phase of the battle was again targeted on the high grounds of the Meuse River, specifically Brabant, Samogneux, the Bois d'Haumont, the Bois de Brabant-sur-Meuse, the Bois de Molleville, and the Bois d'Etraye approaching southwest by two roads. The Brabant-Etraye Road rose right away and then dropped a little by Etraye. The Samogneux-Crepion Road, on the other hand, began low and then rose to a higher elevation. The 106th Field Artillery Regiment Batteries C, D, E and F left the Bois de la Ville at 3:30 p.m. on the 27th and moved south of Brabant to relieve the 2nd and 3rd Battalions of the 324th Field Artillery Regiment. On October 28 the ammunition dump of the 106th and 104th Field Artillery Regiments were hit by exploding shells.

On October 29, the 52nd Field Artillery Brigade, on their way to relieve the 322nd Regiment of the 158th Field Artillery Brigade, experienced problems with mud and hilly terrain making it difficult for horses pulling heavy equipment. Moving up Malbrouck Hill, the men often had to push the wheels of the caissons stringing picket lines attached to the guns to help the animals. Whenever the horses needed help, the call "canonneer to the wheel" brought the men running.

Meanwhile, the 102nd Sanitary Department was busy evacuating casualties while under heavy shell fire. Captain Theodore F. Mead of the Medical Corps for the 104th Field Artillery Regiment was mortally wounded and died at Brabant-sur-Meuse while attending to wounded men on October 29. The 79th Division had a dressing station for the 315th Infantry Brigade on the Samogneux-Brabant Road, as well as one for the 314th Infantry Brigade on the road into the Bois de Consenvoye. Men only slightly wounded were aided on the outskirts of Charney.

The 104th Field Artillery Regiment took over the sector bound by the right edge of the Bois d'Ormont and the left edge of the Le Houpy Bois.[34] The thick Ormont Wood, criss-crossed by paths, was infested with machine guns and dug outs. Machine gunners sometimes were located up in trees and other unexpected places. As the enemy moved back, they also often left booby traps behind. Explosives were often attached to things soldiers might pick up as souvenirs such as helmets or rifles. Booby traps were also set in the trenches and single-standing buildings, under ordinary looking planks of wood or food supplies, or on things sticking innocently out of the ground. Taking enemy territory required great care, and detailed divisional warnings listed all the possibilities. The artillery was exposed in this sector, but they nestled under camouflage to stand their ground supporting the 313th and 314th Infantries. Units of the 104th supported a move of the 313th Infantry of the 79th Division to the east through the typical French rural villages of Wavrille and Etraye with their central Roman Catholic church. Both the infantry and artillery were under very heavy shelling as the 313th skirted the difficult woods.

The Allies were getting closer to the defensive line as they pushed forward, forcing the Central powers to fall back. The 52nd Field Artillery Brigade had again sent liaison officers to the brigades, regiments and battalion headquarters of the infantry in order to provide almost immediate response to their needs. There was excellent telephone communication between them. Between October 28 and November 1, the entire 52nd Field Artillery Brigade would perform "sixty-five missions of concentration, area harassing and protective barrages." Throughout their stay in the sector the enemy shelling and gassing was relentless.[35] They remained under direct observation by the enemy in Haramont and the Bois D'Ormont.

October 30 the 52nd Field Artillery Brigade was ordered to take over part of the sector held by the 51st Field Artillery Brigade from Bois de Belleau to the Bois d'Ormont. To accommodate this addition, the 104th Field Artillery Regiment took over the missions of the 105th so the 105th could take on the missions from the 51st. The 106th (howitzer) took the responsibilities of the howitzer regiment of the 51st Field Artillery Brigade. On October 30 and 31, the 106th sent out harassing fire. The entire Allied battle line now extended from Verdun to the North Sea. Within this line, the objective for the 79th Division was the Carignan-Sedan- Mézières Railroad to the north and the heights east of the Meuse with its well placed powerful artillery.[36] The mission remained the same as it was at the beginning: drive the Germans out of northern France and Belgium, thereby ending the war. The Germans still held the hills and the old forts of Verdun, the area east of Samogneux on the Meuse River, and the territory north to la Borne de Cornouiller and beyond. The French Corps had as their objective to remove the enemy from la Borne de Cornouiller (named Hill 378 by the Americans or Corn Willie Hill) which guarded the valley roads leading east to the plains of Woëvre and the German camps at Etraye, Réville and Ecurey. The plains stretch from Toul, France to Luxemburg, Germany. The Germans had masses of troops and stores of material at Etraye, Réville and Ecurey. The hill had a commanding view at a bend of Meuse River that allowed sighting of Meuse Valley, both up and down stream. The Germans had emplacements with long range artillery. Once that hill was taken, Allied infantry could strike across the plain of Woëvre into Germany. This was a difficult assignment to be given to the 79th Infantry, as the hill had a bald top, bare of trees and brush, and they would be continually fired upon. The 158th Infantry Brigade, specifically, was given the task of taking the hill. Then the 157th Infantry Brigade would drive towards the Woëvre plain.

By October 31, the Central powers still had 31 divisions fighting and in reserve at the front, but, the Hindenburg Line had been broken and the Argonne Forest was in the hands of the Allies. 18,600 of their soldiers had been captured. They scattered exposed Allied units in the area near Brabant-sur-Meuse through heavy aerial bombing.[37] The men running for cover included 1,442 men in the 104th Field Artillery Regiment, 1,399 in the 105th, 1,467 in the 106th, and 235 in the Trench Mortar Battalion.

The men did not know it yet, but November marked the closing of the war. Allied soldiers were forbidden to circulate rumors in order to keep moral high and to stay focused. Relaxing at this point might cost them their lives. The Central powers were losing their battle in the Middle East, Balkans and Italy. The Bulgarians had left the war in October. The Turkish surrendered on October 31. Austria-Hungary would surrender November 4, but the Germans continued the battle. Yet there was civil unrest in Germany and the German Army was no longer what it had been. The Allies had taken a number of ports as well. As an encouragement to the Allied soldiers at the front, Field Marshal Haig told ranking officers to explain to those men on the front line "the larger picture of their success." It was a wise move with so many of them dirty, hungry, cold, and wet.[38]

On November 1 General Liggett reorganized the 1st Army for the final push towards Sedan to the northwest and the railroad which supplied German troops all the way to the English Channel. The town of Sedan was meaningful to the French because in 1870 Emperor Napoleon III had surrendered there to the Prussian King Wilhelm I during the Franco-Prussian War. The Prussians then besieged Paris. September 2 was an unofficial celebration day each year in Germany until 1919. It was called Sedantag, or Day of Sedan. The French also had lost the provinces of Alsace and Lorraine during that struggle. The same enemy was holding the city now.[39] Taking Sedan back would be cause for great celebration among the French.

The members of the Allied line were now I Corps on the west, made of the 78th, 77th, and 80th Divisions, in the center V Corps with the 2nd and 89th Divisions, and III Corps to the east with the 90th and 5th Divisions, as well as the French XVII Corps with the American 79th, 26th, and 81st Divisions. From November 1 through the 3, the 52nd Field Artillery Brigade, still under Brigadier General George Albert Wingate, responded to calls from the 79th Division and also supported the III Corps in an advance along the Cunel-Brieulle Road and farther to the west of the Meuse River, and northward from Brieulle to Dun-sur-Meuse. They were attempting to force the Germans from the west bank heights in those areas.[40]

The 104th Field Artillery Regiment in particular supported the 313th and the 314th Infantry Regiments, in the 157th Infantry Brigade of the 79th Division. The 313th Infantry Regiment held a line through the Bois d'Ormont and the Bois de Brabant-sur-Meuse. The Ormont Wood was thick, and each time the Americans had previously tried to take it, they had been driven back by enemy fire. Through the rain in an unprotected location, the 75mm guns of the 104th Field Artillery Regiment supported the attack, which was considered "a most important factor in overcoming the enemy resistance at that point."[41] During the first days of November, the entire sector from Haumont to the southern point of the Bois de Consenvoye was shelled repeatedly. The town of Haumont was completely destroyed; the effect of the shelling caused the soil to completely die, never to support crops again.

Carver, Lindstrom and Foster in their book on the 90th Aero Squadron, written in 1920, mentioned that on November 1, 1918, the mist in this area was so thick that planes were forced to "skim the ground" and the risk in a hilly area was very great. They flew low along the barrage lines, just over the infantry. The planes were often tossed by the concussion caused by the exploding artillery shells.[42]

Major-General O'Ryan's book on the 27th Division mentioned in this area, "The enemy was accustomed to deliver bursts of fire consisting of anywhere from 60 to 120 shots, delivered without warning and with great rapidity against a single locality. These bursts of fire during the first five days of occupation of this position were very frequent, but were in descending scale towards the last."[43] The 104th Field Artillery Regiment was called on to deliver "concentration fire, retaliation fire and harassing fire," often using 4,000 projectiles a day. Their concentrated fire near Crepion was effective in lessening the enemy's return fire. The 105th Field Artillery Regiment performed 65 barrages, and other forms of fire, between October 28 and November 1. The 106th Field Artillery Regiment sent out 1,900 rounds of high explosive shells and 75 rounds of gas on November 1 alone, sending harassing fire the next day as well.[44]

The men supporting the guns faced additional dangers. The ammunition dump of Battery C, 105th Field Artillery Regiment, at Brabant-sur-Meuse was hit by enemy shells. Ammunition exploded, causing a fire. On November 1, Private Robert Fennell of the 104th Headquarters Company was attempting to transport liaison officers to the forward infantry positions when the car he drove was shelled at the Bois d'Ormont and he was killed. On November 3 Privates Lewis Conor and Frank O'Neill of Battery F, 104th, were killed trying to repair phone lines under heavy shelling. Men performed heroic feats and tried to help the wounded. Privates Charles Weaver and Earl Wils of Battery C, 104th Field Artillery entered a gun emplacement under shell fire at Brabant-sur-Meuse on November 3 to carry a wounded man to safety. Corporal Matthew S. Fox of Battery F removed the bodies of two comrades from a gun emplacement hit by an enemy shell, extinguished the burning camouflage, and aroused the remaining gun crew while 200 fuses and rounds of shells exploded at the ammunition dump nearby. Private Joseph Lee was killed at his gun post.[45]

On November 2 and 3 there was intense shelling by the enemy on the front line, especially near Brabant which was also gassed. The 52nd Field Artillery Regiment supported infantry reconnaissance into enemy territory. The 75s sent out preparatory fire and a protecting barrage before an attack being made by the 158th Brigade of the 79th Division. The 158th had received intelligence that the Germans were withdrawing from the Meuse Line south of Dun-sur-Meuse, and they sent reconnaissance patrols to verify if that was the case. The standing and protecting barrage became a rolling barrage to precede the advance, covering 100 meters in six minutes. The howitzers hit sensitive places such as a machine gun nest and enemy battery which took 1,023 rounds to destroy.[46] Meanwhile, platoons of American infantry were shelled and gassed by the Germans, with one platoon caught in a box barrage. Both sides were desperate to win, keeping up the firing as darkness fell.

At 5:30 a.m. on November 3 the 316th Infantry Regiment began moving forward against Hill 378, la Borne de Cornouiller, one of the key enemy strongholds along the Haraumont Ridge. The infantry passed through the woods and held the ground at the foot of the hill. The 105th Field Artillery Regiment supported the 158th Infantry Brigade as they attempted to scale the hill with no cover, the woods on their right filled with machine guns. The 105th fired a standing and then rolling barrage in front of them for two hours. The night of the 3rd, the artillery sent out covering fire in preparation of an attack planned by the 158th Infantry for the following day. Preparatory bombardments were thought to demoralize the opponent and clear out enemy trenches. They did not always have that effect, but they were used extensively during the Great War nonetheless. The artillery bombed the area by the hill in front of the infantry for three hours. The 4th dawned under a heavy fog. The infantry advanced against gas shells and shrapnel, while the Germans shot down the observation balloons of the 9th Balloon Company. One gun of Battery D of the 105th was sent forward to neutralize machine gun and trench mortar activity on the right flank. However, the rain made the roads impassible with mud and the horses could not make it up the heavy grade, so they were forced to return.[47]

The 104th Field Artillery Regiment supported the 157th Infantry of the 79th Division in the direction of the Bois de la Grande Montagne as they moved northeast towards Réville and Etraye, while the 15th Col. French Division attacked on the left. This advance developed into an engagement that ended up using the entire 158th Infantry Brigade and a large part of the 157th Infantry Brigade. Some members of the 104th Field Artillery Regiment came under a vicious assault. The men were quick in their responses to danger, and remained cool and calm. While Battery A at Brabant-sur-Meuse was under attack, a high explosive shell with an instant fuse became wedged into the bore of Private Vincent Thompson's field piece. The wooden rammer staff broke in the bore against the nose of the projectile. Acting quickly, he forced the cartridge case into the breech, closed the block, and fired to clear the bore. While this was a very dangerous procedure, it restored the gun to action.[48] The 106th gave supportive fire at key points during the attack. They sent gas and almost 1,000 rounds on the Villeneuve Ferme, the Sillon-Fontaine Ferme, and assorted spots in that region. Throughout the next few days the infantry undertook repeated attacks on enemy batteries, supported by the artillery.

At 5:00 a.m. on November 5, an attack by the 158th Infantry Brigade was protected by the 52nd Field Artillery Brigade with intermittent harassing fire, followed by a standing and rolling barrage which lasted for three hours and fifteen minutes. Two guns of the 2nd Battalion of the 105th were ordered forward to assist the advanced position of the infantry. The German artillery, however, had felled so many trees and so badly damaged the road, that there was no way to get through and the battalion was called back. After night fall, the Allies sent a terrific barrage on the enemy. The first 15–20 minutes were said to sound like a "hurricane." The Allied artillery noticed a decrease in return fire.[49] The enemy sent over gas using only one or two guns. The American divisions reached the hills overlooking Sedan. The 1st American Army shifted its boundaries to the east to allow room for the French 4th Army to capture Sedan.

At Brabant-sur-Meuse on November 5, Privates, 1st Class, Harvey B. Christian, Max Dietzman and Charles McGinty, with Private Lee Woods, 1st Lieutenant Miles W. Castell and Corporal Kenneth F. Adams of Battery B, 104th Field Artillery Regiment rescued two badly wounded comrades under the shelling. Corporal Wilfred K. Brown of Battery A, was also under heavy shelling with an explosion happening directly in front of his gun position. He quickly re-erected the aiming post to enable the gun to return to action. Corporal Patrick J. McMurrough of Battery F carried messages from the battery to Battery Headquarters throughout the night, despite being wounded three times.[50] Battery F had already lost six men between November 3 and 4. The Germans, now disorganized, threw in their reserve units. The American 79th Division was also in trouble. 1st Battalion of the 315th Infantry was considered "used up" from the heavy action and was moved into reserve as the 2nd Battalion stepped forward. The 316th was in even worse condition. Second Battalion had two batteries suffering heavy loss. First Battalion was almost nonexistent.

On November 6, the Germans still held the high ground at la Borne de Cornouiller and their guns fired back with high explosives and shrapnel; there was also gas in the woods south of Borne du Cornouiller. Some members of the 79th Division were caught by high explosives, shrapnel, and gas. From 6:00 a.m. to 11:40 a.m. the 105th Field Artillery Regiment fired harassing fire and a barrage. At 2:15 p.m. they repeated it, ending at 7:55 p.m. The 106th Field Artillery Regiment sent high explosives and gas, moving its Battery C closer to the front. The night of the 6th through 7th, control of the eastern Meuse passed from the XVII French Corps to the II French Corps. At 7:45 a.m. on the 7th, artillery preparatory fire began, aimed at the road to the northeast from Sivry-sur-Meuse to Réville. The infantry advanced under fog, but was met with machine gun resistance in the woods. However, there was a noticeable absence of heavy enemy retaliatory fire. The enemy was hauling back their guns.[51] The enemy then retired from Borne du Cornouillle.

In the morning of the 7th, one barrage of the 52nd Brigade "fell short" because it seemed to the men that they had stopped the Germans and it no longer seemed necessary. Another artillery barrage rolled ahead until 4:10 p.m. Complaints were made by the infantry that it seemed to be falling on them. The artillery was told to cease fire. Everyone checked their positions. The 104th Field Artillery Regiment, which began with Colonel Merritt H. Smith commanding, and then functioned temporarily under Lieutenant-Colonel John T. Delaney, now passed command to Colonel Charles C. Pulis. The 105th Field Artillery Regiment fired from 6:00 a.m. until 11:40 a.m. and then from noon until 2:15 p.m.

On November 7 the drive was made towards the Woëvre valley. At 7:55 a.m. the 105th Field Artillery Regiment had opened fire in support of the 158th Infantry Brigade, beginning with a standing barrage for 15 minutes, then rolling it forward, ending with a standing barrage lasting from 9:50 a.m. to 10:20 A.M.[52] The infantry reached the Kriemhel Stellung. The entire 79th Division then pivoted to its right, advancing its left to Solférino Ferme (farm) to connect with the 15th Colonial French Division. The 15th Colonial French Division had crossed the Meuse at Vilosnes to the north and taken the Haraumont Ridge east of that to reach the ferme. The 79th Division was able to break through the strong enemy line at both the Giselher Stellung and the formidable Kriembheld Stellung. On the night of the 7th, a secret German armistice delegation crossed the French lines. The kaiser had abdicated and revolution was erupting in Germany. The French and Americans continued the offensive, waiting for word of unconditional surrender. On the field, the war was still very much in force. The French XI Corps took control of troops formerly under the French XVII Corps with General Claudel in command.

On November 8, the 79th Division advanced to the Bois de la Grande Montagne, the Bois d'Etrayes, the Bois de Wavrille, the Belleau Bois, the Bois de Chênes, and the Bois d'Ormont. They captured the towns of Réville, Etraye, Wavrille and Crepion from the Germans. The artillery was used to assist this advance in close support. The 106th Field Artillery Regiment had concentrated largely on Buisson Chaumont, Côte de Romagne, and the Côte de Morimont trenches. As a result of all of these efforts, the enemy was driven from the heights of the Meuse River at last, across the Tinte Brook to Hills 328, 319, Côte de Morimont, Côte du Château and Côte d'Orne. The mission of the offensive had finally been met. The Batteries A, B and C of the 104th Field Artillery Regiment moved forward, firing along the Brabant-Etrayes Road and in the woods along on the enemy front line. At 3:00 p.m. the Germans near Hill 360 put forth tremendous artillery shelling on Allied troops, extending right and left and lasting until 6:00 p.m. There was a gas attack on Haumont-Batiue and the Ravine Rechimore. Then the enemy left the Bois d'Ormont.[53]

The 105th Field Artillery Regiment supported an attack of the 158th Infantry northeast by Etraye-Réville. The 2nd Battalion of the 105th assisted using concentrations and harassing fire. The 1st Battalion moved forward near Hill 378, Corn Willy Hill. The battalion was moved forward again the next night, close to the infantry line east of the Villeneuve Ferme.[54]

The morning of November 9 was quiet until 11 a.m. when one gun fired on the high ground near Ormont Ferme. Batteries A and E of the 104th moved nearer to the Ormont Ferme. The Germans had mined their dugouts in the woods, making it very dangerous. The Germans made a stand on Hill 328, and on the high hills of the Côte d'Orne (Hill 356) and the Côte de Château. Hill 328 was a long hill with machine guns placed at the top. The batteries could not move much closer to the farm due to the enemy artillery fire. The Allied commander wanted their guns to try to take out the observation points near Peine Wood by going around the Molleville Ferme, but there was too much shell fire, coupled with more rain, to allow that movement.

Meanwhile, the 75s of the 104th Field Artillery Regiment hammered away at where they expected the Germans to be, using heavier concentration on selected points.[55] By evening the heavy fire of the brigade was focused on Côte 328, and also on Côte 319. The 104th Field Artillery Regiment kept firing as the larger unit "blasted the hills." According to Major-General O'Ryan's book, "The fire of this regiment played a very big part in making possible the successful attack of the infantry against the entrenched hill just north of the town of Chaumont and on the next day the same thing was true of the attack on Hill 319."[56] Major-General Kuhn had directed the artillery preparatory fire on Côte 319 in person. The 79th Division said that their success was "due almost entirely to the magnificent preliminary artillery fire."[57]

The 106th Field Artillery Regiment continued its fire on the Buisson Chaumont, Côte de Romagne, and the Côte de Morimont (Hill 361). During the night, the 1st Battalion of the 105th Field Artillery Regiment moved farther forward following the infantry advance. The enemy lines were clearly visible. An attack was planned on the Côte de Chateau, and the Côte d'Orne beyond the town of Damvillers.⁵⁸ Damvillers was a large town backed by a forest beyond and the Côte d'Orne.

As a republic was being declared in Germany following Kaiser William II's abdication, the American engineers were busy building bridges. On November 10 under the mist, they worked near Côte 319 where La Thinte Rivière (brook) was shallow with a mud bottom. Since the sound of driving nails would have attracted enemy shelling, the bridge was lashed together with rope and wire. It was not evident here that the close of the war was only a day away. At 5:00 a.m. the American artillery aimed heavy harassing fire on the two hills beyond Damvillers, followed by a standing barrage at 6:00 a.m. The 79th Division attacked. The 157th Infantry Brigade advanced on Hills 328 and 319 supported by the 104th Field Artillery Regiment. These were high hills "rising from the plains east of La Thinte Rivière opposite Danvilliers."⁵⁹ The hills were strategic to the enemy, part of the strongly prepared positions in the Kreimheld Stellung.

The 158th Infantry Brigade attacked the Côte de Morimont, supported by the 105th Field Artillery Regiment. The 106 Field Artillery Regiment supported both the 157th and 158th Infantry units. The artillery focused on the Côte du Château trenches at the southern edge of Hill 319, the Côte d'Orne, and Buisson Chaumont. The 157th was successful in capturing Hills 328 and 319. The 158th was unable to take the dominating position of Côte d'Orne on its flank, so an attack on the Côte d'Orne was ordered for the next day.

Battery D of the 104th Field Artillery Regiment moved near Crepion. The 52nd Field Artillery Brigade Headquarters was also moved forward with the 79th Division to Molleville Ferme. In this position, the French 15th Colonial Infantry Division served on their left and the American 26th Division was on their right. The artillery could clearly see the German front lines, deemed "a very risky distance for artillery."⁶⁰

On November 11, the units were told to end hostilities at 11:00 a.m. as part of the armistice agreement which officially ended the war. Under heavy fog, the 52nd Field Artillery Brigade continued firing on the enemy until exactly 11:00 a.m. Angry at the Germans, they were determined to fight to the last minute. They suffered return fire as well. The exception was the 104th Field Artillery Regiment, who fired their last shot at 10:15 a.m. The 104th had one battalion at Crepion, three at Ormont Ferme, and two near Malbrouck Hill. The 105th Field Artillery Regiment began fire at 8:00 a.m. as planned, in support of the 315th Infantry Brigade, and ended fire at exactly 11:00 a.m. The 106th Field Artillery Regiment fired on the west trenches on the Côte Morimont until 11:00 a.m. When the guns stopped, the entire area changed from the deafening noise of explosions to an eerie "dead silence" all at once, exactly on time. One report mentions that the men found the silence so unsettling that it took two days before they acclimated enough to sleep.[61] Soldiers noticed the gradual return of "nature sounds" in the fields and woods. The war, with all of its blasting of artillery and machine guns, had driven out the birds and other small animals. Once that stopped, they began finding their way back.

After the cease-fire, the rest of the day the gun crews kept the guns ready in case they needed to return to fire. They could not sit and relax until they were sure it was truly finished. Later the crews would be first reduced to half and then relieved. In the afternoon of November 11, French, Russian, Belgian and American prisoners released from the German lines came into the 79th Division sector. They were sent to the rear. Over 5,000 were evacuated.[62] Infantrymen went out on patrols collecting Allied and enemy military material of value.

The night of the 11th was cold, but the 52nd Field Artillery Brigade set off pyrotechnic displays in multi-colors. They were called "hilarious" by the 79th Division Infantry men, in a rather judgmental way. Some of the Germans expressed interest in fraternizing with the Americans, but the Americans were forbidden to do so. The members of the 52nd Field Artillery Brigade were not exactly in the mood to forgive them either. The Germans set off their own pyrotechnic displays: "rockets, very candles, red fire, blue fire, green fire, all the night signaling material from its dumps, were sparkling and sizzling in the air." For most of the night, the Germans were singing "Fatherland."[63] The Americans were too exhausted to sing.

Brigadier-General W.J. Nicholson, commanding general of the 157th Infantry Brigade of the 79th Division, would later write a thank you letter to the members of the 104th and 106th Field Artillery Regiments. In it he mentioned that from the very beginning of their work together, they had "assisted materially in maintaining a high standard of morale." He wrote that both units assigned to infantry "proved themselves to be the best supporting artillery which has been associated with us. Their fire has been the most accurate, their action upon request the most prompt, their means of communication with us the most complete and continuous and their cooperation by moving forward with our infantry, the best that has been our fortune to encounter."[64] Brigadier-General George Albert Wingate would also receive acknowledgment for his battle efficiency and thorough knowledge of field artillery as commander of the 52nd. Commanders of the individual regiments mentioned that "The Artillery fire of the Brigade was very good; the guns proved to be accurate, worked well, and the results of fire were extraordinary."[65]

In the report of the 27th Division for their time as part of the A.E.F., it was noted that the 104th Field Artillery Regiment, using the French 75mm guns, had fired 66,782 shells with a combined weight of 1,001,730 pounds.

The 105th Field Artillery Regiment, using the French 75mm guns, had fired 81,096 shells with a combined weight of 1,216,440 pounds. The 106th Field Artillery Regiment, using the howitzers, had fired 33,036 shells with a combined weight of 3,072,348 pounds. The total number of shells for the three regiments was 180,914 shells at 5,290,518 pounds with a cost of $4,939,720. These figures were for just September 8 to November 11, 1918. The Meuse-Argonne Offensive resulted in 122,000 American casualties with 26,277 dead. 28,000 Germans were dead with an additional 92,250 wounded and 26,000 taken prisoner.[66]

Although the Germans had agreed to the armistice on November 11, the German High Seas Fleet did not officially surrender to the British until November 21. The men of the 52nd Field Artillery Brigade, however, were finished with their shelling and they spent their days salvaging material. While walking through enemy territory, they were often amazed at how accurate their fire had been. In some cases they had merely "estimated" where the enemy "ought to be, and hit him," other times shells missed with one man stating that it was "largely a matter of luck." The patrols attempted the daunting task of "cleaning up" the battlefield. Roads were repaired and new ones built; ammunition was piled high and duds were exploded.[67]

During their time at the front, the 52nd Field Artillery Brigade had suffered loss. The infantry suffered higher numbers since they were the ones making the assaults in enemy territory. The total wounded for the three regiments of the 52nd during their tour of duty were sixty eight wounded with six dying from their wounds, and six killed. Burial details were part of the service rendered to the dead. France became the resting place for many of them.

There were still groups of Germans in the area occupied by the 79th Division who were not yet sure if the war was really over. One group presented themselves to the division. "Their officers had left them two days prior, and the non-commissioned officers the preceding day." But if they were taken at that point by the Americans, they would have been called deserters by their army, so the 79th Division turned them around towards Germany and sent them walking. On November 13 the German army began evacuating the areas they held, and on November 17 the 79th Division sent out patrols to check on the abandoned positions. Local citizens also began to filter back, looking for homes now long gone.[68]

From October 28 to November 11 the 52nd Field Artillery Brigade, with the 102nd Ammunition Train, had been stationed on the armistice line that ran from Fresnes-en-Woëvre to Damvillers, and in the area north and west of Verdun-sur-Meuse. From November 23 to December 12, they were assigned to the 1st Army as Army Artillery, quartered in Verdun-sur-Meuse in "windowless and frequently roofless houses in the suburbs of that city"[69] which

Postcard of Montsûrs in the department of Mayenne, the region of Pays de la Loire, France. This village served as headquarters for the 27th Division after the war (courtesy Andrew B. Rankin, Jr., Collection).

were cold in the snow and ice. Yet they experienced very little influenza. They watched streams of prisoners pass by. Some members of the 79th Division had been given leave to southern France and the Rivera. The men of the 52nd who had suffered through both Texas heat and French rain, now watched sleet and snow falling by their bunks. They shivered by their little tin stoves. Their commander had given them an honest appraisal of what the fighting would be like in France. They had been told it would be brutal, and it was. Their experiences in Texas and South Carolina had helped condition them mentally as well as physically for the hardships of war.

From December 12 to 14, the 52nd Field Artillery Brigade, with the 102nd Ammunition Train, was boarded onto trains to join the rest of the 27th Division. From December 1918 to February 1919, the headquarters of the 52nd Field Artillery was established at the Château Le Haut Meral in Montsûrs, France. Through January, the men of the 52nd bunked in neighboring villages in Laval near Le Mans, sleeping in houses, barns, or tents set up in empty lots.

On December 3 the 27th Division was given seven days leave, plus travel time, with small numbers of men leaving daily for St. Malo, a seaside resort on the northern coast of Brittany. It would be the first leave for the brigade, but they first had to join the division in a thorough delousing process to rid them of parasites, and be issued new uniforms and equipment.[70] Regiments held competitions in cleaning and restoration of equipment. During the month of December replacements arrived, and some of the division was broken up. The veteran soldiers welcomed the new members. With the strenuous field exercises being held under the American II Corps, the men felt that a new operation was coming and that they might be assigned to serve along the Rhine River. With the new replacements, the 52nd Field Artillery Brigade numbered 4,302.

The division emblem, the Orion patch, had been adopted but during the war authorization had not come to wear it. After the armistice authorization finally came, and the patches were shipped to France, but men only got one after passing an exam by an officer. The exam was not only based on fulfilling their specific duties, but also on their character. The veterans decided not to resent new recruits receiving them, and the new recruits worked hard to earn them. The men who received the patch wore it with great pride.[71]

The field exercises in December lasted through January under the American II Corps officers. The 30th Division officers served as umpires for the men of the 27th, while the 27th officers served as umpires for the 30th Division. The exercises included competitions, athletics, marching, demonstration of precision, combat exercises, and the conditioning of both transport and animals. The exercises were strenuous and the men were kept under strict discipline. December 20 to 25 there were exercises in liaison work.

On Christmas Day,

The Cathedral at Montsûrs, France (courtesy Andrew B. Rankin, Jr., Collection).

the companies, battalions and regiments held dinners. There were no turkeys, although some had roast beef. Some of the dinners were held in local hotels. Large Christmas trees were set up in the area towns, which was not the custom in France. They were lit with candles by the soldiers, and the local children were given toys by men dressed as Santa Claus. The American traditions seemed very strange to the French locals. Soldiers swelled the area churches, and a choir composed of soldiers sang a combination of excerpts from the Catholic Mass, Protestant hymns, and Jewish songs. The day after the holiday, the men resumed their training.

An assessment of the artillery's action during the Meuse-Argonne Offensive was published in *The Field Artillery Journal* in 1923. It mentioned repeated comments made by enemy prisoners about the effectiveness of the artillery in taking out their positions and in generally intimidating them. In some cases, their retreat was made "impossible," and in others they were forced to move their locations over and over again, as they watched their positions demolished.[72] The combination of defensive and offensive fire contributed greatly to the victory in the Meuse Argonne.

CHAPTER NINE

Mustering Out (1919)

While the 27th Division was still in France following the armistice, the adjutant general in New York was busy working with the Militia Bureau for the reformation of National Guard units. Plans were also made on how to return the men from France. The units needed to comply with federal government requirements. The New York National Guard wanted to retain the well trained officers and any men who were in good physical conditioning and the desired age, dismissing any who were not physically able to meet the new federal requirements. Near the end of the war, the National Guard had been forced to recruit those under 18 and over 45 for service in state, as the overseas draft took men between those ages. Brigadier-General Charles W. Berry, the adjutant general of New York for the year 1919, found that "at no time was the New York Guard properly armed, uniformed and equipped." This caused him great concern and in January of 1919 he sought to reorganize the division with arms, uniforms and equipment.[1]

While the guard was going through inner changes during the month of January, the Paris Peace Settlement was being held. Representatives of four governments collected: President Wilson of the United States; Prime Minister David Lloyd George (1863–1945) of Great Britain; Premier George Clémenceau (1841–1929) of France; and Premier Vittorio Orlando (1860–1952) of Italy. Additional treaties were signed between the Allies and individual Central power countries: the Treaty of Versailles with Germany; the Treaty of St. Germain with Austria; the Treaty of Neuilly with Bulgaria; the Treaty of Trianon with Hungary; and the Treaty of Sèvres with the Ottoman Empire (later known as Turkey). President Wilson had drawn up 14 points to negotiate an end to the war, previously unknown to the Allies. These included free trade, disarmament, and an association of nations which would resolve differences between countries peaceably. The signed treaties redrew European boundaries and new nations were established. The treaties of St. Germain and Trianon dissolved the Austria-Hungary Empire, forming separate nations, each less that ⅓ of their former territory. Some of the former empire territories went to Italy, Romania and the new countries of Czechoslovakia, Poland and what would become Yugoslavia. Mesopotamia (Iraq), Palestine and Syria were taken from the Ottomans. Bulgaria lost territory to Greece and Romania. Germany gave up Belgium, Czechoslovakia, Denmark, France and Poland as well as colonies it controlled overseas. The German coal fields were given to France for 15 years, to make up for what had been stolen. Germany not only lost territory, but had to pay the Allied military occupying the west bank of the Rhine River for 15 years. The size of the German military was limited, and in 1921 a bill was delivered for reparations to be paid to the Allies in the amount of $33 million. The ill-will fostered by these actions would grow in Germany and later contribute to the outbreak of yet another war, World War II. Wilson's League of Nations, a forerunner of the United Nations, was established but the United States Congress refused to let America become a member. Forty-two countries initially joined with a total of 57 eventually in its membership. The league sought to handle disputes between countries, but it was later ineffective during World War II and dissolved in 1946. France was decimated at the end of World War I with one quarter of her young men between the ages of 18 and 30 dead, and one quarter of them maimed. The northern industrial zone was in ruins, and thousands of square miles were pitted by the intense shelling done by both sides. The soil was so damaged that things simply would not grow for a considerable amount of time.[2]

The American Army in France did not have enough ships to bring the soldiers home all at one time. The 102nd Trench Mortar Battalion of the 27th Division set sail from Brest on January 8. They had not been greatly used during the war due to the limit of their range and the placement of the 52nd Field Artillery Brigade in the Verdun area. The rest of the brigade had to wait their turn, the army kept them training, although the long hikes were difficult for the men in their weakened condition. On January 22, the 27th Division underwent a formal review by Generals Pershing, Read, and O'Ryan at the Belgian Camp in Bonnétable, Sarthe, France. Practice reviews were held. Many of the men had to march eight miles to the review field. The day of the review was cold and rainy. The artillery paraded without guns or horses, since those were to be left behind in France.

William F. Clarke of the 104th Machine Gun Regiment told a humorous story about the review in his book titled *Over There with O'Ryan's Roughnecks*.[3] Twenty-five thousand men stood at attention as Pershing paused to speak to individuals with wounds, or those wearing stripes or decorations. The review lasted a very long time with no "at ease" call. Clark's group was the last to be reviewed, and they saw the generals form a tight circle around Pershing, facing outwards. It seems that in the damp weather, "nature called" and there was no place for the general to find relief. The entire division, standing at attention with faces to the front for an extended period of time, did not see the reason for the delay. Clark commented that those witnessing the event, as the bands played Sousa marches, wondered "if the 27th Division was the only division in the A.E.F. to stand at attention while its Commander-in-Chief performed an act of nature." At last, the generals returned to the front of the gathering and the final "at ease" was given.[4]

Humor aside, Major-General John O'Ryan stated in his book that his men performed acts of valor in battle "so numerous, that within the division they came to be regarded almost as common place."[5] In his report, the nearly 2,500 divisional citations given to members of the 27th Division go on for pages in very small print. The citations pertaining to the 104th Field Artillery Regiment, as well as those for the entire 52nd Field Artillery Brigade, almost always have the repeated phrase "while under heavy enemy shell fire" with many adding "under machine gun fire" and "gas concentrations." O'Ryan's respect for the work done by his men during their brutal stay in the European arena was evident. His men seemed to mirror the same respect back to him. In February, the British government gave men medals at the Belgian Camp. Men also received medals from the French government, Belgian government, and the A.E.F. Their contribution is still a focus of study in modern research on World War I.

Back in New York, service medals were designed to recognize service at the Mexican border. They were given to officers and men who spent more than ten days under the order of the governor of New York from June 18, 1916, until April 5, 1917. Fifty designs had been submitted to the adjutant-general of New York State. The one chosen was by the Bailey, Banks and Biddle Company of Philadelphia. The front of the medal had the Aztec god of war, Huitzilopochtli, and the back had the coat of arms of New York State with the words "Mexican Border Service, 1916–1917. Presented by the State of New York." The ribbon had stripes of red, blue, yellow, green, yellow, blue and red. Twenty-five thousand soldiers were presented with the medal.

A service medal was also designed to commemorate service in the Great War. The design, chosen from 100 submissions, was by Captain Charles J. Dieges of the 27th Division, who was from the firm of Dieges and Clust in New York City. The front of the medal had a figure of an American soldier with the words "World War" against a background that included a figure representing liberty and humanity draped in an American flag with battleships, destroyers and transports seen at a distance representing the navy. On the reverse side was the official seal of the state of New York with a wreath of laurel and oak. On the wreath were the names of countries in which the soldiers had fought with the inscription "For service, 1917–1919." The ribbon had the colors blue, white, blue, white, and blue. It was given to 500,000 New Yorkers.[6]

Mustering Out 173

Before leaving France, all soldiers were required to go through the camp at Brest for delousing before departing for the United States. The 27th Divisional Commander was concerned as his men had already gone through an intricate delousing process, and he feared re-infection at Brest. After repeated urgent requests, medical officers from the embarkation point came to the division to do an exhausting examination of the men, with every part of the soldier checked. The men of the 27th were given a clean bill of health to leave.[7] Most of the 27th Division was sent home between February 17 and 26, although the majority of the field artillery regiments did not leave until later.

The men remaining continued with hikes, inspections, gas mask drills, and the cleaning of their billets. Private, 1st Class Dudley Hess, regimental artist, dedicated an illustrated history of the 52nd Field Artillery Brigade to the commander, Brigadier-General George Albert Wingate. Hess attributed their success in that difficult area to Wingate's "keen judgment, high efficiency, and thoro[gh] Generalship," enabling the brigade to achieve their mission with minimum loss.[8] A few regiments of the 52nd Field Artillery Brigade left

The U.S.S. *America* transported members of the 104th Field Artillery Regiment from Brest, France, on March 6, 1919, to the army piers at Hoboken, New Jersey, on March 13, 1919 (courtesy National Archives, photograph no.111-SC-41614-A, taken by Sergeant G.H. Lyon, Signal Corps on 3/13/1919).

Brest, France, on February 24. There was a large wharf with shelters and gang planks onto ships at Brest. The remainder sailed from Brest on March 6, arriving in New York on March 13. There were storms at sea on their return trip and the ocean was choppy with intermittent rain.

The 104th Field Artillery Regiment sailed with the group leaving Brest March 6 on the United States Navy steamship U.S.S. *America*. The ship had been built in 1905 as a passenger ship, christened the *S.S. Amerika,* by the Harland and Wolff Company in Belfast, Northern Ireland, for the Hamburg-American Line based in Germany. At the beginning of the war, the ship had docked in Boston, but in April of 1917, when the United States entered the war, the ship was seized. The crew made an attempt to sabotage the ship, but it was repaired and put into service by the United States Navy to transport about 40,000 troops to France via nine transatlantic trips. The U.S.S. *America* mostly traveled between Hoboken, New Jersey, and Brest, France. It had two

Members of the 52nd Field Artillery Brigade in the 27th Division, including the 104th Field Artillery Regiment, enthusiastically wave to a ferryboat on the Hudson River on their return home after World War I. The U.S.S. *America* carried 2,508 passengers and 577 crew members. The 104th Field Artillery Regiment filled more than half the ship with their numbers (courtesy National Archives, photograph no.111-SC-41616-A, taken by Sergeant G.H. Lyon, Signal Corps on 3/13/1919).

smoke stacks and triangular camouflage patterns painted on its hull. The ship's displacement was about 41,500 tons. It was 687 feet in length and the beam was 75 feet and 5 inches. It could travel at 17.5 knots and carried 2,508 passengers with a crew of 577. The navy armed the ship with machine guns and depth charges. The ship suffered an accidental sinking at the Hoboken pier and an outbreak of severe influenza killing fifty of the men aboard in the fall of 1918, yet it was still able to make cross–Atlantic trips at the end of the war to bring 47,000 troops home from France. Upon their return, the 104th Field Artillery Regiment experienced a grand reception in the Hudson River harbor with area boats sounding horns. At the docks, people cheered, and it was called very moving by the men. The men were sent to the quarantine station for yet more searches for lice.

On March 25, 1919, the 27th Division collected in New York City for a final five mile victory parade. The weather was warm and clear. They formed in rows eighteen across. The parade began by passing under the Victory Arch at Madison Square where Fifth Avenue and Broadway intersect at 23rd Street

Members of the 104th Field Artillery Regiment disembarking onto the pier at Hoboken, New Jersey, from the U.S.S. *America* on March 13, 1919 (courtesy National Archives, photograph no.111-SC-41613-A, taken by Sergeant G.H. Lyon, Signal Corps on 3/13/1919).

in Manhattan with Major-General John O'Ryan and his staff mounted and the men marching. The arch had been specially built for the occasion, and was covered with sculptured weapons and the names of the battles in which the division had participated. The soldiers marched north to 110th Street at the northern edge of Central Park. This direction was the reverse of the direction they had marched at the beginning of the war. The New York Public Library at 5th Avenue by 42nd Street had an "Altar of Liberty" placed in front of it with long battle pikes sticking into the air and shields behind it with the 27th Division's new logo.[9] Arms were symbolically laid down on the altar as a sign of the end of the struggle.

A memorial caisson with flowers and wreaths was pulled by eight black horses in honor of the men who had lost their lives. About seventeen picked men followed carrying poles and ropes attached to a huge flag with 1,900 gold stars representing those who were killed in action or died of their wounds. The wounded were carried in automobiles in two columns which covered two miles. Thousands and thousands of people watched and cheered as the remaining men marched in their regiments following their commander who was on horseback. It was said to have been the largest gathering of people in America up to that time. Major-General O'Ryan and his staff turned at the plaza by 110th Street and reviewed the men as they passed. At the end of the parade the men disbanded, slipping into side streets to proceed to luncheons being held all over the city to accommodate the 25,000 men. The officers ate at the Waldorf-Astoria at 301 Park Avenue.

Some members of the division returned to their armories for a day or two and some marched to the Atlantic Avenue station of the Long Island Railroad, headed north to Camp Upton in upstate New York. The rest of the division joined them there. No leave was granted, which was frustrating for men who had loved ones longing to spend time with them. The period at Camp Upton also became an annoyance for what some felt were meaningless drills. For the artillerymen, drilling with empty cartridges after blasting real enemy locations in real offensives seemed pointless. In addition, marching and hiking after routinely starving in the trenches with little or no sleep felt disrespectful. The soldiers were given opportunities to take classes in a wide variety of subjects which were deemed beneficial, but, most of them just wanted to go home. On March 28 the camp was hit by a snow storm bringing their tour of duty to a cold, wet close.

On April 1, 1919, the 27th Division was demobilized and left federal service, while returning to the New York National Guard. The day before, Major-General O'Ryan had been discharged from the 27th Division and returned to the guard. He would be relieved from active duty on May 16, 1923, and join the guard reserves. O'Ryan would go on to later found the American

Legion, serve as New York State transit commissioner, become a partner of Pan American Airways, and eventually be president of Colonial Airlines. In 1934, he would run as a candidate for New York City mayor but withdraw to support LaGuardia, and then serve as police commissioner. During World War II he would be the civil defense director of New York City, and later the national commander of the Military Order of Foreign Wars.

Under the New York National Guard, the 104th Field Artillery Regiment became the 1st Field Artillery Regiment once more. Those units which had served as depot batteries, temporarily covering New York State while the other units were overseas, were disbanded. There was a general reshuffling of men as some were honorably discharged and some retained. Healthy, young men were generally kept, along with those who had combat experience, and those who were older or lacked skills were dropped. The size of the regiments was reduced, and by December of 1919 the 1st Field Artillery Regiment numbered 664 men. The regiment commander was Colonel John Thomas Delaney with Lieutenant-Colonel James Edward Austin, and Majors Charles Gray Blakeslee and Fred A. Petersen. Battery A was commanded by Captain Oscar J. Brown with 1st Lieutenants William J. Night and Stuart E. Hosler, and 2nd Lieutenants Frank J. Ferry and Donald P. Gorman. Battery B was commanded by Captain William C. Stone with 1st Lieutenants George O. Thorp, Effingham Nicoll Lawrence and William H. Merrick. Battery C was commanded by Captain Francis Johnston Hopson and Charles J. Mangan with 1st Lieutenants Howard E. Taylor and William H. Spring, and 2nd Lieutenant Harry J. Keegan. Battery D was commanded by Captain Walter E. Hegeman with 1st Lieutenant Arthur Vinton Lyall, and 2nd Lieutenants John J. O'Reilly and Francis W. Sutherland. Battery E was commanded by Captains Robert Law Russell and Arthur Crawford Stoney with 1st Lieutenants Richard S. Vreeland and Ralph R. Finney, and 2nd Lieutenants Willard C. Striffler and Ranson Hughes. Battery F was commanded by Captain Arthur W. Hofmann with 1st Lieutenant Robert F. Smith and Leon J. Weil. The battery adjutants were Captains Francis P. Gallagher and Arthur Edward Kaeppel. Supply Company was commanded by Captain George E. Wolfe with 1st Lieutenant Bernard S. Charlin. The band leader was 2nd Lieutenant Joseph Frankel.[10]

Beginning on October 9, 1919, the New York National Guard, was assigned to inspection and inventory of property. When in federal service, all federal property in individual states transferred to the United States government. Once out of federal service, the items needed to be transferred back. The property was in a chaotic condition since the mobilization in 1916 first for Mexico and then 1917 for France had happened rapidly one after the other. Most of the officers who would have kept the inventory under normal circumstances had been in federal service. It took several months to accomplish the catalog of equipment. The National Guard requested war service records for its men from the Regular Army. Initially the request was refused, stating the time it would take to compile that information, and the labor required. Finally, Congress appropriated funds in the amount of $3,500,000, for a report to be furnished to the adjutant-generals of several states.[11]

The men who had served along the Mexican border were interested to learn that on April 10, 1919, Mexican President Venustiano Carranza had Emiliano Zapata assassinated in Mexico. Carranza would be assassinated one year later after fleeing Mexico City during a revolt led by General Álvaro Obregón. Pancho Villa negotiated a peace with the interim president Adolfo de la Huerta and agreed to retire to the Hacienda Canutillo in Durango. Obregón then became president, and July 8, 1920, Pancho Villa finally surrendered to the Mexican government. Three years later, on July 20, 1923, Pancho Villa was assassinated in Parral, Mexico. The American Army disbanded troops stationed along the Mexican border, which finally brought the tensions between the two countries to a close.[12]

On December 10, 1920, Wilson, the former president of the United States, won the Nobel Peace Prize for his part in helping the Allies during the "war to end all wars," which did not, unfortunately, end all wars. In America, the country seemed to breathe a sigh of relief as the 1920s roared in with their "good times." The assembly line was perfected. There were improving working conditions for workers, and consumerism was launched with households seeking to own refrigerators, toasters, radios, telephones, washing machines, vacuum cleaners, phonographs, supermarket foods, retail clothing and cosmetics. Cars were more available and the public flocked to watch silent films. Women won the vote through the passing of the 19th Amendment. Some women even opted to become flappers and led more liberated lifestyles.

Meanwhile, the Graves Registration Service of the New York National Guard continued to use piers 2–4 in Hoboken, the United States Army Piers, for the process of returning the bodies of deceased New York servicemen from France. Each soldier had a card in the adjutant-general's office with the following: soldier's name, his serial number, the Graves Registration Cemetery Code number, rank, and organization, full name of next of kin, address of same, the name and date of the transport returning the soldier to the United States, the name and address of the person authorized by the next of kin to receive the remains of the late soldier, and the date the body was shipped to that person from Hoboken, New Jersey. For those wishing to leave their deceased loved one in Europe, the card held the date and cause of death with the name and location of the cemetery. Ceremonies were held at the pier by chaplains from various traditions and loved ones grieved their loss. On November 15, 1921, the piers were then turned over to the United States Shipping

Board and the Graves Registration Service was moved to an army base in Brooklyn to continue their work.[13]

In the spring of 1921, the 27th Division had receptions and a dance at the Waldorf-Astoria. It would become an annual event. The men had experienced something that changed them forever. The stated function of the yearly event was to help the men of different companies doing different service "become better acquainted, and to renew friendships made during the summer field training."[14] The division also began a magazine in April 1924, which ran until August 1940, called the *New York National Guardsman*. It cost fifteen cents per copy. The initial editor was, once again, Lieutenant-Colonel Fred M. Waterbury. It contained news about those in service, but also about those who were veterans of the Great War. There were photographs from the war scattered throughout each issue.

A large reunion was planned for September 26 to 27, 1924, in Troy, New York, to commemorate the anniversary of the division's attack on the Hindenburg Line. Those who lost their lives or were wounded were remembered. That particular gathering featured the following speakers: Secretary of War John W. Wecks, General J.J. Pershing, Governor Alfred E. Smith, United States Senator J. W. Wadsworth, Jr., and the honorary president of the veteran's group Major-General O'Ryan. Pershing would be called a "true friend of the National Guard."[15] The veteran's group officers included President General George Albert Wingate, 1st Vice President General Franklin W. Ward, 2nd Vice President Brigadier-General Edgar S. Jennings, 3rd Vice President Colonel William J. Donovan, Secretary Lieutenant-Colonel J.A.S. Mundy, and Assistant Secretary Capt. James A. Walsh.[16] These gatherings were considered healing for the men, and held respectfully by those who had served through such a difficult period. Some American servicemen still stood guard along the Rhine River until January of 1923. For them, it had been a long and tiresome tour of duty.

The 1st Field Artillery Regiment veterans would meet yearly for a dinner dance.[17] They would read in the *New York National Guardsman* how their comrades continued to train at Tobyhanna, Pennsylvania, and at the State Camp of Instruction in Peekskill, New York. Later the regiment would also use Montauk Point, New York. In 1923, the armory on Broadway in New York City, bound by Broadway, Columbus Avenue, 67th and 68th Streets, would be deemed unsatisfactory. It had been built to house 10–12 units and regiments now called for 19 units plus a regimental headquarters. The land was very valuable, and the plan was to sell it, which was accomplished in 1929. Austrian immigrant Max Verschleiser won the bid of $3,375,000 for the property in January of that year. The regiment then moved to a $1,000,000 property in Jamaica, Queens. Verschleiser had come to America in 1886 and owned a number of hotels and amusement centers.[18] The division assessed properties whose leases were coming to an end, and made plans to develop its armories and the 2,000 acre State Camp at Peekskill. The 1st Field Artillery Regiment move was part of that overall plan.[19] In the early 1920s, the soon to be famous baseball player George Herman "Babe" Ruth joined the regiment.

During World War II, the regiment would be reorganized for federal service on October 15, 1940, as the 249th Field Artillery Battalion of the 27th Division. They served in the Pacific 2nd Battalion and became the 104th Field Artillery Battalion of the 27th Division on September 1, 1942, serving in the Pacific until December 31, 1945. July 24, 1947, they were reactivated as the 104th Field Artillery Battalion in the 42nd Division of the New York National Guard, and on March 16, 1959, they were reorganized as the 104th Field Artillery Regiment. In the early 1990s, the regiment was still based in Jamaica, Queens, New York, and named the 2nd Battalion, 104th Regiment, New York National Guard.[20] Today 104th DECON Battalion still maintains the long tradition of service of the regiment under capable leadership and dedicated personnel.

Between the years of 1916 and 1919, the 104th Field Artillery Regiment made transitions reflective of those being made in the United States Army. Military technology and battle preparedness were moving towards modern warfare. Prior to this period, the National Guard had largely been used to suppress riots in-state and only served for a number of months at a time outside of state. With the involvement in both border patrol in Texas and World War I, the regiment became part of the American Army. Beginning with the three-inch field pieces in Texas, the regiment later used the larger French 75mm field pieces. Barrage techniques improved due to the reliability of the pieces which needed no adjustment after fire. The men used new strategies and acquired great skill. Much of their success in their missions was due to the careful training designed by their commander, Major-General John Francis O'Ryan and the capable officers serving the regiment. The 104th Field Artillery Regiment endured Spartan-like training and suffered through terrible conditions in both in the United States and in France, yet they completed each mission with little complaint. The sacrifices they made during their term of service should be remembered as the nation enters the centennial of the Great War.

Appendix I: Deaths

Deaths, 6th Division, N.Y.N.G., Mexican Punitive Expedition (July 19, 1916–November 25, 1916)

More than 20 men from the New York National Guard's 6th Division died in Texas while serving on border duty during the Mexican Punitive Expedition. They did not die in combat. Three drowned in an irrigation canal, two died from gunshot wounds, one died from pneumonia, 5 died from the typhoid/paratyphoid "A" epidemic, three died of tuberculosis, one died of meningitis, two died of dysentery, two died of gastroenterocolitis/intestinal obstruction, two died from interstitial nephritis, one from endocarditis, and one was kicked by a horse. An additional man from the 1st Field Artillery Regiment was accidently killed on route from Camp Whitman to McAllen, Texas, and a few men had died at their home stations prior to border duty. Illness was the largest cause death.[1]

Deaths, 104th Field Artillery Regiment, 27th Division, N.Y.N.G., A.E.F. (World War I, September–November 1918)

During World War I the regiment lost the following men:

Battery A

Private Schuyler R. Smith	October 19	Was in an exposed observation post without protection when mortally wounded by an enemy shell.

Battery E

Sergeant Peter F. Kelly	September 29	Voluntarily cleaned out a recently evacuated and mined dugout in the Bois de Forges. He was seriously wounded by an explosion and later died.

| Private William Sieven | October 19 | Delivered ammunition to the battery under shelling and gas by the enemy. He was wounded and died by Consenvoye. |

Battery F

Battery F lost six men between November 3 and 4. The end of the war was just a week away. They were very close to the German last stronghold, under constant heavy shell fire at Brabant-sur-Meuse. November 3 the ammunition dump of the battery was set on fire by enemy shells. A number of men also were killed at their gun posts.

Private John Brandino	November 4	Killed in the Brabant-sur-Meuse area
Private, 1st Class, Lewis S. Connor	November 3	Killed repairing phone lines at - Brabant-sur-Meuse area.
Private Thomas Delaney	November 4	Killed in the Brabant-sur-Meuse area
Private John J. Finan, Jr.	November 4	Killed at post under heavy fire at Brabant-sur-Meuse area
Private Joseph P. Lee	November 4	Killed by enemy shell at his gun post under heavy fire at Brabant-sur-Meuse area.
Private Thomas J. Tracy	November 4	Killed in the Brabant-sur-Meuse area

Headquarters Company of the 104th Field Artillery

| Private Robert Fennell | November 1 | Drove a car over roads being shelled in an attempt to deliver liaison officers to a forward position held by the 79th Infantry by the Bois d'Ormont. He did this work until killed. |
| Private Martin Schneider | October 19 | Killed at his forward observation post at night by heavy shelling. He had improvised protection, but was killed at Dannevoux. |

Medical Officers and Staff of the 104th Field Artillery

| Captain Theodore F. Mead, M.C | October 29 | Killed at Brabant-sur-Meuse while attending to the wounded under heavy shell fire. |

Appendix II: Awards and Citations, World War I1

Regimental Honors for Service at Lorraine, 1918, and the Meuse-Argonne Offensive

Distinguished Service Cross

GEORGE A. DUPREE, Corporal, Battery B, 104th Field Artillery. For extraordinary heroism in action near Montzéville, France, September 14, 1918. When a continuous bombardment had set fire to the camouflage covering of a large ammunition dump of 75-millimeter shells and exploded nine of the shells, he, utterly disregarding his personal safety, left a sheltered position and ran to the dump and, with the aid of three other men, extinguished the fire, not only saving the ammunition, but also preventing the exact location of the dump by the enemy.

MATTHEW S. FOX, Corporal, Battery F, 104th Field Artillery. For extraordinary heroism in action near Consenvoye, France, November 4, 1918. While the battery position was being subjected to severe bombardment of gas and high-explosive shells, Corporal Fox, in an effort to rescue two wounded comrades, extinguished a pile of burning camouflage, which was used as a cover for the ammunition and fuses. While fighting the burning camouflage the ammunition was exploded by another bursting shell.

HERBERT M. BRINK, mechanic, Battery B, 104th Field Artillery. For extraordinary heroism in action near Montzéville, France, September 14, 1918. When a continuous bombardment had set fire to the camouflage covering of a large ammunition dump of 75-millimeter shells and exploded nine of the shells, he, utterly disregarding his personal safety, left a sheltered position and ran to the dump and, with the aid of three other men, extinguished the fire, not only saving the ammunition, but also preventing the exact location of the dump by the enemy.

WILLIAM J. NETTE, private, first class, Battery B, 104th Field Artillery. For extraordinary heroism in action near Montzéville, France, September 14, 1918. When a continuous bombardment had set fire to the camouflage covering of a large ammunition dump of 75-millimeter shells and exploded nine of the shells, he, utterly disregarding his personal safety, left a sheltered position and ran to the dump and, with the aid of three other men, extinguished the fire, not only saving the ammunition, but also preventing the exact location of the dump by the enemy.

RALPH B. SULLIVAN, private, Battery B, 104th Field Artillery. For extraordinary heroism in action near Montzéville, France, September 14, 1918. When a continuous bombardment had set fire to the camouflage covering of a large ammunition dump of 75-millimeter shells and exploded nine of the shells, he, utterly disregarding his personal safety, left a sheltered position and ran to the dump and, with the aid of three other men, extinguished the fire, not only saving the ammunition, but also preventing the exact location of the dump by the enemy.

Divisional Citations

COLONEL JOHN T. DELANEY, 104th Field Artillery. 1. For his exceptional military attainments displayed while in command of his regiment during its operations in support of the attack on the Ormont Wood, France, November 4–7, 1918, which were a most important factor in overcoming enemy resistance at that point. 2. For conspicuous gallantry in action during operations of the 52d Field Artillery Brigade, in the vicinity of Brabant-sur-Meuse, France, November 4 to 8, 1918. This officer voluntarily maintained his P.C. [post command] in an advanced position, under heavy and constant fire of high explosives and gas shells under direct enemy observation.

COLONEL MERRITT H. SMITH, 104th Field Artillery. For exceptional devotion to duty during the operations of the 52d Field Artillery Brigade in the vicinity of La Claire Farm[2] and Bois de Forges, France, September 9 to October 18, 1918, before and during the Meuse-Argonne offensive. This officer rendered conspicuous services and, although seriously ill, continued in the performance of his duties until completely prostrated.

MAJOR GEORGE W. AUGUSTIN, M.C., 104th Field Artillery. For exceptionally meritorious service during operations in the vicinity of Bois de Forges, Brabant-sur-Meuse and Crepion, France, September 25 to November 11, 1918, in his efficient care of the wounded and supervision of their evacuation from the front.

MAJOR JAMES E. AUSTIN, 104th Field Artillery. For conspicuous gallantry in action during the operations of the 104th Field Artillery in the vicinity of Consenvoye, France, October 11, 1918, when he boldly crossed the Meuse River under heavy enemy shell fire, reconnoitered a position and later brought his battalion over the river and rendered effective shell fire, in support of the infantry, his battalion being the first American artillery to cross the Meuse north of Verdun.

CAPTAIN CHARLES G. BLAKESLEE, 104th Field Artillery. For skillful and determined handling of his battery during the operations of the 104th Field Artillery in the vicinity of Le Claire, France, September 9 to 26, 1918, until severely wounded by a machine gun bullet.

CAPTAIN FRANCIS P. GALLAGHER, 104th Field Artillery. For conspicuous gallantry in action in the vicinity of Drillancourt, France, October 1918, when under heavy enemy shell fire and direct observation he repaired and placed in action against the enemy a captured German battery of 77 mm guns and fired them effectively against enemy positions.

CAPTAIN GEORGE B. GIBBONS, 104th Field Artillery. For exceptionally meritorious and efficient services as a battery commander during active operations of his regiment in France, and for the high standard of discipline and professional skill attained by the field battery, constituted of student officers under his instruction and command during the period of the Third Officers' Training Camp at Camp Wadsworth, S.C.

CAPTAIN WALTER E. HEGEMAN, 104th Field Artillery. For exceptional devotion to duty and conspicuous gallantry in action in the vicinity of Consenvoye and Brabant-sur-Meuse, France, during October 1918, when, with untiring effort, he personally supervised the delivery of rations to the firing batteries under heavy enemy shell fire over almost impassable roads.

CAPTAIN ARTHUR W. HOFMANN, 104th Field Artillery. For conspicuous gallantry in action in the vicinity of Consenvoye, France, when after being wounded and rendered unconscious by a shell explosion, he, after medical treatment, refused to be evacuated but remained on duty adjusting the fire of his battery. This October 19, 1918.

CAPTAIN HAROLD LAWSON, 104th Field Artillery. For conspicuous gallantry in action in the vicinity of Bois d'Ormont, France, November 9, 1918, in completing a reconnaissance of enemy positions, although knocked down and badly bruised from the explosion of a mined dugout.

CAPTAIN WALTER C. McCLURE, 104th Field Artillery. For exceptional devotion to duty and skillful reconnaissance and occupation of positions under heavy enemy shell fire during operations in the vicinity of Dannevoux and Brabant-sur-Meuse, France, during October 1918.

CAPTAIN THODORE F. MEAD, M.C. 104th Field Artillery (Deceased). For conspicuous gallantry in action in the vicinity of Brabant-sur-Meuse, France, October 29, 1918, in attending wounded under heavy enemy shell fire until himself mortally wounded.

CAPTAIN FRED A. PETERSON, 104th Field Artillery. For exceptional devotion to duty during operations in the vicinity of the Bois Burrus, Bois de Forges and Brabant-sur-Meuse, France, during September and October 1918, as Regimental Operation Officer, in which he displayed marked ability and efficiency.

CAPTAIN ROBERT L. RUSSELL, 104th Field Artillery. For exceptional devotion to duty during operations in the vicinity of the Bois D'Ormont, France, November 9, 1918, when, although having been knocked down by the explosion of a mined German dugout he successfully completed the reconnaissance of enemy positions.

CAPTAIN SYLVESTER SIMPSON, 104th Field Artillery. For exceptional devotion to duty and efficient handling of a battalion during operations in the vicinity of Brabant-sur-Meuse, France, and for skillful reconnaissance of battalion position. This during October 1918.

CAPTAIN CHANNING R. TOY, 104th Field Artillery. For exceptional devotion to duty during operations in the vicinity of the Bois Burrus, Bois de Forges, and Brabant-sur-Meuse, France, during September and October 1918, as Regimental Intelligence Officer, in which he displayed marked efficiency.

FIRST LIEUTENANT ARTHUR ATCHESON, 104th Field Artillery. For exceptional devotion to duty during operations in the vicinity of Dannevaux and Brabant-sur-Meuse, France, October 1918, in aptly commanding his battery in action in the absence of his battery commander, displaying meritorious conduct under fire.

FIRST LIEUTENANT MILES W. CASTEEL, 104th Field Artillery. For gallantry in action during operations in the vicinity of Brabant-sur-Meuse, France, November 5, 1918, in rescuing two badly wounded comrades under heavy enemy shell fire.

FIRST LIEUTENANT ARCHIBALD B. CLARK, 104th Field Artillery. For gallantry in action and exceptionally meritorious service in the vicinity of Malbrouck Hill, France, October 31 to November 11, 1918, in establishing and maintaining telephone communication between Regimental Headquarters and a forward observation post under heavy enemy shell fire.

FIRST LIEUTENANT ARTHUR E. KAEPPEL, 104th Field Artillery. For exceptional devotion to duty during operations in the vicinity of Bois de Forges and Consenvoye, France, during October 1918, when his battery commander having been wounded, he ably commanded his battery in action, frequently with no other officer to assist him.

FIRST LIEUTENANT GEORGE W. MARTIN, 104th Field Artillery. For gallantry in action in the vicinity of Brabant-sur-Meuse, France, October 29, 1918, in supervising the placing of his battery in position under heavy enemy shell fire and gas concentrations.

FIRST LIEUTENANT ROBERT F. SMITH, 104th Field Artillery. For exceptional devotion to duty during operations in the vicinity of Vacherauville, France, November 1, 1918, in proceeding to the forward position of his battery from the echelon through heavy enemy shell fire.

FIRST LIEUTENANT H. F. THOMAS, 104th Field Artillery. For conspicuous gallantry in action in the vicinity of Malbrouck Hill, near Brabant-sur-Meuse, France, October 28 to 31, 1918, in reconnoitering the entire enemy front line and establishing an observation post in an abandoned French tank in the Ormont Wood under heavy enemy shell fire.

FIRST LIEUTENANT FREDERICK A. WILLIS, Battery A, 104th Field Artillery. For exceptional courage, and devotion to duty in voluntarily carrying a message to the forward line through heavy shelling and machine gun fire and in evacuating a wounded solder in his regiment. This during the operations of his regiment near Etraye, France, November 11, 1918.

SECOND LIEUTENANT JAMES ANDREWS, 104th Field Artillery. For exceptionally meritorious service during operations in the vicinity of Bois de Forges and Bois de Septsarges, France, September 26 to November 11, 1918, in supervising the hauling of ammunition to forward battery positions, traveling day and night under great fatigue and with short rations until badly injured and evacuated.

SECOND LIEUTENANT ARMSTRONG CRAWFORD, 104th Field Artillery. For gallantry in action and exceptional devotion to duty in the vicinity of Brabant-sur-Meuse, France, October 29, 1918, in constantly patrolling his battery column while enroute to position under heavy enemy shell fire.

SECOND LIEUTENANT RALPH REGAN FINNEY, 104th Field Artillery. For extraordinary heroism in action in the vicinity of La Claire Farm, France, October 8, 1918, when two cases of hand grenades dropped from a runaway limber and exploded, causing about twelve casualties, he, disregarding the bursting grenades, rushed to the aid of the wounded directing and helping their removal from danger and rendering first aid at great personal risk.

SECOND LIEUTENANT HOWARD HUMPHREY, 104th Field Artillery. For conspicuous gallantry in action in the vicinity of Brabant-sur-Meuse, France, November 5, 1918, in personally repairing a broken telephone wire to Battalion Headquarters under heavy enemy shell fire.

SECOND LIEUTENANT McALLISTER MARSHALL, 104th Field Artillery. For exceptionally meritorious service during operations in the vicinity of the Bois de Forges and Brabant-sur-Meuse, France, where, as Artillery Liaison Officer with infantry units, he rendered services of conspicuous worth. This on September 20 to November 11, 1918.

SECOND LIEUTENANT WILLIAM N. MCLUNG, 104th Field Artillery. For conspicuous gallantry in action in the vicinity of Brabant-sur-Meuse, France, November 4, 1918, in rescuing wounded men, clearing away debris and maintaining the fire efficiency of his battery while subjected to a concentration of enemy artillery fire.

SECOND LIEUTENANT WILLIAM H. MERRICK, 104th Field Artillery. For conspicuous gallantry in action during operations in the vicinity of Montzéville, La Claire Farm, Forges, Béthincourt, Consenvoye and Brabant-sur-Meuse, France, September 26 to November 11, 1918, in conducting caissons loaded with ammunition to forward battery positions over congested roads under heavy enemy shell fire.

SECOND LIEUTENANT SIDNEY N. RIGGS, 104th Field Artillery. 1. For conspicuous gallantry in action in the vicinity of the Bois de Chaume, near Consenvoye, France, September 26, 1918, in continuing on duty as Liaison Officer with the infantry front line under heavy enemy shell fire, although severely gassed, until evacuated. 2. For conspicuous gallantry in action in the vicinity of the Bois de Forge, France, September 26, 1918, in advancing with the first infantry line and maintained telephone communication back to Artillery and Division Headquarters under heavy enemy machine gun and shell fire.

SECOND LIEUTENANT GASTON F. M. SCHREIBER, 104th Field Artillery. For gallantry in action and exceptional devotion to duty in the vicinity of Brabant-sur-Meuse, France, October 29, 1918, in constantly patrolling his battery column while enroute to position under heavy enemy shell fire.

SECOND LIEUTENANT FRANCIS W. SUTHERLAND, 104th Field Artillery. For exceptional devotion to duty and efficiency in assembling and conducting the combined bands of the division at Spartanburg, S.C., and during the review by the Commander in Chief of the A.E.F. at Montfort, France.

SECOND LIEUTENANT GEORGE E. WOLFE, 104th Field Artillery. For conspicuous gallantry in action in the vicinity of the Bois de Forges, France, October 2, 1918, in remaining at his post under heavy enemy shell fire, supervising the distributing rations until he was severely wounded.

REGIMENTAL SUPPLY SERGEANT HARRY J. BRUCE, Supply Company, 104th Field Artillery. For conspicuous gallantry in action in the vicinity of the Bois de Forges and Brabant-sur-Meuse, France, September 1 to November 11, 1918, in bringing rations and supplies over roads subjected to heavy enemy shell fire and gas concentrations to forward battery positions.

REGIMENTAL SUPPLY SERGEANT JOHN S. MURPHY, 104th Field Artillery. For conspicuous gallantry in action in the vicinity of the Bois de Forges and Brabant-sur-Meuse, France, September 1 to November 11, 1918, in bringing rations and supplies over roads subjected to heavy enemy shell fire and gas concentrations to forward battery positions.

FIRST SERGEANT ADRIAN J. JACQUES, Battery B, 104th Field Artillery. For gallantry in action and devotion to duty in the vicinity of Montzéville, France, September 9, 1918, in bringing urgently needed rations to forward positions under heavy enemy shell fire.

FIRST CLASS SERGEANT ROLAND SUTHERLAND, Sanitary Department, 104th Field Artillery. For conspicuous gallantry in action in the vicinity of Brabant-sur-Meuse, France, October 29 to November 11, 1918, in repeatedly and with great coolness evacuating casualties from areas almost constantly under heavy enemy shell fire.

SERGEANT FRANK ARMSTRONG, Battery E, 104th Field Artillery. For gallantry in action during operations in the vicinity of Brabant-sur-Meuse, France, October 14, 1918, in repairing and maintaining the telephone lines under heavy enemy shell fire.

SERGEANT WARD O. BROWN, Battery C, 104th Field Artillery. For gallantry in action in the vicinity of Montzéville Farm, France, September 9, 1918, in voluntarily repairing broken telephone lines under heavy enemy shell fire.

SERGEANT CLAUDIUS D. BUSH, Headquarters Company, 104th Field Artillery. For exceptional courage and determination in the sector northeast of Brabant, France, October 30 to November 6, 1918, in constantly maintaining the regiment's liaison line under heavy fire and direct observation by the enemy.

SERGEANT JOHN F. BYRNES, Supply Company, 104th Field Artillery. For conspicuous gallantry in action in the vicinity of Bois de Forges, France, when, although wounded himself, he refused medical attention and conducted a detachment from the Bois de Forges to Cumières, secured rations and forage and returned while under heavy enemy shell fire to the gun positions near Chattancourt. This on October 12, 1918.

SERGEANT EDWARD M. EDGETT, Headquarters Company, 104th Field Artillery. For exceptional courage and determination in reconnoitering an entire day from an advanced observation station, under constant enemy fire. This during the operations of his regiment near Brabant, France, October 30, 1918.

SERGEANT GEORGE J. GINGERICH, Battery B, 104th Field Artillery. For exceptional devotion to duty during operations in Verdun sector, France, from September 26 to November 11, 1918, in conducting accurate fire of his piece under heavy enemy shell fire.

SERGEANT HENRY W. GINITHEN, Battery B, 104th Field Artillery. For exceptional devotion to duty during operations in Verdun sector, France from September 26 to November 11, 1918, in conducting accurate fire of his piece under heavy enemy shell fire.

SERGEANT STEPHEN W. HALTON, Battery A, 104th Field Artillery. For conspicuous service in action in the vicinity of the Bois de Forges, France, September 29 and October 3, 1918, as a member of a gun crew in repairing and operating against the enemy a group of captured enemy 77mm field guns.

SERGEANT CHARLES HULL, Battery C, 104th Field Artillery. For gallantry in action in the vicinity of Montzéville, France, September 9, 1918, in voluntarily repairing broken telephone wires under heavy enemy shell fire.

SERGEANT PETER F. KELLY, Battery E, 104th Field Artillery (Deceased). For exceptional bravery in action during operations in the vicinity of the Bois de Forges, France, September 29, 1918, in voluntarily cleaning out a recently evacuated mined dugout during the performance of which duty he was seriously wounded by an explosion and later died.

SERGEANT CHARLES LEVY, Headquarters Company, 104th Field Artillery. For gallantry in action in the vicinity of Consenvoye, France, October 14, 1918, in laying a telephone cable across the Meuse River under heavy enemy shell fire.

SERGEANT JAMES MINOR, Headquarters Company, 104th Field Artillery. For conspicuous gallantry in action in the vicinity of Ormont Wood, France, November 2, 1918, in laying a telephone wire from the Battery Commander's station to a forward observation post in an abandoned French tank in the Ormont Wood, and maintained it intact for several days under heavy enemy shell fire.

SERGEANT WILLIAM H. ROACH, Headquarters Company, 104th Field Artillery. For conspicuous gallantry in action in the vicinity of Bois de Forges, France, October 8 and 9, 1918, establishing a forward observation post in a tree and maintaining same throughout the night under heavy shell fire and gas concentrations.

SERGEANT GUY F. WILLIAMSON, Battery D, 104th Field Artillery. For exceptional courage and determination in remaining at his post during heavy shell fire and gas concentration while acting battery non-commissioned gas officer, near Brabant, France, November 2, 1918.

SERGEANT EDWIN WORKS, Battery D, 104th Field Artillery. For great courage and determination near Brabant-sur-Meuse, France, October 28, 1918, in a sectional ammunition dump caused by an exploding shell.

SERGEANT LOUIS B. WRIGHT, Battery B, 104th Field Artillery. For exceptional devotion to duty during operations in Verdun sector, France, from September 26 to November 11, 1918, in conducting accurate fire of his piece under heavy enemy shell fire.

SUPPLY SEARGEANT JAMES W. BANNON, Battery F, 104th Field Artillery. For conspicuous gallantry in action during operations in the vicinity of Ormont Farm, France, November 10, 1918, in bringing his detachment to forward battery positions over roads subjected to heavy enemy shell fire.

SUPPLY SEARGEANT PHILIP TATTER SALL, Battery E, 104th Field Artillery. For conspicuous gallantry in action during operations in the vicinity of Ormont Farm, France, November 10, 1918, in bringing his detachment to forward battery positions over roads subjected to heavy enemy shell fire.

STABLE SERGEANT WILLIAM C. DEACON, Battery B, 104th Field Artillery. For gallantry in action and devotion to duty in the vicinity of Montzéville, France, September 9, 1918, in bringing urgently needed rations to forward positions under heavy enemy shell fire.

CORPORAL KENNETH F. ADAMS, Battery B, 104th Field Artillery. For gallantry in action during operations in the vicinity of Brabant-sur-Meuse, France, November 5, 1918, in rescuing two badly wounded comrades under heavy enemy shell fire.

CORPORAL HERMAN D. BECKMAN, Battery D, 104th Field Artillery. For great courage and determination in laying a telephone line in the Bois de Consenvoye, France, a distance of two kilometers, under extremely heavy shell fire on October 28, 1918.

CORPORAL WILFRED K. BROWN, Battery A, 104th Field Artillery. For conspicuous gallantry in action in the vicinity of Brabant-sur-Meuse, France, November 5, 1918, in voluntarily exposing himself to heavy enemy shell fire in front of his gun position and re-erecting the aiming post to enable his gun to continue in action.

CORPORAL JOHN BUSH, Battery A, 104th Field Artillery. For extraordinary heroism in action in the vicinity of the La Claire Farm, France, October 8, 1918, when two cases of hand grenades dropped from a runaway limber and exploded, causing about twelve casualties, he, disregarding the bursting grenades, rushed to the aid of the wounded, directing and helping their removal from danger and rendering first aid at great personal risk.

CORPORAL LEONARD S. COLYER, Headquarters Company, 104th Field Artillery. For gallantry in action in the vicinity of Bois de Forges, France, September 28, 1918, in laying telephone lines between battery and Regimental Headquarters and infantry positions under heavy enemy shell fire.

CORPORAL RICHARD M. COTT, Headquarters Company, 104th Field Artillery. For exceptional devotion to duty during operations in the vicinity of La Claire Farm, Bois de Forges and Brabant-sur-Meuse, France, September 26 to November 11, 1918, during the Meuse-Argonne offensive, in preparing and maintaining with great accuracy the regimental battle map under difficult and adverse conditions.

CORPORAL JOHN DALY, Battery A, 104th Field Artillery. For conspicuous service in action in the vicinity of the Bois de Forges, France, September 28 to October 3, 1918, as a member of a gun crew in repairing and operating against the enemy a group of captured enemy 77 mm field guns.

CORPORAL GEORGE H. EBELING, Battery D, 104th Field Artillery. For gallantry in action, when, as a battery agent, he went through heavy shell fire and gas on several occasions, carrying important orders to and from Battalion Headquarters. This in the Verdun sector, France, September 6 to November 11, 1918.

CORPORAL WILLIAM L. B. FARRELL, Headquarters Company, 104th Field Artillery. For conspicuous gallantry in action and devotion to duty throughout the night of October 8–9, 1918, in a forward observation post in a tree in the Bois de Forges, France, under heavy shell fire and gas, observing barrage signals and reporting accurately by telephone to the Battalion Headquarters.

CORPORAL RICHARD FLYNN, Battery B, 104th Field Artillery. For gallantry in action, when as a battery agent he went through heavy shell fire and gas, carrying important orders to and from Battalion Headquarters, France, September 26 to November 11, 1918.

CORPORAL MATTHEW S. FOX, Battery F, 104th Field Artillery. For conspicuous gallantry in action in the vicinity of Barbant-sur-Meuse, France, November 4, 1918, in rescuing the bodies of two comrades from a gun emplacement hit by an enemy shell, extinguishing the burning camouflage and arousing the remainder of the gun crew while about two hundred fuses and rounds of shell were exploding at a nearby ammunition dump.

CORPORAL LELAND B. HALL, Battery F, 104th Field Artillery. For conspicuous gallantry in action in the vicinity of Germonville, France, September 25, 1918, in bringing down a German aeroplane by the fire of a machine gun with which he was guarding an ammunition dump, being later wounded himself.

CORPORAL WILLIAM A. HAYES, Headquarters Company, 104th Field Artillery. For gallantry in action in the vicinity of the Bois de Forges, France, September 28, 1918, in laying telephone lines between battery and Regimental Headquarters and infantry positions under heavy enemy shell fire.

CORPORAL LOUIS HORN, Headquarters Company, 104th Field Artillery. For gallantry and extraordinary heroism in action in the vicinity of Samogneux, France, November 2, 1918, in repairing telephone lines between Regimental Headquarters and forward infantry positions under heavy enemy shell fire, although repeatedly knocked down by high explosive shells.

CORPORAL JESSE W. HOWARD, Battery C, 104th Field Artillery. For gallantry in action in the vicinity of Montzéville, France, September 9, 1918, in voluntarily repairing broken telephone wire under heavy enemy shell fire.

CORPORAL JAMES J. LAWLOR, JR., Battery F, 104th Field Artillery. For exceptional devotion to duty during operations in the vicinity of Dannevoux, France, while acting as a machine gun corporal attached to infantry units, he rendered exceptional services in the performance of difficult and dangerous duties under fire.

CORPORAL ALBERT LIPTAX, Headquarters Company, 104th Field Artillery. For exceptional devotion to duty during operations in the vicinity of La Claire Farm, Bois de Forges and Brabant-sur-Meuse, France, during the Meuse-Argonne offensive, in preparing and maintaining with great accuracy the regimental battle map under difficult and adverse conditions.

CORPORAL PATRICK J. McMURROUGH, Battery F, 104th Field Artillery. For conspicuous gallantry in action in the vicinity of Brabant-sur-Meuse, France, November 6, 1918, in carrying important messages between his battery and Battalion Headquarters throughout the night, and although wounded three times, declining to be relieved.

CORPORAL JOHN J. O'CONNELL, Battery C, 104th Field Artillery. For gallantry in action in the vicinity of Montzéville, France, September 9, 1918, in voluntarily repairing broken telephone wires under heavy enemy shell fire.

CORPORAL FRANK REILLY, Headquarters Company, 104th Field Artillery. For conspicuous gallantry in action and devotion to duty, when he remained on duty throughout the night of October 8 and 9, 1918, in a forward observation post in a tree in the Bois de Forges, France, under heavy enemy shell fire and gas, observing for barrage signals and reporting accurately by telephone to Battalion Headquarters.

CORPORAL CLIFFORD W. SAMPTON, Headquarters Company, 104th Field Artillery. For gallantry in action in the vicinity of Ormont Hill, France, October 28, 1918, in reconnoitering enemy front line positions under heavy enemy shell fire.

CORPORAL GEORGE O. SCHOONOVER, Headquarters Company, 104th Field Artillery. For conspicuous gallantry in action in the vicinity of Ravin du Rapilleux and Le Mort Homme, France, September and October 1918, in serving as a runner between Battalion Headquarters and battery positions under heavy enemy shell and machine gun fire.

CORPORAL FRANK TURNER, Battery B, 104th Field Artillery. For gallantry in action during operations in the vicinity of Barbant-sur-Meuse, France, November 5, 1918, in the repairing of broken telephone lines under heavy enemy shell fire.

CORPORAL WILLIAM WARD, Headquarters Company, 104th Field Artillery. For gallantry in action in the vicinity of Barbant-sur-Meuse, France, November 8, 1918, in laying telephone wires between battalion and regimental headquarters for 250 meters under heavy enemy shell fire and gas concentrations.

CORPORAL GEORGE WARREN, Battery C, 104th Field Artillery. For gallantry in action in the vicinity of Montzéville, France, September 9, 1918, in voluntarily repairing broken telephone wires under heavy enemy shell fire.

CORPORAL EDGAR W. WORMELL, Battery B, 104th Field Artillery. For gallantry in action during operations in the vicinity of Barbant-sur-Meuse, France, from October 30 to November 11, 1918, in carrying messages to forward infantry positions under heavy enemy shell fire.

PRIVATE, FIRST CLASS, HARVEY B. CHRISTIAN, Battery B, 104th Field Artillery. For gallantry in action during operations in the vicinity of Barbant-sur-Meuse, France, November 5, 1918, in rescuing two badly wounded comrades under heavy enemy shell fire.

PRIVATE, FIRST CLASS, JAMES T. CLUNE, Batter B, 104th Field Artillery. For gallantry in action during operations in the vicinity of Barbant-sur-Meuse, France, November 5, 1918, in repairing broken telephone lines under heavy enemy shell fire.

PRIVATE, FIRST CLASS, AARON J. CUFFEE, Headquarters Company, 104th Field Artillery. For gallantry and extraordinary heroism in action in the vicinity of Consenvoye, France, October 14, 1918, in voluntarily swimming the Meuse River with a telephone cable under heavy enemy shell fire and gas concentrations.

PRIVATE, FIRST CLASS, MAX DIETZMAN, Battery B, 104th Field Artillery. For gallantry in action during operations in the vicinity of Barbant-sur-Meuse, France, November 5, 1918, in rescuing two badly wounded comrades under heavy enemy shell fire.

PRIVATE, FIRST CLASS, JOHN W. FLEET, Headquarters Company, 104th Field Artillery. For gallantry in action in the vicinity of Bois de Forges, France, September 28, 1918, in laying telephone lines between the battery and the Regimental Headquarters and infantry positions under heavy enemy shell fire.

PRIVATE, FIRST CLASS, HAROLD FULLER, Battery D, 104th Field Artillery. For exceptional courage and devotion to duty near Brabant-sur-Meuse, France, October 29, 1918. In carrying a message to the battalion post of command, a distance of two kilometers, through an enemy barrage and heavy gas concentration.

PRIVATE, FIRST CLASS, KARL KITCHELT, Sanitary Department, 104th Field Artillery. For conspicuous gallantry in action in the vicinity of Malbrook Hill, France, October 29, 1918, in carrying a message to Bras, a distance of five kilometers, to secure an ambulance for the evacuation of casualties, under heavy enemy shell fire, during which he was knocked down several times by shell explosions.

PRIVATE, FIRST CLASS, WALTER McAVINNE, Battery F, 104th Field Artillery. For exceptional courage and devotion to duty near Consenvoye, France, in evacuating wounded under heavy enemy shell fire and gas concentration. This on October 19, 1918.

PRIVATE, FIRST CLASS, ROBERT McCAULERY, Battery A, 104th Field Artillery. For extraordinary heroism in action in the vicinity of the La Claire Farm, France, October 8, 1918, when two cases of hand grenades dropped from a runaway limber and exploded, causing about twelve casualties, he, disregarding the bursting grenades, rushed to the aid of the wounded directing and helping their removal from danger and rendering first aid at great personal risk.

PRIVATE, FIRST CLASS, CHARLES McGINTY, Battery B, 104th Field Artillery. For gallantry in action during operations in the vicinity of Brabant-sur-Meuse, France, November 5, 1918, in rescuing two badly wounded comrades under heavy enemy shell fire.

PRIVATE, FIRST CLASS, ALFRED McGINNESS, Battery E, 104th Field Artillery. For exceptional bravery in action in the vicinity of Bois de Forges, France, September 29, 1918, in voluntarily helping to clean out a recently evacuated mined enemy dugout, in the performance of which duty he was wounded by an explosion.

PRIVATE, FIRST CLASS, JOHN NOLAND, Battery E, 104th Field Artillery. For conspicuous gallantry in action during operations in the vicinity of Consenvoye, France, October 18, 1918, in delivering ammunition to battery positions under enemy shell fire and gas concentrations, in the performance of which duty he was so seriously wounded as to necessitate the amputation of one limb.

PRIVATE, FIRST CLASS, FRANCIS A. PEARCE, Battery F, 104th Field Artillery. For exceptional courage and devotion to duty near Consenvoye, France, October 19, 1918, in evacuating the wounded under heavy shell fire and gas concentrations.

PRIVATE, FIRST CLASS, PAUL PROKOP, Battery D, 104th Field Artillery. For great courage and determination in laying and repairing telephone lines near Brabant-sur-Meuse, France, under extremely heavy shell fire on October 30, 1918.

PRIVATE, FIRST CLASS, C. ROSS, Battery B, 104th Field Artillery. For gallantry in action during operations in the vicinity of Brabant-sur-Meuse, France, November 5, 1918, in repairing broken telephone lines under heavy enemy shell fire.

PRIVATE, FIRST CLASS, GEORGE SEIDEL, Battery A, 104th Field Artillery. For exceptional devotion to duty during operations in the vicinity of Brabant-sur-Meuse, France, November 1, 1918, when, having been ordered to report without loss of time to forward gun positions, he rode through heavy enemy shell fire.

PRIVATE, FIRST CLASS, WILLIAM SIEVEN, Battery E, 104th Field Artillery (Deceased). For conspicuous gallantry in action in the vicinity of Consenvoye, France, October 19, 1918, in delivering ammunition to battery positions under heavy enemy shell fire and gas concentrations, in the performance of which duty he received a wound, which caused his death.

PRIVATE, FIRST CLASS, SILAS SPITZER, Battery D, 104th Field Artillery. For exceptional courage and determination in carrying messages and rations under heavy shell fire and over territory under observation by enemy fire. This at Forges, France, October 4, 1918.

PRIVATE, FIRST CLASS, PAUL STEVENSON, Sanitary Detachment, 104th Field Artillery. For conspicuous gallantry in action in the vicinity of Brabant-sur-Meuse, France, October 29 to November 11, 1918, in repeatedly and with great coolness evacuating casualties from areas almost constantly under heavy enemy shell fire.

PRIVATE, FIRST CLASS, THOMAS F. TIERNEY, Battery B, 104th Field Artillery. For gallantry in action during operations in the vicinity of Montzéville, France, September 9, 1918, in bringing rations to battery positions under heavy enemy shell fire and by great coolness, initiative and without regard to personal risk, saving animals and material from destruction.

PRIVATE RAYMOND BATES, Battery A, 104th Field Artillery. For conspicuous service in action in the vicinity of the Bois de Forges, France, September 28 to October 3, 1918, as a member of a gun crew in repairing and operating against the enemy a group of captured enemy 77mm field guns.

PRIVATE WALTER BEST, Battery D, 104th Field Artillery. For great courage and determination near Brabant-sur-Meuse, France, October 28, 1918, in laying telephone line for a distance of two kilometers under extremely heavy shell fire.

PRIVATE HUGO BONSAING, Battery A, 104th Field Artillery. For exceptional devotion to duty in the vicinity of Brabant-sur-Meuse, France, November 5, 1918, when, in response to a barrage call, he fired his piece accurately and unaided for twenty-four rounds in the absence of other members of the gun crew.

PRIVATE JAMES P. BROW, Battery A, 104th Field Artillery. For conspicuous service in action in the vicinity of Bois de Forges, France, September 28 to October 3, 1918, as a member of a gun crew in repairing and operating against the enemy a group of captured enemy 77 mm field guns.

PRIVATE LEWIS CONOR, Battery F, 104th Field Artillery (Deceased). For gallantry in action in the vicinity of Brabant-sur-Meuse, France, November 3, 1918, in repairing telephone lines under heavy enemy shell fire until killed.

PRIVATE DAVID CREW, Battery C, 104th Field Artillery. For conspicuous gallantry in action and exceptional devotion to duty in the vicinity of Forges, France, October 3, 1918, when, having been sent to secure the fire of a heavy battery against an enemy position causing great loss and finding the fire could not be executed, he proceeded a distance of five kilometers under heavy enemy shell fire and induced another battery to execute the mission.

PRIVATE CHARLES L. CROVAT, Headquarters Company, 104th Field Artillery. For accompanying the 132nd Infantry on the occasion of the assault against Forges Wood, France, September 28, 1918, and establishing wire communication with his regiment, this under heavy enemy shell and machine gun fire.

PRIVATE ALBERT A. DALBERT, Headquarters Company, 104th Field Artillery. For conspicuous gallantry in action in the vicinity of the Bois de Chaume, France, October 13 to 16, 1918, in carrying messages to and from Battalion Headquarters, frequently under heavy enemy shell and machine gun fire and continuing although seriously affected by gas.

PRIVATE HARRY C. DUPREE, Battery B, 104th Field Artillery. For gallantry in action during operations in the vicinity of Verdun, France, September 26 to November 11, 1918, in carrying messages to battery positions under heavy enemy shell fire.

PRIVATE DENIS J. DWYER, Battery D, 104th Field Artillery. For conspicuous gallantry in action in the vicinity of Consenvoye, France, October 11 and 12, 1918, in rescuing a wounded comrade under heavy enemy shell fire and carrying him to a dressing station in time to save his life.

PRIVATE ROBERT FENNELL, Headquarters Company, 104th Field Artillery (Deceased). For conspicuous gallantry in action in the vicinity of Bois d'Ormont, France, November 1, 1918, in driving his automobile over roads subjected to heavy enemy shell fire in an attempt to conduct liaison officers to forward infantry positions, continuing his work until killed.

PRIVATE JOHN O. GILSON, Battery C, 104th Field Artillery. For gallantry in action in the vicinity of Montzéville, France, September 9, 1918, in voluntarily repairing broken telephone wires under heavy enemy shell fire.

PRIVATE HENRY M. HERRERA, Headquarters Company, 104th Field Artillery. For gallantry in action during operations in the vicinity of Brabant-sur-Meuse, France, October 31 to November 11, 1918, in continually carrying messages from Regimental PC to Brigade Headquarters under heavy enemy shell fire.

PRIVATE JOSEPH LEE, Battery F, 104th Field Artillery. For conspicuous gallantry in action in the vicinity of Brabant-sur-Meuse, France, November 4, 1918, in continuing to serve his gun under heavy enemy shell fire until killed at his post.

PRIVATE MAX P. MADSON, Headquarters Company, 104th Field Artillery. 1. For gallantry in action in the vicinity of Brabant-sur-Meuse, France, November 2, 1918, in voluntarily carrying a message to Brigade Headquarters and guiding a truck loaded with supplies over roads and fields under heavy enemy shell fire. 2. For exceptional courage and determination in the sector northeast of Brabant, France, October 30, 1918, in constantly maintaining the regiment's liaison line under heavy fire and direct observation of the enemy.

PRIVATE CLAUDE MURWIN, Sanitary Detachment, 104th Field Artillery. For conspicuous gallantry in action in the vicinity of Brabant-sur-Meuse, France, October 29 to November 11, 1918, in repeatedly and with great coolness evacuating casualties from areas almost constantly under heavy enemy shell fire.

PRIVATE DENIS J. NEWMAN, Battery F, 104th Field Artillery. For meritorious service during operations in the vicinity of Brabant-sur-Meuse, France, November 3, 1918, in rendering assistance to a gun crew whose ammunition dump was set on fire by enemy shells.

PRIVATE FRANK O'NEILL, Battery F, 104th Field Artillery (Deceased). For gallantry in action in the vicinity of Brabant-sur-Meuse, France, November 3, 1918, in repairing telephone lines under heavy enemy shell fire until killed.

PRIVATE GEORGE R. RUSSEL, Headquarters Company, 104th Field Artillery. 1. For exceptional courage and determination in the sector northeast of Brabant, France, October 30 to November 6, 1918, in constantly maintaining the regiment's liaison line under heavy fire and direct observation of the enemy. 2. For gallantry and extraordinary heroism in action during the operations of the 104th Field Artillery in the vicinity of Samogneux, France, November 2, 1918, in repairing telephone lines between Regimental Headquarters and forward infantry positions under heavy enemy shell, although repeatedly knocked down by high explosive shells.

PRIVATE MARTIN SCHNEIDER, Headquarters Company, 104th Field Artillery (Deceased). For conspicuous gallantry in action in the vicinity of Dannevoux, France, October 19, 1918, in remaining at his observation post at night through continuous heavy enemy shell fire with only improvised protection until killed.

PRIVATE JAMES SMALL, Battery A, 104th Field Artillery. For conspicuous gallantry in action in the vicinity of Brabant-sur-Meuse, France, November 5, 1918, in relaying firing data, as telephone operator, to a platoon of his battery under heavy enemy shell fire, thereby enabling the guns to remain in action.

PRIVATE SCHUYLER R. SMITH, Battery A, 104th Field Artillery (Deceased). For conspicuous gallantry in action in the vicinity of Dannevoux, France, October 19, 1918, in remaining on duty in an exposed observation post without protection under heavy enemy shell fire, until mortally wounded.

PRIVATE MATTHEW SOLINSKI, Battery A, 104th Field Artillery. For conspicuous service in action in the vicinity of Bois de Forges, France, as a member of a gun crew in repairing and operating against the enemy a group of captured enemy 77mm field guns. This September 28 to October 3, 1918.

PRIVATE STANLEY I. STILES, Sanitary Detachment, 104th Field Artillery. For conspicuous gallantry in action in the vicinity of Brabant-sur-Meuse, France, October 29 to November 11, 1918, in repeatedly and with great coolness evacuating casualties from areas almost constantly under heavy enemy fire.

PRIVATE MATTHEW J. STOTTHARD, Battery D, 104th Field Artillery. For conspicuous gallantry in action in the vicinity of Consenvoye, France, October 13, 1918, in going for and returning with his battery kitchen across the Consenvoye Bridge under heavy enemy shell fire and gas concentrations.

PRIVATE VINCENT THOMPSON, Battery A, 104th Field Artillery. For conspicuous gallantry in action in the vicinity of Brabant-sur-Meuse, France, November 4, 1918, when during an attack by his battery a high explosive shell with an instantaneous fuse became wedged in the bore of his field piece, and a wooden rammer staff broke in the bore against the nose of the projectile, he forced the cartridge case into the breech, closed the block and fired the piece, clearing the bore and restoring the gun to action at great personal risk.

PRIVATE JARVIS F. TURNER, Headquarters Company, 104th Field Artillery. For gallantry in action in the vicinity of Chattancourt, France, October 26, 1918, in establishing and maintaining telephone communications between the Regiment Headquarters and forward infantry positions under heavy enemy shell fire.

PRIVATE CHARLES WEAVER, Battery C, 104th Field Artillery. For conspicuous gallantry in action in the vicinity of Brabant-sur-Meuse, France, November 3, 1918, in entering a gun emplacement under heavy enemy shell fire and assisting in carrying a wounded comrade to safety.

PRIVATE EARL WILS, Battery C, 104th Field Artillery. For conspicuous gallantry in action in the vicinity of Brabant-sur-Meuse, France, November 3, 1918, in entering a gun emplacement under heavy enemy shell fire and assisting in carrying a wounded comrade to safety.

PRIVATE LEE F. WOODS, Battery B, 104th Field Artillery. For gallantry in action during operations in the vicinity of Brabant-sur-Meuse, France, November 5, 1918, in rescuing a wounded comrade under heavy shelling.

Chapter Notes

Preface

1. Drew Rankin's father was June Rankin, sportswriter/baseball editor of the *New York Herald* and *New York Sunday Mercury*, and later golf editor for other papers including the *New York World*. His uncle, Will Rankin, was baseball editor of the *New York Clipper*. See Pamela A. Bakker. *Eyes on the Sporting Scene, 1870–1930: Will and June Rankin, New York's Sportswriting Brothers* (Jefferson, NC: McFarland, 2013) for more details on Drew's childhood.
2. The term Boche, meaning beast, was used by the French for the Germans who had invaded their country.

Chapter One

1. James A. Roberts. *New York in the Revolution as Colony and State* (Albany: Brandow, 1898), 9–10.
2. Frederick Phisterer. *New York in the War of the Rebellion, 1861 to 1865*, 3d ed. (Albany: J.B. Lyon, 1912) gives more information on the New York National Guard during the Civil War. Also see Gus Person, "Answering the Call: The New York State Militia Responds to the Crisis of 1861," *Civil War History Journal* (May/June 2008), available online at http://dmna.ny.gov/historic/reghist/civil/Answeringthecall_Person.pdf//.
3. C. Wendell, *Third Annual Report of Military Statistics of the State of New York* (Albany: The Bureau, 1866), and http://dmna.ny.gov/historic/reghist/civil/infantry/12thNYSM/12thNYSMmain.htm.
4. *Annual Report of the Adjutant General of the State of New York* (Albany: Argus, 1869), 17–19.
5. Major Albert A. Nofi's history of the 104th DECON Battalion on http://www.88ny.net/2-104.htm.
6. A caisson is a two-wheeled cart designed to carry artillery ammunition. It also carried a spare wheel on the back, an extra limber pole, pick axes, a felling axe and a shovel used to build emplacements for field pieces. There was one caisson for each field piece which attached to a limber. Limbers were two-wheeled carts which supported the end trail of the field piece. The field piece had an iron ring on its trail which fit over a pintle hook on the limber and then locked in place. The limber had a central pole with horse harnesses on either side. Usually six horses pulled a limber. They were harnessed in pairs on either side of the limber pole. A driver rode on the left horse, called the near horse, and also controlled the right horse, called the off horse. The limber also had an ammunition chest. Limbers were used to pull caissons, artillery pieces, a battery's wagon, and the forge which was used to repair items as needed.
7. *Annual Report of the Adjutant General of the State of New York: 1868* (Albany: Argus, 1869), 53.
8. http://www.cwartillery.com/FA/FA.html//.
9. John F. O'Ryan. *The Story of the 27th Division, Vol. I* (New York: Wynkoop, Hallenbeck, Crawford, 1921), 13–15.
10. *Annual Report of the Adjutant General of the State of New York: 1916* (Albany: J. B. Lyon, 1917), 60.
11. Richard W. Stewart, ed., *American Mil-*

itary History, Vol. I: The United States Army and the Forging of a Nation, 1775–1917 (Washington, D.C.: Center of Military History, 2005), 345.

12. Steward, 351. Also see First Lieutenant G. Bagnall, N.Y.N.G., *Brooklyn Guardsman, 1903: An Authentic and Authorized Register and Record of the Local Land and Naval Forces of the State of New York* (Brooklyn: New York National Guard, 1903).

13. O'Ryan, 17.

14. James W. Hurst. *Pancho Villa and Black Jack Pershing: The Punitive Expedition in Mexico* (Westport, CT: Praeger, 2008), xx.

15. Edward G. Lengel, *To Conquer Hell: The Meuse-Argonne, 1918, The Epic Battle That Ended the First World War* (New York: Henry Holt, 2008), 26.

16. Brooklyn Auxiliary of the 105th Field Artillery, *A.E.F., A Brief History of the Activities of the 105th Field Artillery, American Expeditionary Forces: On Active Service in France, 1918–1919* (New York, 1919), 16.

Chapter Two

1. Robert S. Thomas and Inez V. Allen, *The Mexican Punitive Expedition Under Brigadier General John J. Pershing, United States Army, 1916–1917* (Washington, D.C.: War Histories Division Office of the Chief Of Military History, Department of the Army, 1954). I-9. Also see James W. Hurst. *Pancho Villa and Black Jack Pershing: The Punitive Expedition in Mexico* (Westport, CT: Praeger, 2008), xi and I-11.

2. See Mitchell Yockelson, "The United States Armed Forces and the Mexican Punitive Expedition: Part 1 and Part 2," *Prologue Magazine* 29, no. 3 (Fall 1997) for more details on the expedition.

3. John F. O'Ryan, *The Story of the 27th Division, Vol. I* (New York: Wynkoop, Hallenbeck, Crawford, 1921), 16; *Annual Report of the Adjutant General of the State of New York: 1916* (Albany: J. B. Lyon, 1917), 18; and Major Edward Olmsted, "Organization of the N.Y. Division," in Henry Hagaman Burdick, ed., *New York Division, National Guard, War Record* (New York: Burdick & King, 1917), 22.

4. *Annual Report of the Adjutant General of the State of New York: 1916* (Albany: J.B. Lyon, 1917), 20–21.

5. "Capital's Leaders Will March Today; New York's Drafted Men Will Parade," *New York Times,* September 4, 1917.

6. James W. Hurst, *Pancho Villa and Black Jack Pershing: The Punitive Expedition in Mexico* (Westport, CT: Praeger, 2008), 106; O'Ryan, 569; and *Annual Report of the Adjutant General of the State of New York: 1916,* 39–40.

7. *Annual Report of the Adjutant General of the State of New York: 1916,* 20, and Brooklyn Auxiliary of the 105th Field Artillery, *A.E.F., A Brief History of the Activities of the 105th Field Artillery, American Expeditionary Forces: On Active Service in France, 1918–1919* (New York, 1919), 16–17.

8. O'Ryan, 572.

9. The 2nd Lieutenant for this battery was not listed in the 1916 Adjutant General report.

10. O'Ryan, 18.

11. "Major General William S. McNair." *The Field Artillery Journal* XXII, no. 6 (November–December 1932), 575. This particular issue is a tribute to the passing of Brigadier-General William S. McNair.

12. Andrew B. Rankin, Jr., "A Soldier's Life on the Border," *The Owl,* October 5, 1916, 6. *The Owl* newspaper was published at Rockville Center on Long Island, New York, from March 30, 1912, to November 14, 1919. It became the *Long Island News and the Owl* from November 21, 1919, to December 28, 1995. Its name then changed a number of times: *The Owl; The News and Owl; Rockville Center News & Owl; Long Island News & the Owl.*

13. Lieutenant William Welsh, "The First Field Artillery," in Burdick, 71.

14. Rankin, "A Soldier's Life on the Border," 6.

15. Ibid., 5.

16. O'Ryan, 63–64, 71–72.

17. *Annual Report of the Adjutant General: 1916,* 46.

18. Rankin, 6.

19. O'Ryan, 583.

20. *Annual Report of the Adjutant General,* 67, and Rankin, 6.

21. Welsh in Burdick, 73; *Annual Report of the Adjutant General: 1916,* 23; and Rankin, 6.

22. Rankin, 6.

23. Olmsted in Burdick, 25.

24. *Annual Report of the Adjutant General: 1916,* 147–149.

25. Rankin, 7.

26. Lieutenant-Colonel Franklin W. Ward,

"The Entertainments of the Division," in Burdick, 41.
27. Rankin, 7.
28. Ibid.
29. O'Ryan, 21–22.
30. Welsh in Burdick, 73.
31. Rankin, 7.
32. *Rio Grande Rattler* 1, no. 13, September 6, 1916, 6.
33. Rankin to Davenport, August 12, 1916.
34. O'Ryan, 24.
35. Ibid.
36. Welsh in Burdick, 71.
37. Ibid., 37.
38. Lieutenant-Colonel E.L. Gruber, *Notes on the 3 Inch Gun Material and Field Artillery Equipment* (The Reserve Officer's Training Corps of Yale University, 1918), 16.
39. Lieutenant C. E. Bregenzer, "The 22nd Corps of Engineers," in Burdick, 57, and O'Ryan, 575–577.
40. *The Rio Grande Rattler*, August 23, 1916, and O'Ryan, 577–580.
41. *Annual Report of the Adjutant General: 1916*, 27.
42. Welsh in Burdick, 75.
43. *Annual Report of the Adjutant General: 1916*, 39–40.
44. Herbert W. Congdon, *Mexican Border* (unpublished), Chapter XXXIV, available online at http://dmna.ny.gov/historic/reghist/mexBorder/mexBorder_history_Congdon.htm.
45. Brooklyn Auxiliary, 17–18.
46. *Rio Grande Rattler*, issue 7, October 4, 1916, 7.
47. *Rio Grande Rattler*, issue 8, October 11, 1916, and issue 9, October 18.
48. Lieutenant-Colonel Franklin W. Ward, "The Entertainments of the Division," in Burdick, 44.
49. *Annual Report of the Adjutant General: 1916*, 153.
50. Welsh in Burdick, 73.
51. Letter: Rankin to Davenport, August 12, 1916.
52. David Allen Glenn, *A Reanalysis of the 1916, 1918, 1927, 1928 and 1935 Tropical Cyclones of the North Atlantic Basin*, Thesis, Mississippi State University, Department of Geosciences, August 2005, 18, available online at http://www.aoml.noaa.gov/hrd/hurdat/Glenn_Thesis.pdf.
53. *Annual Report of the Adjutant General of the State of New York: 1916* (Albany: J. B. Lyon, 1917), 166.
54. Olmsted in Burdick, 29; Brooklyn Auxiliary, 17; and Herbert W. Congdon, *Mexican Border*, (unpublished), Chapter XXXIV, available online at http://dmna.ny.gov/historic/reghist/mexBorder/mexBorder_history_Congdon.htm.
55. Ward in Burdick, 41–42.
56. Major William R. Wright in Burdick, 67.
57. *New York National Guardsman* XI, no. 9 (December 1934).
58. Lieutenant-Colonel F. M. Waterbury in Burdick, 38.
59. Waterbury in Burdick, 39. In 1916 Frank M. Waterbury was a major serving with the New York Division in Texas. His report on border activities, however, was published in 1917 after he had earned the rank of lieutenant-colonel.
60. Olmsted and Ward in Burdick, 26–42, and O'Ryan, 42, 581.
61. O'Ryan, 58.
62. *Handbook of the 4.7-inch gun Materiel, Model of 1906, With Instructions for its Care* (Washington: Government Printing Office, 1917), and Burdick, 30, 74–76.
63. Jim Bond, "Little Tanks: The Development of the American Field Shoe [Boot] During the World War," available online at http://www.worldwar1.com/dbc/1_tanks.htm.
64. Ward in Burdick, 43.
65. *Rio Grande Rattler*, issue 7, October 4, 1916, and Burdick, 42–43.
66. Olmsted in Burdick, 29–32.
67. O'Ryan, 573.
68. Ward in Burdick, 43, and *Rio Grande Rattler*, issue 15, November 29, 1916.
69. *Wadsworth Gas Attack and the Rio Grande Rattler*, January 19, 1918.
70. *Rio Grande Rattler*, issue 16, December 6, 1916, 5.
71. Hurst, 174.

Chapter Three

1. Mitchell Yockelson, "The United States Armed Forces and the Mexican Punitive Expedition: Part 2." *Prologue Magazine* 29, no. 3 (Fall 1997); Brooklyn Auxiliary of the 105th Field Artillery, *A Brief History of the Activities of the 105th Field Artillery, American Expeditionary Forces: On Active Service in France, 1918–1919* (New York, 1919), 18; and Robert

S. Thomas and Inez V. Allen, *The Mexican Punitive Expedition Under Brigadier General John J. Pershing, United States Army, 1916–1917* (Washington, D.C.: War Histories Division Office of the Chief of Military History, Department of the Army, 1954), IV-18.

2. *Annual Report of the Adjutant General of the State of New York: 1916* (Albany: J.B. Lyon, 1917), 8–9, and Major-General John F. O'Ryan, *The Story of the 27th Division, Vol. II* (New York: Wynkoop Hallenbeck Crawford, 1921), 583.

3. Howard Spodek, *The World's History* (New York: Prentice Hall, 2010), 662.

4. Henry Hagaman Burdick, ed., *New York Division, National Guard, War Record 1916 by the Officers and Men of the Division* (New York: Burdick and King, 1917), 105, available online at http://www.dmna.ny.gov/historic/mil-hist.htm//.

5. Edward G. Lengel, *To Conquer Hell: The Meuse-Argonne, 1918, The Epic Battle That Ended the First World War* (New York: Henry Holt, 2008), 18.

6. William F. Clarke, *Over There with O'Ryan's Roughnecks: Reminiscences of a Private 1st Class Who Served in the 27th U.S. Division with the British Forces in Belgium and France* (Seattle: Superior, 1968), 24.

7. O'Ryan, 17, 35, and James H. Hallas, ed., *Doughboy War: The American Expeditionary Force in WWI* (Mechanicsburg, PA: Stackpole, 2000), 2, 9–12, 20.

8. O'Ryan, 584.

9. Susan Turpin, Carolyn Creal, Ron Crawley and James Crocker, eds., *When the Soldiers Came to Town: Spartanburg's Camp Wadsworth (1917–19) & Camp Croft (1941–45)* (Spartanburg, SC: County Historical Association, 2004), 4.

10. Clarke, 23.

11. *Annual Report of the Adjutant General of the State of New York: 1916*, 15–16.

12. Turpin, 47, and *Annual Reports of the Secretary of War: United States War Department, 1918, Vol. I* (Washington, D.C.: Government Printing Office, 1918), 183.

13. Hallas, 197, and O'Ryan, 109, 954.

14. Letter: Ruth Rankin Leaper to Pamela A. Bakker, April 1, 2013.

15. Clarke, 25.

16. *Wadsworth Gas Attack and the Rio Grande Rattler*, January 19, 1918.

17. Turpin, 3–4, 57.

18. Brooklyn Auxiliary of the 105th Field Artillery, 23.

19. O'Ryan, 125.

20. http://www.firstworldwar.com/weaponry/grenades.htm//.

21. O'Ryan, 131.

22. Clarke, 67–68.

23. O'Ryan, 553–554.

24. Brooklyn Auxiliary of the 105th Field Artillery, 20.

25. *Wadsworth Gas Attack and Rio Grande Rattler*, November 23, 1917, 6, 12.

26. Ibid.

27. John H. Eggers, *The 27th Division: The Story of Its Sacrifices and Achievements* (New York: John H. Eggers, 1919), 5.

28. http://www.schistory.net/campwadsworth/Chapter5.html//.

29. Turpin, 6.

30. Brooklyn Auxiliary of the 105th Field Artillery, 20; http://www.schistory.net/campwadsworth/chapter6.html//; and Turpin, 6.

31. O'Ryan, 598–601.

32. Brooklyn Auxiliary of the 105th Field Artillery, 20.

33. O'Ryan, 71–72.

34. O'Ryan, 93, and Clarke, 18.

35. O'Ryan, 94.

36. *Wadsworth Gas Attack and Rio Grande Rattler*, November 27, 1917, 3–4.

37. Turpin, 32–37.

38. Brooklyn Auxiliary of the 105th Field Artillery, 22, and Hallas, 56.

Chapter Four

1. *The Wadsworth Gas Attack and the Rio Grande Rattler*, February 2, 1918, 3.

2. Ibid., February 9, 1918, 6.

3. http://www.worldwar1.com/dbc/overseasc.htm//.

4. *The Wadsworth Gas Attack and the Rio Grande Rattler*, April 13, 1918, 16.

5. Edward Coffman, *The War to End All Wars: The American Military Experience in World War I* (Lexington: University Press of Kentucky, 1998), 81, and *The Wadsworth Gas Attack and The Rio Grande Rattler*, January 12, 1918, 6.

6. *The Wadsworth Gas Attack and the Rio Grande Rattler*, March 2, 1918, 34.

7. Ibid., April 6, 1918, 8, and John F. O'Ryan, *The Story of the 27th Division, Vol. II* (New York: Wynkoop, Hallenbeck, Crawford, 1921), 411.

8. *The Wadsworth Gas Attack and the Rio Grande Rattler,* January 9, 1918, 29–30.
9. Ibid., January 26, 1918, 18.
10. Edward G. Lengel, *To Conquer Hell: The Meuse-Argonne, 1918, the Epic Battle That Ended the First World War* (New York: Henry Holt, 2008), 36.
11. O'Ryan, 152–3.
12. Susan Turpin, Carolyn Creal, Ron Crawley, James Crocker, eds., *When the Soldiers Came to Town: Spartanburg's Camp Wadsworth (1917–19) & Camp Croft (1941–45)* (Spartanburg, SC: Spartanburg County Historical Association, 2004), 8.
13. O'Ryan, 147.
14. Ibid., 148.
15. John H. Eggers, *The 27th Division: The Story of Its Sacrifices and Achievements* (New York: John H. Eggers, 1919), 28; Mitchell A. Yockelson, *Borrowed Soldiers: Americans Under British Command, 1918* (Norman: University of Oklahoma Press, 1962) also follows the 27th and 30th Divisions serving under British command, and lists their training locations.
16. William F. Clarke, *Over There with O'Ryan's Roughnecks: Reminiscences of a Private 1st Class Who Served in the 27th U.S. Division with the British Forces in Belgium and France* (Seattle: Superior, 1968), 32.
17. Rankin to Smathews, May 5, 1918. This may have been a motorcycle manufactured by the Indian Motorcycle Manufacturing Company.
18. O'Ryan, 601.
19. Brooklyn Auxiliary of the 105th Field Artillery, *A.E.F., A Brief History of the Activities of the 105th Field Artillery, American Expeditionary Forces: On Active Service in France, 1918–1919* (New York, 1919), 24.
20. Major Albert S. Bowen, M.C., *The Medical Department of the United States Army in the World War: Activities Concerning Mobilization Camps and Ports of Embarkation, Vol. IV* (Washington, D.C.: United States Government Printing Office, 1928), 359–360.
21. Ibid., 361–362.

Chapter Five

1. William F. Clarke, *Over There with O'Ryan's Roughnecks: Reminiscences of a Private 1st Class Who Served in the 27th U.S. Division with the British Forces in Belgium and France* (Seattle: Superior, 1968), 20.
2. John F. O'Ryan, *The Story of the 27th Division I* (New York: Wynkoop, Hallenbeck, Crawford, 1921), 630.
3. James H. Hallas, ed., *Doughboy War: The American Expeditionary Force in WWI* (Mechanicsburg, PA: Stackpole, 2000), 33, 51–52.
4. http://www.history.navy.mil/photos/usnshtp/ap/w1ap-t12//.
5. Dudley Hess, *"Going Thru" with a Golden Spoon; an Illustrated Story of the 52nd Brigade Field Artillery, American Expeditionary Forces* (New York: Hess Brothers, 1923), 3, and Clarke, 28.
6. Letter: Andrew Rankin to Smathews, July 1918.
7. Clarke, 31, and Edward D. Sirois, *Smashing Through the "World War" with Fighting Battery C, 102nd F.A., "Yankee Division" 1917–1918–1919* (Salem, MA: Meek, 1919), 23.
8. O'Ryan, 639.
9. John H. Eggers, *The 27th Division: The Story of Its Sacrifices and Achievements* (New York: John H. Eggers, 1919), 6–8, 13.
10. http://www.oryansroughnecks.org/engagements.html//.
11. O'Ryan, 655, and Arthur Lloyd Fletcher, *History of the 113th Field Artillery, 30th Division* (Raleigh: The History Committee of the 113th Field Artillery, 1920), 52.
12. Eggers, 9.
13. O'Ryan, 133, and Hallas, 215–216.
14. Robert Lowry Moorhead, *The Story of the 139th Field Artillery, American Expeditionary Forces* (Indianapolis: Bobbs-Merrill, 1920), 60.
15. Hallas, 49.
16. Lt. C.J. Hansen, *Regimental History 342nd Field Artillery, 89th Division,* 6–7. This was a document on World War I, submitted March 9, 1919, and posted on http:www.//garybhansen.com/pdfs/mil/342nd.pdf//.
17. James M. Howard, *History of the 304th Field Artillery in the World War* (New York: James M. Howard, 1920), 56–57, and Hess, 15, 17.
18. *Being a Narrative of "Battery A of the 101st Field Artillery"* (Boston: Loomis, 1919), 37, and Hess, 15, 17.
19. Brooklyn Auxiliary of the 105th Field Artillery, *A Brief History of the Activities of the 105th Field Artillery, American Expeditionary Forces: On Active Service in France, 1918–1919*

(New York: Brooklyn Auxiliary of the 105th Field Artillery, A.E.F., 1919), 24.
20. Howard, 60–64.
21. Hallas, 180–182.
22. Fred McKenna, ed., *Battery A, 103rd Field Artillery in France* (Providence, RI: Livermore and Knight, 1919), 144–146.
23. John Norris, *Artillery: A History* (Gloucestershire: Sutton, 2000), 172.
24. Lengel, 75.
25. Sirois, 17.
26. Letters: Rankin to Smathews, November 12, 1918, and July 1918.
27. Sirois, 37.
28. *Being a Narrative of "Battery A of the 101st Field Artillery*," 43.
29. McKenna, 133.
30. *The Stars and Stripes* (Paris) 2, no. 10, April 11, 1919, 3.
31. C. Deems, Jr., R.S. Pratt and N.B. Behkopt, "Forms of Artillery Fire Support," *The Field Artillery Journal* XIII, no. 1 (January–February 1923): 74–80.
32. Norris, 173–174; C. Deems, 79; and Sirois, 67¬–68.
33. *Being a Narrative of "Battery A of the 101st Field Artillery*," 60.
34. Ibid., 43–44.
35. Maurise F. DeBarneville, "The Remount Service in the A.E.F.," *The Cavalry Journal* XXX, no. 123 (April 1921), and Thomas Irving Crowell, ed., *A History of the 313th Field Artillery, U.S.A* (New York: Thomas I. Crowell, 1920), 33.
36. McKenna, 108.
37. Sirois, 44, and McKenna, 109.
38. O'Ryan, 660.
39. Ibid., 661–663.
40. Brooklyn Auxiliary, 24, and O'Ryan, 444.

Chapter Six

1. John J. Pershing, *Final Report of Gen. John J. Pershing* (Washington, D.C.: Government Printing Office, 1919), 38–43.
2. Edward Coffman, *The War to End all Wars: The American Military Experience in World War I* (Lexington: University Press of Kentucky, 1998), 273, and Edward G. Lengel, *To Conquer Hell: The Meuse-Argonne, 1918, The Epic Battle That Ended the First World War* (New York: Henry Holt, 2008), 50.

3. Max Roesler, *The Iron-Ore Resources of Europe: United States Geological Survey Bulletin 706* (Washington, D.C.: Government Printing Office, 1921), 16–56.
4. John F. O'Ryan, *The Story of the 27th Division, Vol. II* (New York: Wynkoop, Hallenbeck, Crawford, 1921), 25.
5. James H. Hallas, ed., *Doughboy War: The American Expeditionary Force in WWI* (Mechanicsburg, PA: Stackpole, 2000), 293–295.
6. Ibid., 444–5.
7. Ibid.
8. Thomas Irving Crowell, ed., *A History of the 313th Field Artillery, U.S.A.* (New York: Thomas I. Crowell, 1920), 19, 20, 104. The 313th served the 80th Division in this sector.
9. O'Ryan, 458.
10. Charles Lynch, Joseph H. Ford, and Frank W. Weed, *The Medical Department of the United States Army in the World War, Volume VIII, Field Operations* (Washington, D.C.: Government Printing Office, 1925), 614–723.
11. Le Claire is masculine in French, however, when referring to the farm at the town, La Claire Ferme, the article changes to the feminine "La" to accompany the gender of the word farm.
12. The reference to "D" shells in the field journals most likely referred to high explosive shells with the longest delay fuse possible. Shells were also marked with "75 DE C" which stood for the "75 mm canone de campagne [field] gun."
13. Frederick Louis Huidekoper, *The History of the 33rd Division, A.E.F., Vol. III* (Springfield: Illinois Historical Library, 1921), 22; O'Ryan, 446, 449; and Brooklyn Auxiliary of the 105th Field Artillery, *A.E.F., A Brief History of the Activities of the 105th Field Artillery, American Expeditionary Forces: On Active Service in France, 1918–1919* (New York, 1919), 26.
14. Ashby Williams, *Experiences of the Great War: Artois, St. Mihiel, Meuse-Argonne*, 2012 ed. (Roanoke: Stone, 1919), 81.
15. Brooklyn Auxiliary, 26, 29.
16. O'Ryan, 912, 915, 920.
17. Crowell, 28.

Chapter Seven

1. Edward G. Lengel, *To Conquer Hell: The Meuse-Argonne, 1918, the Epic Battle That*

Ended the First World War (New York: Henry Holt, 2008), 4.
2. Ibid., 60.
3. Ibid., 420.
4. Center of Military History United States Army, *United States Army in the World War, 1917–1919: Organization of the American Expeditionary Forces, Vol. 1* (Washington, D.C.: Center of Military History United States Army, 1988), xix.
5. Brooklyn Auxiliary of the 105th Field Artillery, *A.E.F., A Brief History of the Activities of the 105th Field Artillery, American Expeditionary Forces: On Active Service in France, 1918–1919* (New York, 1919), 28.
6. Ibid.
7. Michelin & Cie, *The Americans in the Great War, Vol. III, Meuse-Argonne Battle (Montfaucon, Romagne, St. Menehould)* (Milltown, NJ: Michelin Tire Company, 1920), 9. This was part of the pictorial Michelin Illustrated Guides to the Battlefields dated from 1914 to 1918.
8. John F. O'Ryan, *The Story of the 27th Division, Vol. II* (New York: Wynkoop, Hallenbeck, Crawford, 1921), 458.
9. Frederick Louis Huidekoper, *The History of the 33rd Division, A.E.F.* (Springfield: Illinois State Historical Library, 1921), 61–62.
10. O'Ryan, 458. The field diaries of the 52nd Field Artillery Brigade, found at the end of volume I of O'Ryan's book on pages 450–481, and the diaries of the individual regiments that followed are used as the outline for this chapter and the next. They contain field orders and reports on specific forms of fire and locations. They have been fleshed out to help the reader feel the process of the battle using material included in the citations given to men for heroic acts under pressure. Material from the divisional reports of the 33rd and Seventy-Ninth Divisions is added as well as those of the 4th and 29th Divisions who were assisted by the brigade during the offensive.
11. Ashby Williams, *Experiences of the Great War: Artois, St. Mihiel, Meuse-Argonne.* 2012 ed. (Roanoke: Stone, 1919), 72. Williams was commander of the 320th Infantry of the 80th Division which served next to the 33rd Division at this point.
12. O'Ryan, 989.
13. Ibid., 954.
14. Ibid., 458.
15. Huidekoper, 58.
16. Thomas Irving Crowell, ed., *A History of the 313th Field Artillery, U.S.A* (New York: Thomas I. Crowell, 1920), 28. The 313th served the 80th Division.
17. Captain Arthur E. Hartzell, *Confidential Meuse-Argonne Battle (Sept. 26–November 11, 1918): For the Use of American Officers Studying the Battle Fields* (General Printing Plant Q.M.C., J8-9-23-19-2m, March 24, 1919), available online at http://www.archive.org/stream/meuseargonnebatt00hartrich/meuaseargonnebatt00hartrich_djvu.txt//.
18. O'Ryan, 450–470. The field diary of the 80th Division listed the weather.
19. Ibid., 447, 458, 459.
20. Ibid., 472.
21. Ibid., 458.
22. Ibid., 448–449.
23. American Battle Monuments Commission, *33rd Division, Summary of Operations in the World War* (Washington, D.C.: United States Government Printing Office, 1944), 26.
24. O'Ryan, 459.
25. Huidekoper, 62.
26. Brooklyn Auxiliary, 29.
27. Edward Coffman, *The War to End All Wars: The American Military Experience in World War I* (Lexington: University Press of Kentucky, 1998), 306–307.
28. O'Ryan, 459.
29. Ibid., 448–9.
30. Ibid., 449.
31. *Annual Report of the Adjutant General of the State of New York: 1919* (Albany: J.B. Lyon, 1920), 26.
32. O'Ryan, 449.
33. Brooklyn Auxiliary, 30.
34. O'Ryan, 459.
35. Ibid., 942.
36. Coffman, 314.
37. The German 7th Reserve Division orders for October 1, 1918, instructed their artillery to destroy the 33rd Division's artillery moving in the area and to use gas whenever possible. See Rexmond C. Cochrane, *The 33rd Division Along the Meuse October 1918: Gas Warfare in World War I, Study Number 8* (Washington, D.C.: U.S. Army Chemical Corps Historical Studies, July 1958), 22, 37.
38. Cochrane, 24.
39. O'Ryan, 465.
40. Ibid., 450.
41. O'Ryan, 449–450.
42. Ibid., 466.
43. Ibid.
44. Lengel, 148.

45. O'Ryan, 969, 985, 1024, 1026, 1056.
46. Ibid., 1030.
47. James H. Hallas, ed., *Doughboy War: The American Expeditionary Force in WWI* (Mechanicsburg, PA: Stackpole, 2000), 266–269.
48. Fred McKenna, ed., *Battery A, 103rd Field Artillery in France* (Providence, RI: Livermore and Knight, 1919), 64, 106.
49. Ibid., p. 243.
50. Edward D. Sirois, *Smashing Through the "World War" with Fighting Battery C, 102nd F.A., "Yankee Division" 1917-1918-1919* (Salem, MA: Meek, 1919), 47–49.
51. O'Ryan, 450.
52. Huidekoper, 88–89.
53. O'Ryan, 971, 1017.
54. Ibid., 450.
55. Coffman, 341.
56. O'Ryan, 452.
57. Hallas, 242.
58. Ibid., 66–67.
59. William F. Clarke, *Over There with O'Ryan's Roughnecks: Reminiscences of a Private 1st Class Who Served in the 27th U.S. Division with the British Forces in Belgium and France* (Seattle: Superior, 1968), 74.
60. O'Ryan, 452.
61. Ibid., 466.
62. Ibid., 955.
63. Ibid., 1005.
64. Ibid., 955.
65. Ibid., 452.
66. Ibid., 1047.
67. Letter: Andrew Rankin to Annie Rankin, October 3, 1918. Ashby Williams of the 320th Infantry, 80th Division mentioned the same attack on an Allied balloon as happening about Sept. 30, 1918. He added that the German pilot used a machine gun with incendiary bullets. Ashby Williams, 91.
68. Lengel, 192.
69. Ibid., 452–454.
70. Huidekoper, 95–96.
71. Cochrane, 28.
72. O'Ryan, 454.
73. Ibid., 454, 461.

Chapter Eight

1. American Battle Monuments Commission. *33rd Division, Summary of Operations in the World War* (Washington, D.C.: United States Government Printing Office, 1944), 33.
2. Frederick Louis Huidekoper, *The History of the 33rd Division, A.E.F.* (Springfield: Illinois State Historical Library, 1921), 100.
3. John F. O'Ryan. *The Story of the 27th Division, Vol. II* (New York: Wynkoop, Hallenbeck, Crawford, 1921), 468, 475.
4. Ibid., 461.
5. Ibid., 455.
6. Ibid.
7. Ibid., 961, 988, 1017.
8. Ibid., 937, 976, 987, 998. Leland M. Carver, Gustaf A. Lindstrom, and A.T. Foster, *The Ninetieth Aero Squadron, American Expeditionary Forces* (Hinsdale, IL: E. Harold Greist, 1920), 46, mentions rain and hail on October 8, 1918, in this sector.
9. Rexmond C. Cochrane, *The 33rd Division Along the Meuse, October 1918: Gas Warfare in World War I, Study Number 8* (Washington, D.C.: U.S. Army Chemical Corps Historical Office, July 1958), 52.
10. O'Ryan, 468.
11. Ibid., 461.
12. Ibid., 462.
13. Robert H. Ferrell, ed., *A Soldier in World War I: The Diary of Elmer W. Sherwood* (Indianapolis: Indiana Historical Society Press, 2004), 94.
14. Brooklyn Auxiliary of the 105th Field Artillery, *A.E.F., A Brief History of the Activities of the 105th Field Artillery, American Expeditionary Forces: On Active Service in France, 1918-1919* (New York, 1919), 32, O'Ryan, 499.
15. O'Ryan, 932.
16. Huidekoper, 126, 128.
17. O'Ryan, 963.
18. Leland M. Carver, Gustaf A. Lindstrom, and A.T. Foster, *The Ninetieth Aero Squadron, American Expeditionary Forces* (Hinsdale, IL: E. Harold Greist, 1920), 46.
19. Ibid., 1057.
20. Edward Coffman, *The War to End All Wars: The American Military Experience in World War I* (Lexington: University Press of Kentucky, 1998), 337.
21. James H. Hallas, ed., *Doughboy War: The American Expeditionary Force in WWI* (Mechanicsburg, PA: Stackpole, 2000), 277.
22. O'Ryan, 972, 1011.
23. Ibid., 462.
24. Huidekoper, 150.
25. O'Ryan, 974.
26. Ibid., 455, 481.
27. Ibid., 938, 1017, 1019, 1021, 1054, 1056.
28. Brooklyn Auxiliary, 42.

29. Letter to the 52nd Field Artillery Brigade Commander from Maj.-General George Bell, Jr., as recorded in O'Ryan, 485.
30. O'Ryan, 455.
31. Seventy-Ninth Division Association History Committee, *History of the Seventy-Ninth Division, A.E.F. During the World War: 1917–1919* (Lancaster, Pennsylvania: Steinman & Steinman, 1922), 197.
32. Brooklyn Auxiliary, 37 and 38; and O'Ryan, 478.
33. O'Ryan, 478–479.
34. Ibid., 462, 939.
35. Ibid., 463, 469, and Brooklyn Auxiliary, 38.
36. Ibid., 1028.
37. Ibid.
38. Ibid., 469, and Edward G. Lengel, *To Conquer Hell: The Meuse-Argonne, 1918, The Epic Battle That Ended the First World War* (New York: Henry Holt, 2008), 384.
39. Ferrell, 87.
40. O'Ryan, 455.
41. Ibid., 930.
42. Carver, Lindstrom, and Foster, 49.
43. O'Ryan, 463, 479.
44. Ibid., 463, 479.
45. Ibid., 988, 1029, 1034, 1043, 1049, 1050, 1060, 1061.
46. Seventy-Ninth Division Association, 223, and O'Ryan, 479.
47. O'Ryan, 470, 471.
48. Ibid., 1058.
49. Ibid., 463.
50. Ibid., 944, 981, 988, 994, 1011, 1012, 1017, 1062.
51. Ibid., 480, and Seventy-Ninth Division Association, 251.
52. Ibid., 471.
53. Ibid., 456, 480.
54. Ibid., 471.
55. Ibid., 290, 465.
56. Ibid., 465.
57. Seventy-Ninth Division Association, 300.
58. O'Ryan, 471.
59. Brooklyn Auxiliary, 39.
60. Ibid., 40.
61. O'Ryan, 456, and Brooklyn Auxiliary, 42.
62. O'Ryan, 456.
63. Seventy-Ninth Division Association, 318.
64. Letter to the 52nd Field Artillery Brigade from Brig.-General W. J. Nicholson, Commanding General of the 157th Infantry Brigade of the Seventy-Ninth Division, recorded in O'Ryan, 486.
65. O'Ryan, 930, and Brooklyn Auxiliary, 42.
66. O'Ryan, 484, and Lengel, 419.
67. Brooklyn Auxiliary, 42; and Seventy-Ninth Division Association, 331–332.
68. Seventy-Ninth Division Association, 328.
69. Brooklyn Auxiliary, 43; and Seventy-Ninth Division Association, 333.
70. Ibid., 44.
71. O'Ryan, 411.
72. Maj.-General Edward F. McGlachlin, "Results of Artillery Action in the Meuse Argonne Offensive," *The Field Artillery Journal* XIII, no. 1 (January–February 1923).

Chapter Nine

1. *Annual Report of the Adjutant General of the State of New York: 1919* (Albany: J.B. Lyon, 1920), 3.
2. Alexander Swanston and Malcolm Swanston, *Historical Atlas of World War II* (New York: Chartwell, 2011), 12.
3. *The New York National Guardsman*, May 1924, 31.
4. William F. Clark, *Over There with O'Ryan's Roughnecks: Reminiscences of a Private 1st Class Who Served in the 27th U.S. Division with the British Forces in Belgium and France* (Seattle: Superior, 1968), 126.
5. John H. Eggers, *The 27th Division: The Story of Its Sacrifices and Achievements* (New York: John H. Eggers, 1919), 29–30.
6. *Annual Report of the Adjutant General: 1919*, 28–29.
7. John F. O'Ryan, *The Story of the 27th Division, Vol. II* (New York: Wynkoop, Hallenbeck, Crawford, 1921), 426.
8. Dudley Hess, *"Going Thru" with a Golden Spoon; an Illustrated Story of the 52nd Brigade Field Artillery, American Expeditionary Forces* (New York: Hess Brothers, 1923; Nabu Public Domain Reprints, 2013 ed.), i. Hess did not include page numbers. This was the dedication page which might be called page i.
9. O'Ryan, 431.
10. *Annual Report of the Adjutant General: 1919*, 152–161.
11. Ibid., 20–21.
12. Mitchell Yockelson, "The United States Armed Forces and the Mexican Punitive Ex-

pedition: Part 1," *Prologue Magazine* 20, no. 3 (Fall 1997).
13. *Annual Report of the Adjutant General of the State of New York: 1921* (Albany: J. B. Lyon, 1926), 47.
14. *The New York National Guardsman*, May 1924, 31.
15. Ibid., January 1925, 6.
16. Ibid., August 1924, 6.
17. Ibid., February 1929, 2.
18. Ibid., 6.
19. *Annual Report of the Adjutant General of the State of New York: 1923* (Albany: J.B. Lyon, 1926), 17–18.
20. http://www.88ny.net/2-104.htm.

Appendix I: Deaths

1. *Annual Report of the Adjutant General of the State of New York: 1916* (Albany: J.B. Lyon, 1917), 107.

Appendix II: Awards and Citations

1. The complete list of divisional citations is in John F. O'Ryan, *The Story of the 27th Division, Vol. II* (New York: Wynkoop, Hallenbeck, Crawford, 1921), 930–1063. Maj.-General John F. O'Ryan, commander of the 27th Division, earned the Distinguished Service Medal; British decoration of the Knights Commander of the Order of St. Michael and St. George; French decorations of the French Legion D'Honneur and the French Croix de Guerre with Palm; and Belgian decoration of the Order of Leopold and the Belgian Croix de Guerre with Palm. Brig.-General George Albert Wingate, commander of the 52nd Field Artillery Brigade earned a Distinguished Service Medal, and two Divisional Citations. These citations focus on the 104th Field Artillery Regiment and were extrapolated from the larger list. Addresses, where mentioned, were deleted. A soldier obtaining multiple citations has them designated by numbers under his name. The citations were made uniform. French accent marks on a particular village were kept consistent in all, and the country of France was added to a few citations to match the pattern of most.
2. It is the town of Le Claire, France but the La Claire Ferme. A farm is feminine in French and the article is changed to reflect that

Bibliography

American Battle Monuments Commission. *27th Division, Summary of Operations in the World War.* Washington, D.C.: Government Printing Office, 1944.

American Battle Monuments Commission. *29th Division: Summary of Operations in the World War.* Washington D.C: Government Printing Office, 1944.

American Battle Monuments Commission. *33rd Division, Summary of Operations in the World War.* Washington, D.C.: Government Printing Office, 1944.

American Battle Monuments Commission. *79th Division, Summary of Operations in the World War.* Washington, D.C.: Government Printing Office, 1944.

Annual Report of the Adjutant General of the State of New York: 1868, 1869, and 1870. Albany: Argus. 1916, 1917, 1919, 1921, and 1926. J.B. Lyon.

Annual Reports of the Secretary of War: United States War Department, 1918, Vol. I. Washington, D.C.: Government Printing Office, 1918.

Bagnall, G.P. *Brooklyn Guardsman, 1903: An Authentic and Authorized Register and Record of the Local Land and Naval Forces of the State of New York.* Brooklyn: New York National Guard, 1903.

Bakker, Pamela A. *Eyes on the Sporting Scene, 1870–1930: Will and June Rankin, New York's Sportswriting Brothers.* Jefferson, NC: McFarland, 2013.

Being a Narrative of "Battery A of the 101st Field Artillery." Boston: Loomis, 1919.

Brooklyn Auxiliary of the 105th Field Artillery. *A.E.F., A Brief History of the Activities of the 105th Field Artillery, American Expeditionary Forces: On Active Service in France, 1918–1919.* New York, 1919.

Burdick, Henry Hagaman, ed. *New York Division, National Guard, War Record 1916 by the Officers and Men of the Division.* New York: Burdick and King, 1917.

Carver, Leland M., Gustaf A. Lindstrom, and A.T. Foster. *The Ninetieth Aero Squadron, American Expeditionary Forces.* Hinsdale, IL: E. Harold Greist, 1920.

Center of Military History United States Army. *Order of Battle of the United States Land Forces in the World War, American Expeditionary Forces: Divisions, Volume 2.* Washington, D.C.: Center of Military History United States Army, 1988.

Center of Military History United States Army. *United States Army in the World War, 1917–1919: Organization of the American Expeditionary Forces, Volume 1.* Washington, D.C.: Center of Military History United States Army, 1988.

Clark, George B. *The American Expeditionary Forces in World War I: A Statistical History.* Jefferson, NC: McFarland, 2013.

Clarke, William F. *Over There with O'Ryan's Roughnecks: Reminiscences of a Private First Class Who Served in the 27th U.S. Division with the British Forces in Belgium and France.* Seattle: Superior, 1968.

Cochrane, Rexmond C. *The 33rd Division Along the Meuse October 1918: Gas Warfare in World War I, Study Number 8.* Washington, D.C.: U.S. Army Chemical Corps Historical Studies, July 1958.

Coffman, Edward. *The War to End all Wars: The American Military Experience in World War I*. Lexington: University Press of Kentucky, 1998.

Crowell, Thomas Irving, ed. *A History of the 313th Field Artillery, U.S.A*. New York: Thomas I. Crowell, 1920.

Eggers, John H. *The 27th Division: The Story of its Sacrifices and Achievements*. New York: John H. Eggers, 1919.

Ferguson, Rebecca. *The Handy History Answer Book*. Detroit: Visible Ink, 2006.

Ferrell, Robert H., ed. *A Soldier in World War I: The Diary of Elmer W. Sherwood*. Indianapolis: Indiana Historical Society Press, 2004.

Fletcher, Arthur Lloyd. *History of the 113th Field Artillery, 30th Division*. Raleigh: The History Committee of the 113th Field Artillery, 1920.

Grinder, R. Dale, ed. *The World War I Survey: Papers Compiled from the United States Army Military History Institute Collection, Carlisle Barracks*. Frederick, MD, n.d.

Gruber, E.L. *Notes on the 3 Inch Gun Material and Field Artillery Equipment*. The Reserve Officer's Training Corps of Yale University, 1918.

Hallas, James H., ed. *Doughboy War: The American Expeditionary Force in WWI*. Mechanicsburg, PA: Stackpole, 2000.

Handbook of the 4.7-inch gun Materiel, Model of 1906, With Instructions for its Care. Washington, D.C.: Government Printing Office, 1917.

Hansen, C.J. *Regimental History 342nd Field Artillery, 89th Division*. (March 9, 1919). http:www.//garybhansenwww/pdfs/mil/342nd.pdf//.

Hartzell, Arthur E. *Confidential Meuse-Argonne Battle (September 26–November 11, 1918), for the Use of American Officers Studying the Battle Fields*. General Printing Plant Q.M.C., J8-9-23-19-2m, March 24, 1919.

Hess, Dudley. *"Going Thru" with a Golden Spoon; an Illustrated Story of the 52nd Brigade Field Artillery, American Expeditionary Forces*. New York: Hess Brothers, 1923.

Howard, James M. *History of the 304th Field Artillery in the World War*. New York: James M. Howard, 1920.

Huidekoper, Frederick Louis. *The History of the 33rd Division, A.E.F., Vol. III*. Springfield: Illinois State Historical Library, 1921.

Hurst, James W. *Pancho Villa and Black Jack Pershing: The Punitive Expedition in Mexico*. Westport, CT: Praeger, 2008.

Jacks, Leo Vincent. *Service Record: By an Artillery Man*. New York: Scribner's, 1928.

Lengel, Edward G. *To Conquer Hell: The Meuse-Argonne, 1918, The Epic Battle That Ended the First World War*. New York: Henry Holt, 2008.

Lynch, Charles, Joseph H. Ford, and Frank W. Weed. *The Medical Department of the United States Army in the World War, Volume VIII, Field Operations*. Washington, D.C.: Government Printing Office, 1925.

McKenna, Fred, ed. *Battery A, 103rd Field Artillery in France*. Providence, RI: Livermore and Knight, 1919.

Michelin & Cie. *The Americans in the Great War, Vol. III, Meuse-Argonne Battle (Montfaucon, Romagne, St. Menehould)*. Milltown, NJ: Michelin Tire Company, 1920.

Moorhead, Robert Lowry. *The Story of the 139th Field Artillery, American Expeditionary Forces*. Indianapolis: Bobbs-Merrill, 1920.

Norris, John. *Artillery: A History*. Gloucestershire, England: Sutton, 2000.

O'Ryan, John F. *The Story of the 27th Division, Vol. I and II*. New York: Wynkoop, Hallenbeck, Crawford, 1921.

Pershing, John J. *Final Report of Gen. John J. Pershing*. Washington, D.C.: Government Printing Office, 1919.

Phisterer, Frederick. *New York in the War of the Rebellion, 1861 to 1865*, 3d ed. Albany: L.B. Lyon, 1912.

Roberts, James A. *New York in the Revolution as Colony and State*. Albany: Brandow, 1898.

Roesler, Max. *The Iron-Ore Resources of Europe: United States Geological Survey Bulletin 706*. Washington, D.C.: Government Printing Office, 1921.

Seventy-Ninth Division Association, History Committee. *History of the Seventy-

Ninth Division, A.E.F. During the World War: 1917–1919. Lancaster, PA: Steinman & Steinman, 1922.

Sirois, Edward D. *Smashing Through the "World War" with Fighting Battery C, 102nd F.A. "Yankee Division," 1917–1918–1919.* Salem, MA: Meek, 1919.

Spodek, Howard. *The World's History.* New York: Prentice Hall, 2010.

Steward, Richard W., ed. *American Military History, Vol. I: The United States Army and the Forging of a Nation, 1775–1917.* Washington, D.C: Center of Military History, 2005.

Swanston, Alexander and Malcolm Swanston. *Historical Atlas of World War II.* New York: Chartwell, 2011.

Thomas, Robert S. and Inez V. Allen. *The Mexican Punitive Expedition Under Brigadier General John J. Pershing, United States Army, 1916–1917.* Washington, D.C.: War Histories Division, Office of the Chief of Military History, Department of the Army, 1954.

Turpin, Susan, Carolyn Creal, Ron Crawley, and James Crocker, eds. *When the Soldiers Came to Town: Spartanburg's Camp Wadsworth (1917–19) & Camp Croft (1941–45).* Spartanburg, SC: County Historical Association, 2004.

Verlag, Chronik, ed. *The Chronicle of World History.* Old Saybrook, CT: Konecky and Konecky, 2008.

Wendell, C. *Third Annual Report of Military Statistics of the State of New York.* Albany: The Bureau, 1866.

Williams, Ashby. *Experiences of the Great War: Artois, St. Mihiel, Meuse-Argonne.* 2012 ed. Roanoke: Stone, 1919.

Yockelson, Mitchell, A. *Borrowed Soldiers: Americans under British Command, 1918.* Norman: University of Oklahoma Press, 1962.

Letters

Bell, Maj.-General George, Jr., Commander of the 33rd Division, to 52nd Field Artillery Brigade Commander. 1918.

Kenney, Charles H., to Rankin, Andrew. September 9, 1916.

Leaper, Ruth Rankin, to Bakker, Pamela A. August 29, 2012, April 1, 2013.

Nicholson, Brig.-Gen. W. J., Commanding General of the 157th Infantry Brigade of the 79th Division, to the 52nd Field Artillery Brigade. 1918.

Rankin, Andrew, to Davenport, Mr. August 12, 1916.

Rankin, Andrew, to Rankin, Annie. October 3, 1918.

Rankin, Andrew, to Smathews. May 5, 1918, July 1918.

Unpublished Documents

Congdon, Herbert W. *Mexican Border*, Chapter XXXIV. http://dmna.ny.gov/historic/reghist/mexBorder/mexBorder_history_Congdon.htm//.

Hansen, C.J. *Regimental History 342nd Field Artillery, 89th Division.* March 9, 1919. http://www.garybhansen.com/pdfs/mil/342nd.pdf//.

Leaper, Ruth Rankin. *Snippets* (unpublished family history). Eatontown, NJ, 1999.

Journals and Newspapers

"Capital's Leaders Will March Today; New York's Drafted Men will Parade." *New York Times*, September 4, 1917.

DeBarneville, Maurise F. "The Remount Service in the A.E.F." *The Cavalry Journal* XXX, no. 123 (April 1921).

Deems, C., Jr., R.S. Pratt and N.B. Behkopt. "Forms of Artillery Fire Support." *The Field Artillery Journal* XIII, no. 1 (January–February 1923): 74–80.

"Major General William S. McNair." *Field Artillery Journal* XXII, no. 6 (November–December 1932): 575.

McGlachlin, Edward F. "Results of Artillery Action in the Meuse Argonne Offensive." *The Field Artillery Journal* XIII, no. 1 (January–February 1923): 11–17.

The New York National Guardsman, May and August 1924; January 1925; December 1934; and April 1939.

"Plans for Review of 27th Division Made." *The Cornell Daily Sun*, March 12, 1919.

Rankin, Andrew, B. Jr. "A Soldier's Life on the Border." *The Owl*, October 5, 1916, 6–8.

Rio Grande Rattler (New York National Guard, Hidalgo County, Texas), August 23, 1916; October 4, 11, and 18, 1917; November 23, 27, and 29, 1917; and December 6, 1917.

The Stars and Stripes (Paris, France) 2, no. 10, April 11, 1919, 3.

Wadsworth Gas Attack and the Rio Grande Rattler, or *Gas Attack*, January 9, 12, 19, and 26, 1918; February 2 and 9, 1918; March 2, 1918; and April 6 and 13, 1918.

Yockelson, Mitchell. "The United States Armed Forces and the Mexican Punitive Expedition: Part 1." *Prologue Magazine* 29, no. 3 (Fall 1997).

Encyclopedias

"World War I." *New American Encyclopedia*. Vol. 15 (Philadelphia: Publishers Agency, 1972). pp. 5597–5610.

Websites

"American Hand Grenades of W.W.I." *Inert-Ordinances*. http://www.inert-ord.net/usa03a/usa1//.

"Battles & Engagements of the 27th Division." *The 107th New York Infantry in the Great War*. http://www.oryansroughnecks.org/engagements.html//.

Bond, Jim. "Little Tanks: The Development of the American Field Shoe [Boot] During the World War." *Doughboy Center*. http://www.worldwar1.com/dbc/1_tanks.htm//.

Bowen, Albert S. "The Medical Department of the United States Army in the World War, Volume IV: Activities Concerning Mobilization Camps and Ports of Embarkation." *U.S. Army Medical Department, Office of Medical History* (Washington D.C.: U.S. Government Printing Office, 1928). http://history.amedd.army.mil/booksdocs/ wwi/wwivoliv/ Chapter7.htm//.

Burdick, Henry Hagaman, ed. "New York Division, National Guard, War Record 1916 by the Officers and Men of the Division" (New York: Burdick and King, 1917. *Internet Archive*. http://www.archive.org/details/newyorkdivisionburd//.

Burdick, Henry Hagaman, ed. "New York Division, National Guard, War Record 1916 by the Officers and Men of the Division" *New York State Division of Military and Naval Affairs*. New York: Burdick and King, 1917. http://www.dmna.ny.gov/historic/mil-hist.htm//.

Congdon, Herbert W. *Mexican Border* (unpublished). *New York State Division of Military and Naval Affairs*. http://dmna.ny.gov/historic/reghist/mexBorder/mexBorder_ history_Congdon.htm//.

"The Evolution of Artillery." *11th Pennsylvania Regiment*. http://www.11thpa.org/documents/FA-History.pdf//.

"Field Artillery in the Civil War." *Civil War Artillery*. http://www.cwartillery.com/FA/FA.html//.

Glenn, David Allen. "A Reanalysis of the 1916, 1918, 1927, 1928 and 1935 Tropical Cyclones of the North Atlantic Basin: A Thesis Submitted to the Faculty of Mississippi State University Department of Geosciences." *Atlantic Oceanographic & Meteorological Laboratory-Hurricane Research* (Mississippi: Mississippi State University, August 2005). http://www.aoml.noaa.gov/hrd/hurdat/Glenn_Thesis.pdf//.

Gruber, Lieut.-Col. E.L. "Notes on the 3 Inch Gun Material and Field Artillery Equipment" (The Reserve Officer's Training Corps of Yale University, 1918). *Internet Archive*, http://www.archive.org/details/notesom 3inchgunM00grubrich//.

"Handbook of the 4.7-Inch Gun Matériel, Model of 1906: With Instructions for its Care" (Washington: Government Printing Office, 1917). *Internet Archive*. http://www. archive.org/details/handbookof47inch00unitrich//.

Hartzell, Arthur E. "Confidential Meuse-Argonne Battle (September 26–November 11, 1918), for the Use of American Officers Studying the Battle Fields" (General Printing Plant Q.M.C., J8-9-23-19-2m,

March 24, 1919). *Internet Archive.* http://www.archive.org/stream/meuseargonnebatt00hartrich/meuaseargonnebatt00hartrich_djvu.txt//.

"The Left Bank of the Meuse." *World War One Battlefields.* 2007. http://www.ww1battlefields.co.uk/verdun/leftbank.html//.

"The 1918 Overseas Cap." *Doughboy Center.* http://www.worldwar1.com/dbc/overseasc.htm//.

Nofi, Major Albert A. "History of the 104th DECON Battalion." *88 NY.net.* http://www.88ny.net/2-104.htm//.

Sears, Lou Ann. "A Short History of United States' Education 1900 to 2006." *History of Literacy.* http://www.historyliteracy.org/download/sears2.pdf//.

"Tent and Trench: A Web Site Dedicated to the Memory of Camp Wadsworth, Spartanburg, South Carolina." Chapters 5 and 6. *South Carolina History Net.* http://www.schistory.net/campwadsworth/Chapter5.html// and http://www.schistory.net/campwadsworth/chapter6.html//.

"Unit History Project, New York Units at the Mexican Border, 1916–1917: NY State Unit History Project." *New York State Division of Military and Naval Affairs.* http://www.dmna.ny.gov/historic/reghist/mexBorder/mexBorder_history_ORyan.htm//.

"Unit History Project, 12th Regiment: New York State Militia, New York National Guard, Civil War, Independence Guard." *New York State Division of Military and Naval Affairs.* http://dmna.ny.gov/historic/reghist/civil/infantry/12thNYSM/12thNYSMmain.htm//.

"Weapons of War-Grenades." *First World War.com.* http://www.Firstworldwar.com/weaponry/grenades.htm//.

"World War I Era Transports." *Department of the Navy, Naval Historical Center.* http://www.history.navy.mil/photos/usnshtp/ap/w1ap-t12//.

Index

Numbers in **_bold italics_** indicate pages with photographs.

Allies 12, 87, 158
America **_173–175_**
American Expeditionary Forces 65; American Army (1st) 108, 110, 118, 123, 129, 155, 158, 166; (2nd) 149; American I Corps 122, 137, 139, 144, 158; II Corps **_168_**; III Corps 122, 129, 137, 139, 141; IV Corps 89, 139, 158; V Corps 137; American Divisions (1st) 110; (4th) 110, 118, 122–123, 139; (8th) 113; (27th *see* New York National Guard); (29th) 110, 141, 147, 151, 152; (33rd) 107, 108–154; (35th) 122; (37th) 122; (42nd) 72–73, 110; (77th/"Lost Battalion")122, 137, 144; (79th) 116, 122, 123, 154–169; (80th) 118, 122–123, 129, 132, 139; (91st) 122; ethnicity 88
American Indian **_35_**, 36
American Smelting and Refining Company (La Cusi Mine, Mexico) 14
anti–Semitism 71
Antigone 89
Arambula, Maria Micaela 11
Arango, Agustin 11
Argonne Forest 118–122
Armistice **_164–174_**
artillery 6; ammunition 6, 7, **_39_**, 40, 102, 124, 132–133, 150, 159, 165–166; barrages 104–106
artillery field pieces: British Stoker Mortar 75, 76, 103, 104; 4.7-inch howitzer field piece (gun) **_55_**, 80; French 75-mm field gun (Canon de 75, 1897) 80, 99, 102–105, 124, 138, 165, 166; French 155-mm Schneider howitzer 80, 99, 103, 124, 166; German artillery 101–102; 3-inch field piece (gun) **_39_**, 40, **_52_**, 53; 3.67-inch Delafield Branded Iron Rifle (gun) 6, 7
Astor Place Riot (1849) 6
Austro-Hungarian Empire 12

Baker, Newton 15
Bandholtz, Harry H. 18, 82, 110
Bar-le-Duc 107
Battle of Verdun 108, 112–114, 123
Bell, Gearge, Jr. 110, 154
Berry, Charles W. 170
Black, Frank S. 7–8
booby traps 156, 163
boxing 49, **_50_**, 71
Briey Iron Basin 12, 109
British Expeditionary Forces 72, 74, 90, 91
Bullard, Major-General 120, 151

caisson 7, 40
Calamares 89, 93–95
Calder, William M. 87
Cameron, Douglas T. 110
Cameron, George H. 110, 120
camouflage 76, **_117_**, 118
camps: (France) St. Nazaire 95, 96; The School of Fire of Camp de Souge, Bordeaux 98–107; (New York) Citizen's Military Training 62; Mills 82; Montauk Point 179; Peekskill 8, 17, 22, 179, 180; Pine 8; Platsburg 62; Upton 176; Van Cortlandt 22–**_27_**, 73; Whitman 18, 22, **_23_**, **_27_**; (Pennsylvania) Tobyhanna Army Field Artillery School 12, 13, 179; (South Carolina) Wadsworth 60–84; (Texas) La Gloria Artillery and Rifle Range 40, 41, 52–

213

54; McAllen 30–59; (Virginia) Humphreys 89; Stuart 85–92
Carranza, Venustiano 10, 11, 14, 59, 178; Carranziatas 17
Central Powers 12, 87, 112, 122, 148, 158
Chaplin, Charlie 57–*59*
Clarke, William F. 135, 171, 172
Clémenceau, George 170
coastal artillery 10
Columbus, New Mexico 14, 15
Curtis JN-3 airplane 16

Delafield, Richard 6
Díaz, Portirio 10
Dick, Charles W.F. 9, 10
Dick Bill 9, 10
Dickman, Joseph T. 110
disease 49, *59*, 86, 91, 92, 97, 111, 155
Dolphin 11
doughboy 100

Eggers, John H. 78
ethnicity and A.E.F. 88

Ferdinand, Franz 12
Flash/sound rangers 104
Foch, Ferdinand 108
Forges Brook 112–113, 122, 125
Forts (American): Eathan Allen 22; Hancock 36; H.S. Wright 22; Sam Houston *35*, 79; Sill 80, 81
French: army 108–145, 150; forts 112, 115, 124
frontier day *55, 56*
Funston, Frederick 15, 19, *25, 35, 56*, 57, 60, 65

Gadsden Purchase 10
Garde Nationale de Paris 6
gas 76, 78, 79, 100, 101, 116, 130, 135, 141, 143, 147, 148, 150, 151, 157, 160, 163; gas mask 76, 78, 79, 95, 100, 101, 136; horse gas mask 106, 107
Gatling Gun 9
General Orders Number 7 (G.O.No. 7) 36–*38*, 97
George, David Lloyd 170
Gerard, James Watson 64
German Army (5th) 108–169
Glenn Springs, Texas 17
Gourand, Henri 119, 120
Great Northern 89
grenade 74, 75
Guadalupe Hidalgo Treaty 10
Gulf of Mexico 31

Haig, Sir Douglas 90, 112
Hand, Daniel W. 18
Harlingen, Texas *30, 38*
Haskell, William N. 18
haversack 41–43, 84, 95
Hess, Dudley 94, 98, 99, *173*
Hidalgo, Texas 19, 31, 49
Hidalgo County (Texas) 17, 18, 31
Hindenburg Line/Siegfried Stellung 119–169; Freya Stellung 121; Giselher Stellung 120, 121; Hagon/Hagen Stellung 120, 123, 129; Haupt Stellung 120; Kriemhilde Stellung 121, 121, 133, 148, 149; Michel Stellung 120; Volker Stellung 123, 129, 151
Holy Roman Empire 112
Horn, R.E. 45
horses 23, 24, 31, *34, 38, 39*, 40, 92, 103, 105–107, 123
Huerta, Victorio 10, 11, 178
Huntington 89
hurricane (Gulf 1916) *48*

Jewish Welfare Board 71
Johnston, Gordon 18

Knights of Columbus 50, 71
Knox, Henry 5
Kuhn, Joseph 155
Kurtz 89

Lafayette, Marquis de 6, 88
Laguna Seca, Texas *41, 48*
La Thinte 164
League of Nations 171
Le Mort Homme-Côte 304 110, 113, 114, 116, 123, 124
Lewis, Edward M. 57
lice 135, 136, 152, *173*
Liggett, Hunter 110, 122, 149, 151, 158
limber 7
Lorraine 109, 111, 149
Lusitania 13, *63*

MacArthur, Douglas 73
machine guns 75
Madawaska 89
Madero, Francisco, Jr. 10, 11
Madero, Texas 19
Maneuver Division 10
Manifesto for the Mexican People 11
manure 92, 96–98
McAllen, John 31
McAllen, Texas 14–*59*
McKenna, Fred 106, 107
McNair, William S. 18, 22, *38, 54*

Index

Meuse-Argonne Offensive 119–169
Meuse River 108–169
Mexican border 172
Mexican Punitive Expedition 14–*59*
Mexican Revolution 10
Mid Ocean Comin' Thru 89
Military Training Commission (MTC) 62
Mission, Texas *30*, 31, *41*
Moselle River 109
Motormen's Strike (1895) 7
mud 135, 136

Napoleon 95, 96, 111
National Defense Act (1914) 17, 23; (1920) 62
Neuilly Treaty 170
New York National Guard 52nd Field Artillery Brigade officers 67, 91, 107, 121, 125, 129, 139; embarkation to France 93
New York National Guard 102nd Ammunition Train 137, 139, 166
New York National Guard 102nd Trench Mortar 69, 81, 99, 126–7, 149, 171; roster officers (partial 1918) 99
New York National Guard 104th Field Artillery Regiment/1st Field Artillery: armory 12, 19, 179, 180; citations World War I 183–196; current history 177–180; deaths World War I 181, 182; early history 5–13; roster officers (1916) 18–20, (1918) 67, (1919) 177; trip to France 93; trip to U.S.A. 174–175; Veterinary Corps 91; World War II 180
New York National Guard 105th Field Artillery Regiment/2nd Field Artillery: roster officers (partial 1916) 20, (partial 1918) 67, 68; Veterinary Corps 91
New York National Guard 106th Field Artillery/3rd Field Artillery: roster officers (partial 1916) 20, 22, 27, 26, 106, 126, (partial 1918) 67, 68
New York National Guard 6th Division (Mexican border duty) 17–59; training *see* Camp McAllen; deaths 59
New York National Guard 27th Division, A.E.F: band 71, 72, 77; embarkment 88, 89; ethnic mix 88; Graves Registration Service 178, 179; infantry activity World War I 72, 90–96; organization 65, 67, 69; parade New York City (farewell) 73, 74, (victory) 175, 176; raiding of division for World War I 82, 83; receptions/reunion 179; service decorations 86, 87, 172; training *see* Camp Wadsworth
The New York National Guardsman 179

New York State Militia 5, 6; Volunteer Militia Artillery 6
The New York Times 33, 64
Nicholson, W.J. 165
Nobel Peace Prize 178

Obregón, Álvaro 178
Orange Riot (1871) 6
Orlando, Vittorio 170
O'Ryan, John J. 8, 12, 13, 22, 39, 49, 56, 65, 72, 74, 82, 83, 86, 87, 89, 95, 97, 112, 159, 176, 177, 180; patch 87, 168; roughnecks 95, 96
The Owl 14–59

Panama Canal 9
Paris Peace Settlement 170
Parker, James 18
pay (discrepancy) 43–46
Peace of Westphalia 112
Pershing, John J. 15–17, 57, 60, 65, 88, 97, 108, 110, 119, 122, 137, 149, 151, 179
Pétain, Henri 108
Pharr, Texas *30*, 31
Phillips, Charles L. 67, 72, 79, 82
Pierce, Palmer E. 72
Pocahontas 89
Preparedness Movement 62
President Grant 89
President Lincoln 89
Princip, Gaurilo 12
prisoners of war 107, 129, 157, 165, 166
Pulis, Charles 162

racism (15th/369th Infantry Regiment) 16, 71, 119, 120
Rail Splitter 89
railroad lines: (France) Mézières-Sedan-Metz Railroad and Carigan-Sedan-Mézières 118, 122, 157; Paris-Bordeaux 98; Paris-Nancy 109; (New York) Delaware and Hudson 27; Long Island 176; New York Central Line 27; (South Carolina) Piedmont and Northern Eletric 70; Southern 70; (Texas) Grande Valley *30*; San Benito and Rio *30*
Railroad Riot (1877) 6, 7
Rankin, Andrew Brown, IV ix, *1*, 22, 72, 90, 94, 102, 138–139, 197
rations 135, 136, 148, 149, 151, 152
Reynosa, Mexico 19, 31, 49
rifle 75, 95; Springfield musket 6
The Ring of the Nibelung 121
The Rio Grande Rattler 43, 49–52, 77
Rio Grande River 31, *35*, 49, *50*, *58*

riots: Astor Place (1849) 6; Motormen's Strike (1895) 7; Orange (1871) 6; Railroad (1877) 6, 7
Roe, Charles 7, 8
Rogers, Henry H. 19, 53
Roosevelt, Theodore 62
Root, Elihu 62
Rupprecht, Field Marshal 88
Ruth, "Babe" 180

St. Germain Treaty 170
St. Mihiel Salient Offensive 108–118
Salvation Army 71
Schlieffen Plan 12
The Sea Serpent: A Mid-Atlantic Issue of the Gas Attack and Rio Grande Rattler 89
Seille River 109
Sèvres Treaty 170
Sharyland, Texas 38
Shipman, Rev. Herbert 49
Sirois, Edward 133
Slocum, Herbert J. 14, 15
Smith, Alfred E. 179
Smith, Emery 141, 144
Smith, Merritt H. 19, 20, *32*, 53, 62, 124, 152
Somme River 112
Spartanburg, South Carolina 73; *also see* Camp Wadsworth
Spence, Cary F. *30*
Sterling's Ranch (Texas) 40, *41*
Stimson, Henry L. 10, 62
Stimson Plan 10
stoves, Sibley 70, 84
Susquehanna 89

Taft, William Howard 10
Tampico, Mexico 11
tents *35*, *59*, 70, 83, 84, 91, 92
trenches: (France) 131, 133, 143, 146, 148, 150, 151; (South Carolina) 71, 77–79; (Texas) 53
Trianon Treaty 170

uniforms 19, *55*, 85, 86, 95, 135, 136, 152, 170
unterseeboot (U-boat) 64, 95

Vanderbilt, Mrs. Cornelius 45
Veracruz, Mexico 11
Verdun 108–143
Verdun-Fromeréville Sector 110–113
Verdun Treaty 112
Versaille Treaty 170
Villa, Pancho 10, 11, 14, 15–*59*, 178; Villistas 14, 17
von Bernstorff, Johann Heinrich 64
von der Marwitz, Georg 120
von Gallwitz, Max 120, 121
von Hertling, George 134

Wadsworth, James W., Jr. *56*, 57, 70, 179
The Wadsworth Gas Attack and Rio Grande Rattler (The Gas Attack) 52, 77, 78, 83, 85–87
war: American Civil 6, 7; Franco-Prussian 111–113; Mexican 7, 10, *35*; Philippine-American 9, 15, 16; Revolutionary 5, 6; Spanish-American 7–9, 87; World War I (The Great War) 12, 111–165, 172
Washington, George 5
Waterbury, Franklin W. *50–52*, 179
Wecks, John W. 179
Welsh, William 18, *23*, *24*, *28*
White, George H. 18
Whitman, Charles S. *56*, 57, 65
Wilhelm, Kaiser I (1797–1888) 158
Wilhelm II (1859–1941) 164
Wilhelm III (1770–1840) 64
Wilson, Woodrow 11, 14, 15, 17, 57, 64, 170, 178
Wingate, George A. 67, 79, 90, 158
Woëvre plain 109, 112, 130, 135, 141, 152, 157, 162
Wood, Leonard 10, 22, 62
Wright, William *25*

Y.M.C.A. *50*, 71, 95, 97–99
York, Sgt. Alvin C. 144
Young's Ranch (Texas) *41*

Zapata, Emiliano 11, 178
Zimmerman, Arthur *63*, 64

www.ingramcontent.com/pod-product-compliance
Lightning Source LLC
Chambersburg PA
CBHW032053300426
44116CB00007B/726